PORTALS AND CORRIDORS
a visionary guide to hyperspace

Monica Szu-Whitney and Gary Whitney

Frog, Ltd.
Berkeley, California

Portals and Corridors: A Visionary Guide To Hyperspace

Copyright © 1999 by Monica Szu-Whitney and Gary Whitney. All rights reserved. No portion of this book, except for brief review, may be reproduced, stored in a retrieval system, or transmitted in any form or by any means— electronic, mechanical, photocopying, recording, or otherwise—without written permission of the publisher. For information contact Frog, Ltd. c/o North Atlantic Books.

Published by Frog, Ltd.

Frog, Ltd. books are distributed by
North Atlantic Books
P.O. Box 12327
Berkeley, CA 94712

Cover design by Gary E. Whitney
Cover art by Monica Szu-Whitney
Book design by Andrea DuFlon

Printed in Korea.

Distributed to the book trade by Publishers Group West

Library of Congress Cataloging-in-Publication Data

1 2 3 4 5 6 7 8 9 / 00 99 98 97 96

Whitney, G.E. (Gary E.)
    Portals and Corridors : A Visionary Guide To Hyperspace / Gary Whitney, Monica Szu-Whitney.
        p. cm.
    ISBN 1-883319-76-5 (trade paper : alk. paper)
    1. Szu-Whitney, Monica--Criticism and interpretation.   I. Szu-Whitney, Monica. II. Title
ND237.S9487W48   1998
759.13--dc21
                                                       98-4131
                                                         CIP

To
the benevolent unseen forces
overlighting
all of existence.

Contents

	Foreword	vii
	Preface	xi
	Introduction	1
ONE	Electric Eel	18
TWO	Nadash	26
THREE	Shulaz	38
FOUR	Yoru-Yoru	48
FIVE	Hamaaz	56
SIX	Flames	66
SEVEN	Byo-Yuu	74
EIGHT	Lou-E-Ah-Nana	82
NINE	Blue Thunder	92
TEN	Anadra	100
ELEVEN	Ruul	110
TWELVE	A-Mee-Al	122
THIRTEEN	Soul	132
FOURTEEN	Aah-Nuk	148
FIFTEEN	Shafuna	156
SIXTEEN	Tibetan Eggs	168
SEVENTEEN	Mayta	176
EIGHTEEN	Arrion	184
NINETEEN	Eliosath	198

TWENTY	Juules	204
TWENTY ONE	Ray-Shuu	214
TWENTY TWO	Lizardman	222
TWENTY THREE	Shi-Shaa	232
TWENTY FOUR	Aahooomm	244
	Afterword	262
	Notes	287

Foreword

IN 1996 I FIRST BECAME AWARE of the effort of the Whitneys' to create a Who's Who of the hyperspatial realm, a sort of taxonomic bestiary of the denizens of the poetic imagination. My own involvement with shamanism and psychedelics had long ago caused me to realize that one of the peculiarities of Western culture as it has evolved over the past several centuries has been a deepening hostility toward the domain of spirit and imagination. Except insofar as the imagination has been seen as the source of inventions and technical innovations, with a potential for profit and military application, our fantastic inner landscapes have been imaged as a desolate and yet somehow dangerous place. This was the tragedy foreseen by William Blake, that the Divine Imagination would be enslaved by method in "the dark Satanic mill" of industrial science.

Early in the twentieth century Sigmund Freud and Carl Jung supported their psychological theories by showing that active fantasies, the unlimbering of the imagination, brought with it the confrontation with archetypal drives and traumatic material unfit for the parlor room atmosphere that science prefers to maintain. Still later the insistence of the psychedelic culture that arose in the West since the 1960s, an insistence that the imagination-driven experiences induced by plants and hallucinogenic substances could be central to personal spiritual efforts at self definition, further unsettled the issue. And then lastly, and at the other end of the intellectual spectrum from debunking science, are the newly militant cults of ignorance that rally under the tattered banner of the label "New Age." To these fractured and epistomologically naive new faiths all the intuitions of and projections by the unschooled mind are to be taken at face value as genuine and trustworthy information about the nature and organization of the cosmos—a position which renders the universe not grandiose and inspiring but rather simply quite silly, a kind of epistemological cartoon world in which Christ, St. Germain, Bugs Bunny, denizens of a punitive 12th planet, and the ghost of Elvis all compete on an equal footing.

Into this morass of intellectual denial and uncritical and naive belief Gary and Monica Whitney have brought a measure of clarity. Contrary to my own approach to the imagination Monica Whitney is not a user of psychedelic drugs or hallucinogenic plants. These tools are mainstays of the shamanic tool kit to be sure, but so is what Depth Psychologists call "active imagination," that is innocent day-dreaming. This is the method the Whitneys used, it is simple and straightforward; to gather experiences and impressions and to faithfully report them without getting near the claim that these experiences are either true or pathological. This method, to gather facts and to search one's observations for patterns, is not new. It is in fact the Baconian method that informed and guided science in its youth before it became arrogant in its certainty that nature was all atoms and mechanism.

The body of work which the Whitneys have assembled speaks strongly to the fact that the ecologies of the hyperspatial imagination are multitudinous and strange. And while the illustrations presented here are not meant to be construed as great art, their primitivism and lack of visual sophistication is a measure of the uncontrived sincerity of the insights and impressions of Monica and Gary. Naturally the report of any explorer or cartographer of an unexplored domain reflects personal limitations and is couched in the language and the expectations of the culture from which the explorer comes. Nevertheless objectivity, while difficult to achieve, is an ideal which unifies the Whitney's approach and gives *Portals and Corridors* a credibility and a charm that channelers of good news from the Pleiades and those with a direct pipeline to the elders of lost Atlantis may lack.

There is no doubt in my mind that the work of the Whitneys is prefigurative of a new direction in science and phenomenology. The easy questions were the first to be dealt with by science, and indeed mastery of matter and biology is slowly being attained. Now science must look at the most complex and integrated phenomena that nature offers, and this is surely the human mind and the nature of consciousness itself. We are in an early phase of this process. First the unconscious was approached with fear and trepidation, a matter for physicians and psychopathologists, later the most powerful tools for the study of the mind, the psychedelic plants and substances, were made illegal and remain so to this day. This situation recalls for those with long memories that the Church once forbade the dissection of human bodies and forced medical students into the role of ghouls who must steal corpses from the gallows and battlefields in order to advance the knowledge of human physiology.

But Truth wants to be known, and the human journey through time is a journey toward an ever more faithful approximation of that Truth. Those who explore and report their findings without fear and compromise become the ideals and inspiration of those who follow and complete their work. I believe that the Whitneys have made a charming and interesting effort to bring into the life of consciousness and collective discourse some of the denizens of the infinite domain that we call, without knowing what the words mean, the Human Imagination.

>   Terence McKenna
>   September, 1998
>   Honaunau, Hawaii

Preface

THE READERS OF THIS BOOK may have the same first reaction that I did to some of the pictures: an emotional one. I felt uncomfortable when I looked at some of the life forms portrayed by Monica. Some of the pictures looked evil and frightening to me.

I have found that no amount of asking some Spiritual Psychic Artists to stop drawing faces, that in our culture, could be thought of as evil-looking, will stop some of those artists from drawing such pictures. Those artists' psychic experiences are their psychic experiences!

In a private meeting, a prophecy was given through me that Monica had the power to develop as a Spiritual Psychic Artist. Throughout the history of my career as a scientifically tested physical phenomena medium, I have been confronted with the following experience: when a prophecy is given to a student, telling him or her of potential psychic ability, some interpret this as a blanket confirmation of the accuracy of each and every psychic impression he or she will ever receive. No such blanket confirmation is expressed or implied.

Having said these things, I feel (emotional reaction aside), that this book presents a different construct of the Universe that may well be worthy of examination.

If beings from other worlds or dimensions were to accomplish travel to earth, through efforts and skills of their own, they would represent the most assertive and politically powerful groups of their worlds. We also know that human life on our planet is carbon based and that our life forms manifest with two legs, arms, eyes, ears, and a mouth. However, most upright life forms from other worlds would not necessarily look humanoid or even be carbon based.

How much diversity can we tolerate in the centuries ahead? Not all visiting aliens would be genuinely friendly. Nor would they necessarily be hostile. Neither would we necessarily be friendly to them.

What if through genetic manipulation, scientists were to create beings that look like the beings that Monica has drawn? Should these beings be allowed to live? If you let them live once they come out of the womb, or a test tube, could you stand it?

Genetic manipulation is one of the burning issues of our time. Many people are discussing the moral implications of genetic manipulation of a human embryo.

What are the future limits in genetic manipulation? One day there may be laws banning genetic manipulation both in the United States and in many other countries around the world. However, not all countries may pass such laws. In any event, some scientists will continue to experiment in this field regardless of what the laws are. What would the outcome of those experiments be?

What if wars were fought one day over the rights of beings that look like the drawings in Monica and Gary's book? These concepts bear contemplation.

For many years, I have asked my students to examine the question: "What are the limits of tolerance?" In examining what those limits of tolerance might be, I asked myself if I could accommodate a being that looked like one of the drawings in this book.

I have already admitted that I felt uncomfortable with some of the pictures in this book. After deep contemplation I concluded that even if I was personally uncomfortable with some of them, I would have to accommodate beings that looked like this, as long as they radiated virtue and spiritual values. (Having taken a second look at the preceding sentence, I feel there is something wrong with it. Are we to "accommodate" only those beings who are virtuous? Who is totally virtuous?)

Do beings like this exist somewhere?

Throughout history and in modern times, government administrations have perpetrated many lies and frauds upon the public. Many people believe that government administrations are lying even today and are not giving us the real truth about alien civilizations visiting Earth.

For example, I personally believe there are certain highly placed people in government intelligence agencies who have known for a long time that there is water on Mars. They feed this information to us only gradually through the controlled establishment media.

Therefore, it is logical there may be government-known life forms out there, about which we have not been told.

Monica has tuned into strange and diverse life forms that could exist. The reader should draw his or her own conclusions as to the realities of those experiences.

When someone claims that a supernatural communication or phenomenon has occurred, we first look, very carefully, to see if the phenomenon is genuine, or deluded, or fraudulent. If we ascertain that the phenomenon is genuine, we next look, very carefully, to see if the phenomenon is of God and good.

Monica is a genuine psychic artist.

Because of our cultural and personal biases, some of the beings she depicts may not appear to be of God and good. The accompanying communications and experiences should be examined to discern if the spirit is of God and good.

If some of the beings Monica perceived through her mediumship turned out not to be of God and good, it certainly would not make her a bad person; anymore than a photographer would be a bad person for taking photographs of some of the less pleasing faces of the human condition.

I was particularly impressed that Monica supplied me with an affidavit sworn under penalty of perjury that she is sincere and genuine in her spiritual work. She believes that she has a spiritual gift in being able to contact, and to draw portraits, of beings from other dimensions of life.

Monica presented me with testimonials from sincere people who declare under penalty of perjury that they have had remarkable personal experiences with her Spiritual Psychic Art.

The art in this book does not depict traditional Spiritual Psychic Art.

A traditional psychic artist sometimes draws faces of loved ones who have biologically died, thus giving evidence for survival of the soul. More often pictures of Guardian Angels are drawn. The purposes of Spiritual Psychic Art are to comfort the mourner, by giving evidence of the soul's survival, and/or to uplift and inspire a truth seeker and/or to give Spiritual Healing to the person who receives the drawing.

Most of the testimonials written for Monica do not describe experiences with beings like the ones in this book. In the testimonials, descriptions are given of certain evidences of Spiritual Healing and/or contact with those who once lived on Earth and died.

A thinking person would not explain away these heartfelt experiences glibly. Even the concept of freedom of the press affirms one's right to express sincere views that are not commonly held by others.

The reader will naturally be curious as to what type of person Monica is.

Monica is a courteous, loving and friendly person. She is gracious and humble. She has a lovely face and she looks angelic. She is a soft-spoken woman who has a delightfully sweet personality and is somewhat self-effacing.

Gary is eloquent as he presents Monica's spiritual journeys to the reader. Some readers may find difficulty in accepting Monica's experiences as anything except pure fantasy. However, some great minds and thinkers teach us that "creativity and imagination" are a key to unlocking many spiritual truths.

Gary masterfully describes Monica's experiences with words that are colorful and expressive. He encourages the reader to journey further with Monica and her guides in the spiritual realms. Each experience is presented in an innocent and fresh way. Whether or not you believe these beings are real, at least you have had an interesting journey through someone else's sincere and genuine effort to make contact with life forms that are alien to our own.

It is through efforts such as these made by Gary and Monica, that we keep alive the common man's and common woman's desire to learn something new. The freedom to do that which Gary and Monica undertake in this book, may in future centuries, stimulate grassroots movements for good social change. I leave it for the reader to decide what good social change may be, especially in connection with intelligent alien life forms, centuries from now.

These decisions are not going to be easy ones.

       Keith Milton Rhinehart
       1998
       Aquarian Foundation

Introduction

WHEN ALICE FELL DOWN the bunny hole, an amusing and fanciful adventure unravelled in which reality dissolved into sometimes-befuddling, sometimes-hilarious events—always just a whisker away from her normal grasp of reality. The March Hare, the Mad Hatter, the Dormouse, and the whole cast of characters unwittingly began to play pivotal roles in Alice's welfare, challenging her understanding and expanding her mind to allow her to reassess the conclusions she had previously made about consensus reality. What once seemed important now had questionable value—what was once inconsequential began to have the gravest of implications. Such is the effect of a simple shift of perspective on the nature of reality.

With the advent of quantum physics and the expansion of human awareness into new physical and spiritual domains, in many ways our entire culture is presently facing the same predicament Alice faced in her adventures—determining what's real and what isn't...or discerning what we believe and discovering how our allegiance to our beliefs has hypnotized us to our present confines.

In 1990, an incident occurred in the lives of my wife Monica and me that would eventually erode our blind acceptance of everyday reality, shifting our perception forever. At the time, the event's import seemed minor. We were attending a séance given by Keith Milton Rhinehart. Never having met him, we were participating in a private worldwide meeting, via a telephone conference hookup, at San

Francisco Branch Aquarian Foundation. He was completely unaware of our specific participation or our location. While entranced by the famous Count St. Germain (legendary around the courts of eighteenth-century France and communicating today by through mental trance), suddenly, Rhinehart stopped in mid-sentence and, completely out of context, proceeded to address Monica of San Francisco as though he had known her all his life, elaborating on her developed skill as a psychic artist. He claimed she had the same talents as a famous medium in England, who produced evidential psychic renderings of others' dead relatives and friends after talking to each inquirer over the phone. Given the fact that Monica wasn't even an artist, this was quite a preposterous assertion. She left the séance that day confused and doubting, dismissing the comment as likely mistaken identity. She had no artistic ability; how could she possibly be a developed or even a developing *psychic* artist?

Because Rhinehart has credibility as a world-renowned medium, having passed rigorous empirical tests, Monica gradually became more and more curious about his bizarre view of her talents. Finally, she rallied her courage to see if she did indeed have an undiscovered mysterious gift, and she began drawing. During her first sittings, mere symbols, colors, and landscapes rushed into her mind's eye with nary a recognizable portrait in sight. Even this was startling, like being plunged into a whirlpool. In time the symbolic imagery gave way to faint impressions of facial characteristics somewhere between the earnest expressions of marginally talented preschoolers and John Lennon's erotic scrawlings. Signatures from elsewhere were beginning to impress themselves through the haze. Gradually, actual personalities began to arrive on her pages, peering out from the chaotic mass of scratches and smudges.

After a period of Monica's apprenticeship, the nature of the process began to shift, perhaps even change dimensions. Rather than glimpsing images in her mind's eye, Monica began to see vivid black outlines already drawn on her page; all she had to do was begin to trace the line and the rest just flowed. It was as if someone else were drawing the outline of the image on the page, then signaling her telepathically the rest of the image as she attempted to execute it. But, strange and at first startling, the images were no longer of putative humans — they depicted beings from an alien world.

As she continued in her development, Monica became increasingly aware of a specific presence prompting her inner vision. Intrigued by the possibility of an extradimensional intelligence, we found ourselves wanting to discover who exactly was stenciling her from the other side, and we and began focusing on the spirit's identity. One day while riding a bus into San Francisco, Monica received a clear mental flash, revealing a magnificent accomplice wearing a deep midnight-blue turban, stars twinkling and swirling about his presence. She knew intuitively in that instant, "Oh, this is my drawing guide I've been waiting for! Wow, he's handsome and magical!" (Sometimes I imagine writing this whole adventure as a musical. It would fall between *Phantom of the Opera* and *Cats*. Only I think I'd ask Mickey Hart to write the score instead of Andrew Lloyd Webber.) Later that evening in meditation, Monica asked who (by name) had revealed himself to her during the day. Aurora was the word that immediately became impressed on her mind. Well, it wasn't Rembrandt, Rubens, or Van Gogh; they were probably busy elsewhere, but we were sure Aurora was nonetheless an artist of cosmic dimensions.

Progressively, the refinement and content of Monica's drawings developed, and they began to hold incredibly strong energy fields with unusual vibrations. Their power went beyond Monica's training. We sensed that they weren't merely the product of fantasy but had import beyond the obvious images. Naturally we wanted to understand what was transpiring and why these exotic beings and creatures of some far vaster universe were venturing into our living room. What were we supposed to do with the drawings?

We spent time reviewing how the phenomenon arose and why we were involved. But no obvious answers occurred. After investigating the opinions of a number of acclaimed psychics, we tried dabbling with the Ouija board, each time with disappointing or negligible results. As frustrations mounted, we began to wonder if the answers lay in the portraits themselves. They seemed to shimmer, calling one to another plane of reality. Ultimately, we came to view them as explicit windows, portals into another world, and we tried to ride the vibration of each into its own dimension of space and/or time. This became the key that unlocked the drawings' mysteries.

It has been a tenuous, long journey, for Monica at times a bit frightening, but after seven years of exploring more than fifty portraits/portals, we have come to trust that we are forming a multitude of actual relationships (and perspectives) with beings from elsewhere in a multi-faceted universe.

Despite her fascination, Monica often still struggles with the nature of what is happening and is a constant critic of the self-evident nature of the findings. From the beginning, she wanted some type of confirmation or reassurance from the world whereby she could determine that others were experiencing similar events and giving reasonable and compatible explanations for these discoveries. I, on the other hand, was much more accepting, willing to be fascinated with the events as they transpired. Maybe because I was primarily a voyeur, not being emotionally bounced around within, it was easier for me to keep a more objective perspective. I believed something was happening for a reason, and I wanted also to discover what it was, yet without risking dispelling it as pure fantasy. Monica and I had known each other for eight years, having been married for five, and I'd never experienced anyone with a more dormant imagination. Flaky imaginative escapes weren't her tendency. She lived among real trees, on real streets, relating to real people. So were these real people in other dimensions, planes, on other worlds around other stars, galaxies; or on other time lines?

As events evolved, we continued to seek confirming data in various traditions, we investigated non-Western realms of shamanic journeying. Here we discovered many points of commonality. Whenever we found material related to what we thought was happening, we would present our hypothesis psychically to Aurora for confirmation. After the initial meeting with her "guide" on the bus to San Francisco, Monica had begun developing an in-depth relationship with Aurora, both by meditation and during the actual drawing process; she could access his consciousness readily. This relationship has blossomed solely out of Monica's gift and has not been experienced first-hand by me. But, even with my lack of direct access to him, Aurora has become a sort of co-conspirator assisting both of us in understanding the odyssey that is transpiring. In meditation Monica posits questions and Aurora agrees or disagrees, but never does he flat-out give us information, insisting we stretch our minds in an attempt to discover distinctions and meanings for ourselves. Even though Monica consistently railed to him about her so-called fantasizing, he insisted she was not spinning tales of fantasy, but peering into other real dimensions of space and time.

"What you are experiencing is real," he declared. "It's a journey into the nature of reality. The experiences transpire in the realm of hyperspace, exhibiting the multi-dimensional nature of existence which goes on and on into infinity!"

Throughout Monica's experience I have been her accomplice, supporting and reassuring her, bolstering her confidence in visions, because I intuitively know they are real. Although the journeys chronicled in these pages are solely Monica's excursions, the interpretation and understanding of them came out of the two of us continually grappling for answers. Much of what you are reading is my interpretation of what is at play during Monica's journeys, mainly because it has been exasperating for her to dissect her own experiences and also not her nature to over-analyze. During the journeying, Monica has been conscious, relating the inter-dimensional experience to me as though we were dialoguing, while I tape-record and take notes on her itinerary and commentary.

Like the fictional Alice, Monica has come upon a type of rabbit hole, but rather than falling, she shifts vibration, triggering a transformation and an expansion of consciousness beyond her normal range. In effect, she has refocused her attention into another aspect of her being—or, shall we say, a different vehicle of perception. With the vibrational shift, she is endowed with deep and widened vision—like an astronomer charting the stars and galaxies through telescopes of higher magnitude and different radiation sensitivities—and immediately a new configuration of the universe presents itself.

Having faced the radically alien phenomena of other dimensions, Monica and I now realize that most of us are frozen into linear time like a river wedged into a gorge. Like the river, we flow with the historical path of least resistance, seeing only the predetermined course the gorge provides. This confining perspective creates the illusion of a solely three-dimensional mechanical-physical universe in unilinear space-time. Our encounters in journeying through the multi-dimensional universe have inspired us to stop clinging to past orientations, and to break the hypnotic trance generated by beliefs formed and adopted in the past. As we refocus our vision and challenge our stubborn beliefs, other possibilities unravel and the voyage begins, taking us out of the narrow straits of our personal gorge.

Mystics, shamans, trippers, and science-fiction writers have given us snapshots of bizarre dimensions, some of their characteristics alluded to by recent discoveries of particle physics. But even with their revelations our daily culture has not strayed far from the historical model of the nature of reality. We do not entertain relationships in other dimensions and we still count on NASA to get us to other worlds, though they will accomplish a smidgen of this in our lifetime. Through Monica's journeying we have found that when one is willing to entertain the notion of letting go of the familiar lock on reality, undreamed-of possibilities appear here and now, completely reshuffling commonly accepted realities and opening psychic tourism to regions well beyond the Moon, Mars, and the moons of Jupiter. Dimension after dimension stack like dominoes out into infinity, shattering one's usual relationship with space and time. At some point humans may board vehicles that slip through the thresholds of bent space and travel among Monica's "friends and acquaintances" and others like (and unlike) them. But at present the physical technology for such remains undiscovered, even unconsidered, as space travel is still confined to the mechanics of the physical plane. So if the unseen worlds of the mystic and shaman exist, how do we chart their locations and propel ourselves through their corridors? Even privileged as Monica is, this was always a question for us—what is the mechanism that switches on the journey? For a long time the answers remained an enigma, eluding our understanding. But slowly the nature of the process has come more into focus.

Monica found, "As I sat quietly, I could detect a shift in the vibration of my consciousness and then I knew this was the indication I had slipped into the realm of non-ordinary reality. But I spent years wandering through the disorienting foreign landscapes and sitting with countless alien beings before I discovered it was a twist in the role of my imagination and intuition that actually triggered and guided the journey." The imagination though was a famously unreliable trigger for true paranormal excursions. "Was I making it all up? For a long time I thought so; but I've never possessed an active imagination, so I knew this was unlikely. Gary and I had searched for some other mechanism that triggered my experiences, then finally we began to look at the imagination as something much broader than I had originally conceived. Could the imagination somehow join with my intuition to form a type of intelligent navigational 'organ' which I utilized while journeying through hyperspace? Could it direct and creatively interact with that which already exists in its own right? In other words, could it act as a tuning fork, and through resonation, magnetize existing realms in a creative interactive manner towards my consciousness? Over time this is what I've come to believe. It's my active engagement and focusing of the imaginative organ that drives the experience as I move through the odd sensations of hyperspace reality. I've come to understand this organ as a separate vehicle of consciousness, which one can activate in order to perceive non-ordinary realities."

We believe that, as hyperspacial realities become better understood, the imagination will be increasingly acknowledged as a true perceiver of phenomena, playing a key role in uncloaking the unusual properties of other dimensions, ultimately being assigned greater stature as an organ of true sense perception. It is our experience that without the enactment of the imagination in symphony with the intuition, the nature of non-ordinary reality remains lost behind a mysterious fog. For it is the imaginative will which assists in negotiating the landscapes of hyperspace, though one must recognize that the will doesn't generate their existence—these landscapes exist in their own right in the other dimensions of reality with or without the play of imagination. One only employs the imagination to navigate, creatively interact with, and interpret the hyperspacial domain, not to create it. The imaginative will is the genius which takes the raw materials of the inner landscapes and fuses them into new meaningful compositions. It is that historically we haven't realized that the imagination is real and imaginal as well as "imaginary," leading to actual places beyond the ken of the other five senses. And in its spare time it traipses off in idle fantasizing; in fact, its fantasies may themselves carry elements of untaken journeys or inner promptings calling out for adventurers.

The word "Imaginality" seems to best describe the perceptual experience of the multi-dimensional worlds encountered by our inner vision. It melds the domain of psychology to the visions of mediums, Sufis, and shamans. Imaginality defines the imagination as "reality," not a mere subjective projection of the mind—but rather the unifying of one's consciousness with the independent nature of the cosmos. With this word and concept, we wish to point to a new understanding of how our brains process and interpret one integrative experience out of the fountain of perceptions flowing from within and without. The imagination is finally the agent connecting the transcendental dots of hyperspace, rendering its imaging understandable. It draws on our past experiences, joining subjective impulses to that which is presently being perceived. It symbolizes the marriage of the mind's consciousness to independent expressions of nature. In redefining the imagination in this way, we shed our past inclinations to view it as merely a source of idle fantasy, uplifting our vision to allow it to assume its true revelatory nature.

The imagination (so redefined) has played a more instrumental role in the creation of reality and its development through history than most people are willing to acknowledge. It was a central value during the Romantic Period and fueled much debate over the nature of its role in relationship to the creative processes in the fields of literature, philosophy, religion, and even science. During the past couple of centuries the imagination has received an increasingly bad rap. Certain belief systems and individuals have rendered it delusionary—pure fantasy or the product of madmen. Often children are scolded for imaginary drifts in consciousness, and through the years many adults have been derided as flakes and dreamers for reporting imaginary interludes.

The poet William Blake referred to the imagination unambiguously as an organ of perception like our other sensory organs. The clearer the imagination organ, the more prophetic its revelatory vision. Blake states, "The imagination is not a State: it is the Human Existence itself. It receives prophetic vision messages, words and images, from the unfallen Paradise within."[1] How far from our present materialistic obsessions! It is clear that Blake saw the imagination as Reality and a vital tool in negotiating and interpreting the nature of our reality. Blake's certainty and faith along with our personal experiences of transdimensional realities have led us to believe we live in a universe governed by the nature of our imagination every bit as much as one governed by linear logic. The notion of "Imaginality" attempts to merge the two divergent paradigms. The experience molding our lives is a product of imagination as much as it is a set of external constructs.

It is a well-known fact that many scientists, including Albert Einstein, experienced intuitive and imaginative insights upon reaching mental impasses regarding a hypothesis. Many resulting theories, unlocked by the intuition in concert with the imaginative organ, have impacted the very foundation of our lives, resulting in mathematical formulas, medicines, agricultural products and even domesticated animals; yet we refuse as a culture to acknowledge the true import of this organ. It is time to reinterpret the character of our imagination and give it the same credence we ascribe to any of our organs of perception. It must be brought out of the shadows and reintegrated into our experiences of life, playing a legitimate role in shaping the nature of our existence. We have lost too much already by giving our imaginations over to those who attempt to control both our culture and our reality through politics and the media. We have become pawns in the play of *their* imaginations because we have forfeited our own. Individually and culturally we have become enslaved by their self-serving fantasies because we no longer trust our ability to imagine for ourselves. Certainly the boredom which allows many of us to sign control of our lives over to government, science, and the media would come screeching to a halt if we reenlivened the reality behind our imaginations.

We have been creatures who allow our biological envelopes to encase our consciousness, tethering it to our immediate five senses. It is Monica's and my feeling that the time is rapidly approaching when we will all live our lives both in and out of ordinary reality, letting our sense organs transcend their perceived capabilities—soaring into new terrain. As we do we may understand new possibilities offered by our Earthly and Spiritual existence. Do we really think we are limited to five senses stymied by a gravitational field? Can we not see with our touch or smell through our sight like the synesthetics who have their normal sense perceptions crossed with one another? Is not the imagination itself a sort of sixth sense soaring through unlimited universes, gathering explosive revelations? Where do new concepts come from? Do they spring from the minds of some humans or are they part of a larger library of common information percolating through space and time, awaiting the beings who dare breach the biological envelope and come upon virgin thought-scapes? Is the genesis of human thought determined solely by the process of rational, linear logic or by a more loosely knit random framework, more akin to the spinning out of nonlinear fractal patterns? Might it be both? Could there be countless archetypes scripting drama after drama from other dimensions, prompting us to act out cosmic plays? Are there currents one can ride like white-water rapids, whisking one through dimension after dimension lickety-split into parallel time-scapes? We suggest there are! But need these spaces be actual light-years into the distance? Definitely not! They may lie as close as swirls of air-borne pollen, poised for our inbreath to seed their unfoldment.

In our culture, mythological beings tend to delight the imagination and capture our attention like eerie foghorns enticing us beyond the concrete into dimensional mists. This fascination has played an active role in many of the mythological backgrounds of Earth's cultures. In *The Mayan Factor*, José Argüelles discusses how Dogon, Egyptian, Mayan, and Aboriginal Australian peoples have recorded visitations and legends of dimensional and extraterrestrial beings which significantly influenced both the religious and temporal concerns of their times. To us, these accounts portend a future (and reveal a past) when space and time are viewed from a much different vantage—by peoples whose consciousness is unfettered by our consensus beliefs. It seems likely that many shamans of past and present cultures created a dynamic rapport with galactic or dimensional intelligences, similar to that of Monica's inter-dimensional journeys. Argüelles speaks of mandalas, possibly encoded with a language describing a passage leading to and from different worlds, a galactic thread or lifeline connecting different inter-dimensional and star systems. These resonant thread-like pathways provide an ongoing channel of communication, facilitating instantaneous transmissions.[2]

We found that when Monica attuned to each portrait, she was able to journey into the being's dimension, vividly experiencing its reality. The portraits did truly seem to act as portals or cosmic corridors, to serve as resonant pathways into the other dimensional realities of the beings represented in the renderings, opening up fantastic worlds completely alien to our understanding of space and time. Often Monica's encounters seemed to synchronize with her own evolving consciousness, presenting opportunities for personal transformation around lingering issues while opening new possibilities of experience. The encounters also have a certain synchronicity, paralleling events that may be transpiring in our own physical reality—emphasizing the bleed-through nature of space and time. Many of these inter-dimensional experiences are recreational, but just when one thinks one is on a joy ride, issues buried deeply in one's subconscious come rising to the surface. One can engage the experiences on a very superficial level or actively work on the evolution and transformation of one's spirit. By this we mean to interact with the journey's images and import thoughtfully, reconciling their content in a way which confronts one's present development or self-understanding—physically, mentally, emotionally, vibrationally, and spiritually. They may also present critical information, grasped perhaps by receptive individuals, for our culture as a whole.

Therefore this collection of "portals and corridors" is an invitation to journey. We want people to feel the aliveness of the drawings, to attune to the unique vibration of each portrait, then slip into the altered rapture of an alien universe, which they may find surprisingly familiar! Arising out of this mystifying and wondrous experience is a new yet ancient vision, endless worlds looking for explorers, hungry for new company—individuals ready to step into their cosmic makeup. We call out to each reader to join us in this exploration, letting his or her spirit move to the rhythm of the inner dimensions.

The experiences one might encounter through the use of these portraits arise from an innocence and ability to suspend any preconceived notions regarding the nature of reality and judgments surrounding the images as art. The portraits are not meant to be mere esthetic objects or perfect snapshots of other realities, but to represent vibrational renditions and to create symbolic images one can use as portal magnets—vibrational vortexes that draw one away from the gravitational pull of the Earth, propelling one into the stars and the dimensional beyond. They portray only a smattering of the infinite possible dimensions, but they are an excellent place to begin one's journeying into the mystery of the multi-dimensional nature of reality.

If one wants to start journeying, we recommend first setting a spiritual context. Begin with intention, an intention to deepen one's understanding of oneself and the nature of the universe. One could call it setting a sacred intention. By sacred we mean respectful—respectful to the majesty of the universe, respectful to our own magnificence, and respectful to our play in the ever-expanding nature of ourselves and the cosmos. And yet it will behoove us to be cognizant that we're each individual souls, moving in the field of infinity and eternity—sometimes narrow in our vision and other times vast, but always inextricably woven into the fabric of the grand universe.

With each and every journey it is wise to invoke the presence of one's personal guides, inviting them to journey along in camaraderie and support. If you aren't aware of your guides this may serve as a first step in finding them and getting to know them. There are many realms one can venture into, so we always surround and seal ourselves in white light, affirming that only God and goodness manifest. The beings introduced in this book, as alien as they may look, are all aligned with forces of good. So if one is to err, it is prudent to err on the side of caution. Here we wish to emphasize being mindful during your preparation for journeying. Prepare yourself as you would for any journey which traverses great distances—pay attention to detail and invoke friendly forces. Remember tourists can be at risk. If you are going to foreign lands, stay alert and observe local customs.

Monica and I are somewhat ritualistic in our approach—we light candles and burn our favorite incense to set a mood while creating a sense of order and harmony with the environment. It also sends a kind of spiritual telegram, informing one's guides that we are preparing for departure. Some may want to do more elaborate ceremonies in the tradition of American-Indian groups or other aboriginal cultures by introducing music or the drumming favored by shamanic voyagers. It's best that voyagers attune to what suits their personality and preferences, following their inner guidance and intuition. Monica generally blindfolds herself and uses ear plugs to isolate herself completely from the immediate physical surroundings. She finds this is a great aid in directing her attention inward.

Once you have set a sacred context, sit quietly in meditation, focusing the mind on your intentions. Start journeying by giving yourself a time period for the excursion, and at the end of approximately ten to fifteen minutes, affirm that you will be back in the room fully conscious of immediate surroundings. This instruction is two-fold. First, it sets a strong intention to return, and second, if one does not actively engage in a dimensional experience, it promotes a focusing—creating a stronger intention to stay on course. There's only a limited amount of time to experience each dimension, so this approach curbs a natural tendency to drift. When you progress in journeying experience, you can extend the duration, eventually dropping the timed aspect altogether.

Now, either choose a portrait with which to work, or bring to mind using your imagination a destination of your own choosing. The portraits are vibrational fields exuding chords that actively signal to one's consciousness a vibration to which one might attune. At first you may find them to be good tools in assisting your shifts into dimensional realities, for they represent a wide gamut of dimensional destinations and give a feel for the unlimited possibilities. But if you are not inclined to use the portraits, you can launch yourself in a multitude of other ways. Monica's journeys chronicle many different methods by which Aurora has coached her to shift from present physical focus into transdimensional realities. When you focus your mind in any suggested fashion, you are actually shifting your attention into the vibrational vehicle of consciousness. A second launch into the dimension occurs through this vehicle. Below we introduce a couple of methods, but to obtain a richer understanding, it would be advantageous to read how Aurora has worked with Monica throughout her episodes. In the chapters that follow, you can pick up many additional instructive hints.

Begin by gazing into the portrait that most attracts you; relax and gently focus your sight on the image while gradually letting the eye's focus go soft, then out of focus. Finally, let yourself merge or blend into the portrait, closing your eyes while retaining the image in your mind's eye or imagination. At this point the imagination is activated, and the imagination becomes the key to a complete shift into the portrait's dimension and full inhabitation of one's vibrational body. Insofar as the imagination instinctually activates during this process, just let it carry you.

It is precisely at this juncture where a tunnel or some version of a corridor often appears, catapulting one through its interiors and out into the new dimension, into the land inhabited by the consciousness behind the portrait. For some journeyers this tunnel will automatically appear and the journey will naturally carry on from there. For others, just focusing on the portrait may carry them directly into the domain of the being in the portrait. Still others may want to visualize the portrait reappearing at the end of the tunnel—this will help project them into the landscape inhabited by the being of focus, wherever it might be.

For some the tunnel might not easily appear, so in this case one actively employs and exerts the imagination. If the imagery doesn't come easily, then pretend. Pretend you are seeing a tunnel and moving down its corridors. Feel the feelings associated with moving swiftly down a corridor, then let the feelings carry you away. Just flow with it. The imaginal and the real are linked. Soon you won't have to pretend. Don't feel foolish—this can be like developing any new muscle or skill, requiring repetition and practice. Do it again and again, and what is real will become obvious!

There are those of us who do not visualize easily—and frankly I'm one who has some difficulty with visualization. Monica clearly has a gift and journeys somewhat effortlessly. While I seem to intuit experiences, I am not able to journey so easily. But when we have attended shamanic journeying classes, we have found that the majority of participants have the ability to experience journeying or non-ordinary reality after applying themselves.

Over time Monica and I have created an exercise to assist me in experiencing the journeys. It is a method some may want to explore, aiding in stimulating the development of the ability to travel via the vibrational body. We partner up in a shared excursion, whereby Monica narrates to me her encounter, creating an opportunity for me to experience journeying. I get sort of a kick-start—piggybacking with a naturally gifted journeyer. We start the journey by sitting together, bringing to mind a destination or focusing on one of the portraits with which we wish to communicate. Then we close our eyes and slip into meditation. Monica begins to narrate the experience she is having. It goes something like this: "I'm holding your hand and you are walking along my left side. We are entering a tunnel and walking very slowly. The tunnel's walls arch over us, radiating rainbows of dazzling colors, blasting us with cosmic light. Take a moment to bask in the light, absorbing its nurturing emanations. This light will assist us in sustaining the focus of our bodies throughout the duration of the journey. Now we start to walk a little faster; feel the coolness of the cave and the compacted earth beneath the soles of our feet. There's a dark opening way up in front and we are moving closer and closer. Soon we are running full-tilt, and hand-in-hand we leap out into the dark opening."

This juncture can act as a departure point or the narrator can carry on from there if it's still necessary. There are of course no guarantees, but many will find these techniques helpful in becoming more adept in journeying to the stars. This process has surely helped me. Once one slips into another dimension, one finds there's a vibrational passageway left in the wake — a kind of stellar breadcrumb trail. In the future it becomes easier to return to this dimension, as the traveled passageway reduces the resistance the mind may have initially experienced and now there exists a more effortless flow.

Just remember to stay focused and relaxed. Let yourself sink into the portrait, directing your imagination to carry you onward. This is not an exercise in effort, but merely a gentle concentrating and focusing of the mind, so as not to let the mind drift aimlessly. Soon the walls will shimmer, dissolving into the landscape, then into the sky and then into you, taking you into the very depths of "Imaginality," freeing you from the slavery of the body forever.

BRIEFLY I WOULD LIKE TO REMIND readers that in both the Introduction and Afterword my voice is primarily interpreting and attemtpting to come to an understanding of what has transpired for Monica. We are extremely close. I have sat with Monica on each journey, so to some extent it is my experience as well, but clearly I am not as gifted in my ability to journey. I have drawn conclusions and deductions based on my collaboration with her during our odyssey together. Throughout the journey episodes I am merely giving form to her experience in short-story format, so the adventure will be entertaining for the reader. But all stories are fundamentally true to how they transpired for Monica with no invention on my part.

AURORA

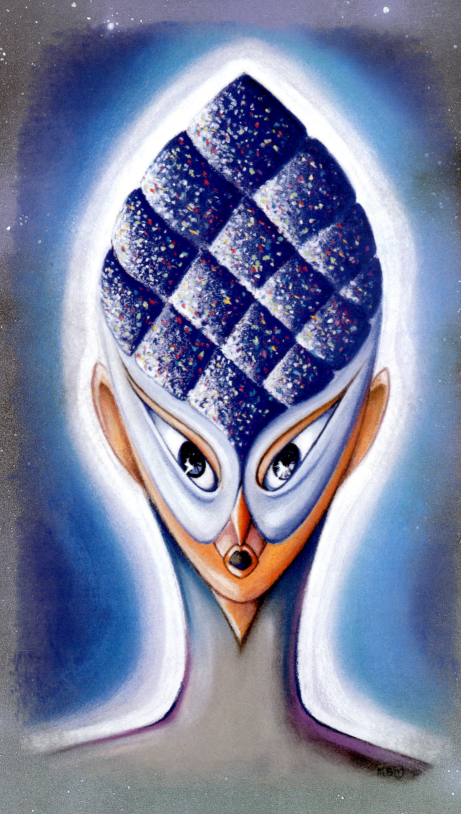

ELECTRIC EEL

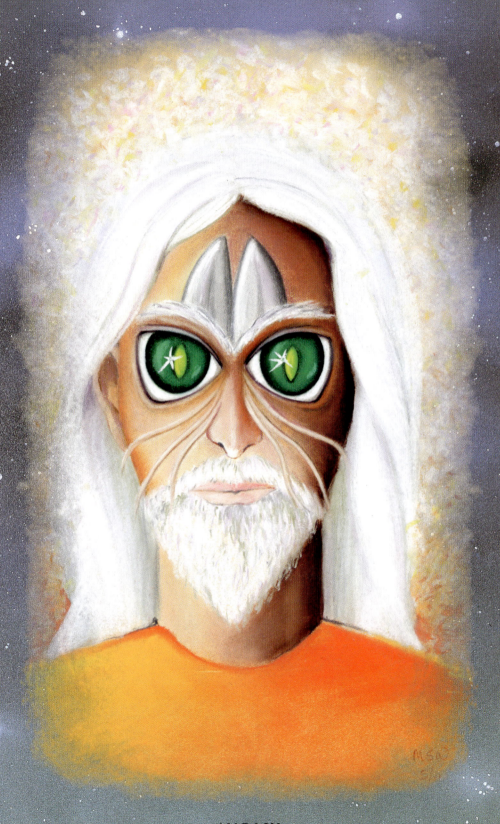

NADASH

SHULAZ

YORU-YORU

HAMAAZ

FLAMES

BYO-YUU

LOU-E-AH-NANA

BLUE THUNDER

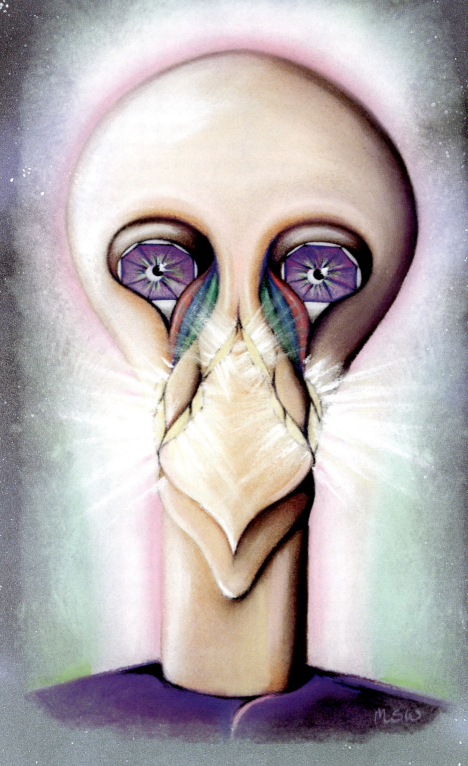

ANADRA

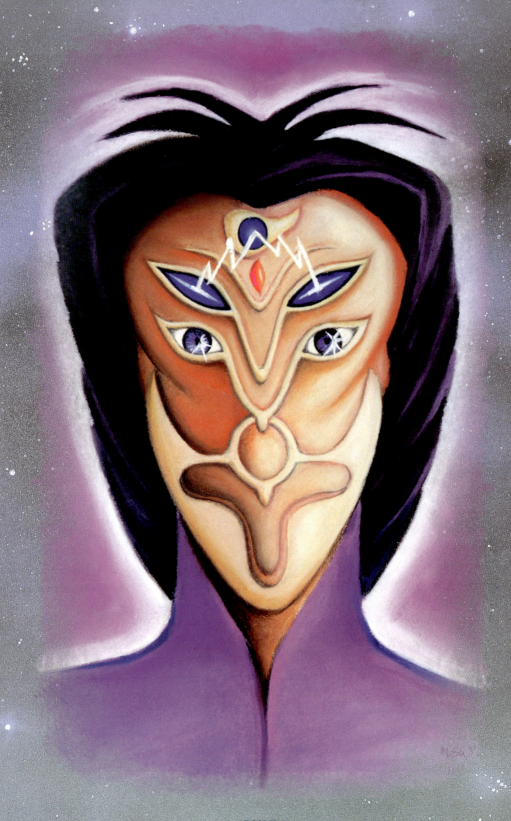

RUUL

A-MEE-AL

SOUL

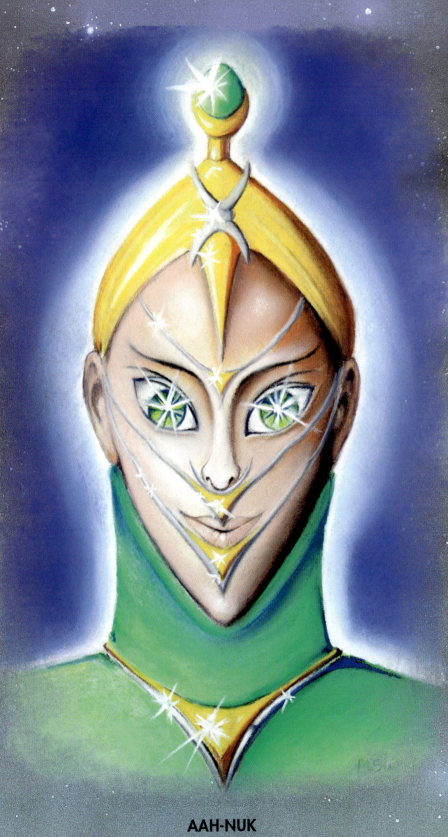
AAH-NUK

SHAFUNA

TIBETAN EGGS

MAYTA

ARRION

ELIOSATH

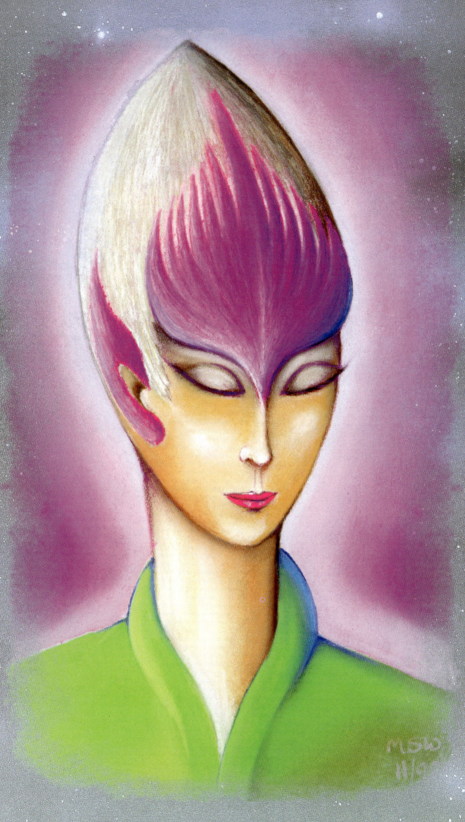

JUULES

RAY-SHUU

LIZARDMAN

SHI-SHAA

AAHOOOMM

AAHOOOMM MASKED

AURORA

FIRST PSYCHIC PORTRAIT, MAY 1990

EARLY ATTEMPT AT PSYCHIC ART

HOW MONICA SEES OUTLINE PROJECTED ON THE PAGE

ANOTHER EXAMPLE OF PROJECTED OUTLINE

WORKING OUT THE DETAILS

ONE

ELECTRIC EEL

oceanic brethren

I'M SITTING IN THE LIVING room in my usual position next to Gary and wham, I'm underwater, swim-walking along the ocean floor. The shift is dramatic and I find myself temporarily overwhelmed. Shortly after regaining my composure, I come upon a huge rock barrier blocking my advance. Brownish areas somewhat camouflage an underlying grey rock material in the wall. Faces and figures are appearing then submerging back in the brownish rocks—in and out, in and out they move. It's a bit eerie, perhaps something akin to viewing an animated exercise like "find the ten creatures hiding in this painting." But in this case, I'm uncertain as to whether or not I want to find them. What are they doing down here? Entire beings seem to reside in this brownish zone as though they were carved right into the rock. As I watch for a moment, it appears they are breathing, wholly unified as a living element within the rock, yet individualized. Extremely human, they seem like ancient ancestors, stationed eons ago to keep vigil over our oceans—Neptune's eternal sentries.

Proceeding up to the wall, my body effortlessly slips right into it—I'm amazed. No longer underwater, I'm standing on a small ledge looking down into a cavernous room. The walls are bright red/orange with intermittent flows of bluish-green metallic rock shimmering as it emits dazzling glints of light. At the floor of the cave a group of beings sits around a large circular table. The table is roughly hewn from slate rock, designed to accentuate its unusual central feature of polished clear glass. I peer into it and immediately I'm swept away to distant oceans with colorful, unfamiliar varieties of fish and coral. Intuitively, I understand the table is a window into another dimension of the Earth's oceans. This is so fascinating—entire worlds are in full motion, seemingly just a magnifying glass away. I wonder where these water worlds are actually located—are we somehow related? Now I get my first good look at the beings around the table. They are clothed in sharkskin bodysuits. The older members of the circle don watery, shimmering capes, draping around their svelte bodies. Each have mysterious pinecone-like skulls—rippling, vibrant, aquatic finials. Even though they exist in a different dimension of our oceans, it is clear they are symbiotically connected to our oceans in some unknown fashion. We are linked and exist to support each other, like sister cities located in different time zones. In staying with this thought, I sense that one of their missions is to heal and purify our oceans. As supportive siblings, they act as a filtering system buffering us from even greater pollution than we already endure.

The circle of beings is focused; all their energy and power are being directed through the center of the table into the oceans. I watch as they diligently apply their powers to the task of healing our oceans. The love and devotion flowing from them is overwhelming. I hear faint words somewhere in my mind, which become louder and more distinct—an elder is transmitting to me a message. He is relating that many of the younger members of their world are extremely discouraged. Earth's oceans are so contaminated with impurities! They work to purify—we immediately pollute, nullifying their earnest gains. Purify-pollute, purify-pollute has become an endless cycle, and the younger generation is dispirited. It has become a challenging task for the elders to keep the younger ones encouraged.

The elder says, "Even though it seems we exist in a dimension far away, we are actually situated very close to each other! So close that crisis situations in your dimension affect the environment in our dimension. This is why the young ones are so discouraged. We have been transmitting thought forms to your dimension for a long while. Some appear to be getting the message, taking up the banner to protect the oceans, but that effort is not nearly enough. We would like more education about the negativity of pollution, both how it affects your physical dimension and ours, trans-dimensionally. The rippling of unconscious actions has drastic ramifications in both domains. Negativity begets negativity. Your waters are destroyed—all the living creatures and plants are poisoned. We fail to comprehend your lack of concern and your negligence, especially since our welfare is so vitally interlinked. Our focus is to love our environment, respect our living forms, and to become one with our environment. As our task becomes more daunting, we find it more and more arduous to rally our spirits to perform the healing work your dimension so desperately needs.

"In our dimension, all the fish and plant forms of the sea are so charged with energy and light that they possess healing properties. This was once true for the Earth as well, but due to the immense pollution, these properties no longer exist, or at best, exhibit only faint shadows of their potential."

He's projecting to me a fish gliding through clear, pure, sparkling water. The water is pristine and magical, engendering exquisite crystalline beauty—a phenomenon no longer existing on Earth. The beings pump their love into the waters; the living creatures receive so much love and light they radiate a myriad of colors. The waters are so pure, all the coral and seaweeds glow with radiance and energy. For contrast, the elder now shows me the waters of our dimension. I immediately feel embarrassed and humiliated, the contrast is so hideous. Our waters are murky and clouded. The seaweed and coral lie lifeless. The fish are all poisoned. Such a sadness overtakes me. I feel his profound grief and sadness, and I weep. Our arrogance knows no bounds—such confusion! At this moment I feel implicated—a party to this outrageous transgression perpetrated on Nature and the innocent inhabitants of other dimensions. I am shamed, not knowing what to do! In his benevolence the elder wants so desperately to show me the beauty of their waters, to impress upon me the sanctity they ascribe to the living waters and the aquatic creatures. Their water has so much energy that when they swim, they experience the bliss and love of the waters moving through their beings. It appears to be both an internal and external experience—a mystical rapture—whereas for us, swimming is at best an external phenomenon even in our most beautiful waters. I find myself wanting to experience this most magical exhilaration.

It is easy to recognize that it has taken an enormous effort to keep their water so pristine, mostly because of the close proximity to our dimension. His fears that the younger generations will be affected by our lack of awareness and sensitivity I suspect are well-founded and could lead to a sense of futility and potential abandonment of their environmental vigilance.

Again he speaks, longingly.

"I hope the book you are working on fosters a deeper awareness and respect of the oceans, rivers, and all living things. Enjoy the waters and all the beautiful things under the water. We are doing all we can to preserve them, but we need your help—we can't do it alone! Your children love the life underwater; bring the beauty to them, so later they will work to preserve it." He projects a picture of my parents' fish tank: one image when it is clean and clear, another when it's dirty and murky. When the aquarium is clean, my little nephew is very attracted, getting quite excited as he watches the fascinating colors and movements of the fish and underwater plants. But when it's dirty, he finds other activities of interest.

Now the elder shows me a scene from the bottom of our ocean. Enormous craters have been blasted into the ocean floor. Charred coral and rocks encrust the battered bottom of the sea, hinting at a deadly nuclear explosion. Dead fish and broken coral formations are strewn helter-skelter in the devastating upheaval. Much is simply pulverized into black powder; the seaweeds are shredded and ashen, lying in heaps like an oceanic holocaust. The water here is so strange and eerie, the feelings are indescribable—a feeling you might have after not eating for two or three weeks, utterly hollow and profoundly empty.

"This is the damage from an atomic detonation," he says frankly. "The visual havoc and life annihilation are all too obvious, but the dimensional ramifications rippling out are equally severe. The scientists and governments refuse to see, taking no responsibility for their actions, remaining aloof and separate from the interconnectivity of life. Their selective perception is strictly based on self-interest and the belief that dominance is the best solution to life preservation and extension. We ask them to reflect on the costs! We are linked to your oceans, and any time you violate the sacredness of life, we all pay a dear price. We urge you to realize that you are not isolated, but connected to all life. Dimension after dimension, we are all intermingled and interdependent upon each other for the expression and existence of life. Please see and appreciate our plea; without exception, we are all inextricably dependent upon each other! Look to the benefits of this blessing, rather than to your insecurities."

I am back in the cave, attempting to understand who has been guiding me through this unpleasant, shameful experience. I want to deepen my relationship with this candid being and explore some solutions. Playing a part in the events he has portrayed has my heart feeling extremely unsettled. First, I request his name. He presents me a symbolic image of his nature. It's a picture of a gigantic electric eel. As he swims through the waters, the electricity moves through his body out into the water, brightening and purifying it. A scent emanates from him, leaving a trail of his sweetness permeating the waters. Each being of their dimension has a specific mission—this presented scenario captures the essence of his mission and represents his name. His life expression is to purify and clean the waters, educating and organizing his peoples with love and grace. In each case, as the beings of this dimension move through their activities, they enhance their surroundings rather than mindlessly contribute to the decline of the environment to which their welfare is so undeniably tied. I can't help but wonder when we will begin to live in this manner, a way of living that appears only too obvious.

The elder invites me to join them in a session around their intriguing table. I am excited and sense that he is responding to my inner frustration—my wanting to feel a part of our oceans' transformation. He invites Gary as well and suggests that by our visualizing Gary at the table with the others, he will be able to participate. I'm on his right and I visualize Gary on his left. We hold hands with all his companions. I am so pleased, feeling we are contributing—working to rectify our ignorance!

He instructs, "Visualize all the power and positive thoughts you can gather—as you formulate and gather, aggregate the building power. Then release it through the glass in the center of the table, out into the waters. Keep doing this over and over, releasing all the power you can possibly imagine—again and again! Visualize this power moving from us, into the waters, transforming and energizing all the living things to life once again! Now gather all the love you possess, keep aggregating and aggregating all you have and then release it into the glass, visualizing all our love filling the waters."

I feel a buzzing energy coming from him, so powerful—our hands are shaking! I look up at the others; we're all radiating such love. The energy moves from being to being, generating great momentum. We are as one vessel, pumping out our love in unison. It is so beautiful and enlivening! I feel refreshingly alive, knowing that if we really put our minds, hearts, and spirits together, we can accomplish great deeds—reenergizing, reclaiming, and saving our mutual waters.

TWO

NADASH

compassionate commitment through time

GARY HAS THE CASSETTES READY for recording—we're set to go, but today I'm anxious, feeling more on edge than usual. I question to myself whether it's a good day to journey, but then we exchange our usual nods and inward I go.

Images approach, but they present no cohesion or continuity. I struggle to make sense of the influx of imagery, but to no avail. Feeling lost, I reach out to Aurora for help. I'm restless, uneasy—walking here and there inside my mind.

He says emphatically, "Sit down here and meditate. Relax and trust me."

We put our foreheads together and immediately up comes one of the beings looking quite similar to an illustration I did several months ago. Unexpectedly I'm engaged on a planet much like Earth, albeit another dimension. I look to Aurora quizzically with an expression of …"What the heck just happened?"

"I carried you! Usually you project yourself, but there have been times when you've experienced difficulty, so on occasion I've intervened. But once you're there, it's up to you to interact and establish relationship," he exclaims, then vanishes.

Momentarily, a being comes forward introducing himself as Belush, inviting me to follow. His braided hair is quite long and forms two separate groupings at the back of his head. Unlike the braided hair to which we're accustomed, Belush's hair is lashed together with fleshy tentacles that emerge from the side of his nose and wrap around to the back. Each weaving is beautifully adorned with colorful beads threaded artistically in and out of the braid. It drapes down his backside. As I casually study him, I'm caught off guard by his powerful green-eyed gaze, and I fall quickly into the mysterious deep regions of his eyes. Stunned somewhat, I recompose myself. I intuit that these beings have evolved mesmerizing powers, but in earlier times their powers were often misused. Today they only use their power to assist others in healing. Belush confirms my intuition while we walk aimlessly through the streets.

"I see my eyes have affected you," Belush comments. "At one point in our history we abused our hypnotic gifts, but now we employ them to alleviate the pain of others. By the hypnotic suggestion transmitted through our eyes, we relieve psychological and physiological pain. But because we all have this ability to one degree or another, our innate nature can unconsciously counteract those who are attempting to heal. So some have become specialists, studying and highly developing our gift; perfecting the hypnotic process we call 'HONZIN.' For these practitioners, the laypersons' hypnotic powers are easily overcome."

"That's fascinating." I probe to confirm my understanding, "So you've developed the ability to control the psyche and physiology through invoking trance-like phenomena which alter a patient's mental patterning. This you induce through a process initiated by the eyes."

"Yes, this is essentially true. Once the subject is relaxed, the eyes beam in new attitudinal constellations, transforming the patient's thoughts that are negatively affecting their health. Let's walk this way. I'd like to show you my house—then I have someone special I'd like you to see." Belush obviously has an agenda, so even though I have further questions, I let our topic go for now.

We're off to Belush's, but I'm not focused—I keep wondering who Belush has in mind to visit. Soon we arrive at his home. It's a humble dome-like adobe structure with some variety of leaves simulating a primitive roof. We walk through a simple wooden door. The contrast is shocking. The interior is fabricated out of a brushed copper material, extremely modern in design, totally catching me off balance. Proceeding on, we descend a flight of stairs. Looking back up, I see a central shaft of open space ascending many floors, culminating in a multi-colored skylight, capping the dome. Suddenly I realize that at least half of the exterior is bermed deceptively below ground level, creating an unsuspected visual paradox once one is inside. A dramatic space results, incorporating an intriguing play of light as it filters down through the colored panes, casting muted hues onto the subterranean interior walls. The entire interior is round, displaying four floors with staggering cantilevered balconies hovering above a first floor. Each contours to the curvature of the building. Functionally, each level is designated for certain activities; the meditation area, which interests me most, occupies the bottom level and acts as a cauldron receiving the in-pouring light. The entire structure is architecturally inventive, presenting numerous surprises—quite an impressive display of architectural genius, given its modest, organic exterior. Once Belush has finished showing me around, he says he'd like to show me the temple, so off we go.

We arrive at a huge building similar in design to Belush's house, which I take to be the temple. The building's glistening dome is completely fabricated out of glass, exhibiting a large central lens that incorporates a multitude of colored glass cells spreading out from the crystalline center. It's absolutely spectacular! As we enter, a huge columnless space captures my attention. It is remarkably engineered, featuring numerous cantilevered levels daringly perched over a center stage.

People are arriving. In a sort of foyer, they shed their shoes, depositing them in neat little compartments opening into the wall. Quickly, the shoes disappear. Immediately another compartment presents itself for the next person. Once the shoes are stored, the people begin to locate their seats for the service.

With everyone busy finding seats, Belush escorts me up to the center stage area. We walk across the stage to a door at the back. I begin to feel nervous, emotions stirring unexpectedly. What's going on? I'm feeling so strange for no apparent reason. I hesitate and balk at passing through the door. I know something I cannot articulate. Prescient feelings torment me, crowding my emotions.

Belush is surprised and turns to me. "What's wrong? It's OK to go in—go ahead, there's nothing to be afraid of!"

I am still reluctant but we enter. Lots of people are milling about—a priest is walking away from us. Belush calls out. The priest turns, and I feel an on-rush of heat and emotion flush my body. A kind of cellular knowing spreads through me like dye filling water. He is so familiar. I'm staggered by my uncontainable emotions. He runs to me, we embrace. Tears pour out, I know not why—I am elated and simultaneously confused. I am aware I have known this being for a long, long time. We are gripping each other's hands tightly, almost afraid to let go, heart pounding, vessels throbbing. Ribbons of thought unwind, unreel—feelings so deep, it's as though an uncharted subterranean current suddenly unleashes, inundating my heart. The priest reaches out, softly touching me on the side of my nose where his cords are located. His look is wistfully distant—perplexing. This encounter is so strange, elusive, like reaching for emotional bubbles that burst and evaporate on sight. I'm straining to contain the event.

Belush says with much delight, "This is Nadash! Nadash requires some time to prepare for the worship which is about to begin, so we mustn't linger, but you'll have time to visit later." I don't want to go—my emotions are pinballing through my psyche, scrambling to understand my rampant feeling! Again I balk at proceeding.

Nadash reassures me, "Don't be disturbed, we will talk later—it's so wonderful to see you!" Then he takes my hands in his and touches them to his forehead, rubbing them over his pointed plates. Again I'm overwhelmed, not comprehending what is taking place. We leave and return to the first level of the temple.

Seated, I fidget with my emotions to such an extent the service blurs into the background. Inexplicable feelings keep racing out of control. I feel so unbalanced—I might have to exit the session. Then a deep resonating gong shifts my consciousness. The sound lifts the hairs on my body to attention, evacuating the constant volleys of invading questions from my mind. Again the gong booms, oozing out from behind the priests. Finally I'm present! I notice blessings being distributed by the priests, splashing holy water here and there over the crowds of people. Gradually I'm settling down, but as I relax my body I start to fade, turning nearly transparent—again my mind races. Belush senses my dilemma and takes my hand. His contact is soothing and it comforts me. Eventually I ground myself, becoming solid again.

The service proceeds with beautiful singing accompanied by a kind of tribal drumming sound. Someone brings out a huge tube, similar to the Aborigines' didgeridoo, but at least four times longer. The musician sends out blasts of energy, then begins jamming rhythmically with the drums. The people rise. They are about to dance, and to my amazement the chairs just silently disappear into the floor. Taking to the floor, the worshippers move exuberantly to the lively music, thoroughly enjoying themselves. Belush grabs my hand. Awkwardly, I improvise to keep step. Stumbling along I notice warm smiles flying my way from around the temple, making me feel more and more at home. The music builds, working itself into a raucous climax...tapers off, then quietly softens. We slow our action gently down to delicate micromovements, then we're still. The chairs re-emerge, blue-colored lights shine down, complemented by a beautiful voice guiding us into meditation. Then the service is over.

I've completely exhausted my endurance and must exit the session, disintegrating on the spot without warning. I experience a second session approximately two weeks later.

With little effort I find myself sitting before an elaborate wooden table in a dimly lit room, joined by Nadash, his wife, and son. The wood table features an intricately carved geometric maze just beneath a glass surface. It's quite unusual—light mysteriously emanates from the deep grooves of the maze into the room. It appears my fascination is obvious. Nadash notices my distraction and explains, "The table was designed for meditation, and our family regularly meditates around it. Perhaps you can experience its unique properties, but I have much to show you so we'll see if time permits."

I can't seem to focus—again it takes me a while to get my bearings and to stabilize my vibration in the dimension. I think it is the level of emotions, which are running higher than usual. Slowly, I begin to consciously adjust to the new reality. Once this occurs I feel extremely comfortable with Nadash's family, genuinely experiencing an easy rapport. But as we exchange pleasantries, anticipation begins to creep in—I feel the suspense and mystery of our relationship pressing upon me. But Nadash appears in no hurry to reveal his secrets, and we launch into a discussion regarding an art object hanging on the wall.

At Nadash's request, his son retrieves a six-foot wooden surfboard-like sculpture from the wall. He hands it to Nadash. Nadash smiles fondly at me and says, "Since you're presently working with healing during your incarnation on Earth, I want to demonstrate a healing technique we use. Those of us who are adept at healing, such as myself, don't need this instrument to administer healing, but it is a common instrument that many use—especially those just beginning in the healing arts."

Nadash motions his son to lie on the floor, then he grabs the board by two handles that are positioned about eighteen inches apart. He stations the board horizontally about a foot over his son and begins transmitting tremendous energy into the board, building up the vibration until it reaches a revving pitch. The energy aggregates to such an extent that the surface of the board becomes translucent, glowing pure white. With his eyes closed, Nadash transfers the energy into his son until the boy's entire body is filled with white light. Wow! Nadash's healing power is overwhelming!

Nadash looks up curiously with a twinkle in his eye, saying, "Now it's your turn. I want you to feel the quality of the energy—you'll find it quite stimulating and refreshing."

I assume a prone position on the floor and Nadash pumps his light into the board. Initially the board looks wooden, then a red-orange light appears in the middle of the board, gradually growing until the board becomes so bright I can no longer look. The energy is so intense that the board is actually humming. The soothing hum that emanates slowly moves through my body. My head seems to get bigger and bigger, expanding my consciousness. I feel so light I can't believe it. Suddenly I'm levitating, gently rising— seemingly on a soft cushion of air. It's amazing. Then Nadash retracts the energy, easing me back down. I feel so clear and clean.

"Many people transfer some of their energy into the board when they are vibrantly healthy," he begins explaining. "The board has properties that can store this energy, then release it later. So if we're sick or a bit exhausted, the board is placed into a slot within the framework of our bed; the stored energy then releases into the body as we sleep, refreshing and recharging all the cells back to vigor and health."

Nadash now beckons me to follow. We exit the living quarters, walking out to the backyard. A beautiful garden greets us, lush with beds of gay flowers and healing herbs, creating a charming enclosure. This is not a typical garden. It is obviously cared for by a special hand, the hand of a man who communes easily with the devic realms. Sprites and faeries flit and twirl about leisurely at play. While we're walking Nadash affectionately guides me over towards a pond to the rear of the gardens.

Sitting next to the pond, Nadash's demeanor turns melancholy—he points towards the water. "Look into the pond and gaze at our reflections," he calmly directs.

Peering into the pond, I see Nadash as though he were only thirty years old, much younger than he is today. His hair is dark and thick, his third eye shield whitish and somewhat translucent. But what is really odd is that in the reflection I am only five to six years old, no longer looking anything like my present self! I appear as a young girl displaying the features characteristic of Nadash's species! I look up astonished, with a baffled expression, searching Nadash for answers. Nadash begins to speak in a compassionate, deliberate manner.

"You see, you are very dear to me! Our meeting means so very much! A long, long time ago, you were the daughter of my sister, who was my closest sibling. Both she and your father died quite young of a disease we couldn't cure. Because I was so close to your mother and having had no children of my own, I took you in, becoming your adopted father. I can remember lovingly rubbing my herbs on your third eye shield, fostering your clairvoyance when you were just a pup. We were so fond of each other. Oh, I loved you so—we had such fun together playing silly games! I became so worried that you would contract the dreaded disease that took your parents' lives, I worked night and day consumed with finding a cure—but ultimately, without success. You eventually contracted the disease and died in your late teens. I was grievously crestfallen."

Suddenly I flashed on our first meeting—all of Nadash's actions became so clear. That's why he touched the side of my nose and fondly rubbed my forehead; it's where my tentacles and plates were once attached. Emotions rush in, flooding my being. I just seem to have no control. Now I know why I had the premonition—I so loved this most unusual being. Tears well up and stream forth. Sobbing, I gasp for air, trying to slow my breath to stop my convulsive sobs.

As I catch my composure, my attention shifts back to Nadash as he continues to elaborate.

"I monitored all your food intake, doing endless tests on your physiology for years. You were so good, cooperating as best you could to aid my research. I cared for and nursed you, but it was hopeless. When you died, I made a commitment to find an inoculation before my death, but as I aged it became apparent I was going to fail. I decided to archive all my research and experimentation on herbs in the library, so I could retrieve it upon my next incarnation. In our dimension it's relatively easy for the more advanced among us to remember our past incarnations, so I eventually picked up where I left off when I returned. You know, it took me three lifetimes to finally discover a cure, but in the end I was successful and kept my promise to you! When I finally did, a deep sadness filled me, knowing I had been too late for you. I can't tell you how pleased I am you're doing healing work—it's a great and rewarding work!"

Sitting at the pond, I reflect on all Nadash has said. I'm so emotionally overwhelmed and moved by his deep love and devotion, and happy once again to be face to face with this incredible being. I feel so much love pulsing in my heart and gratitude for our reconnection; yet still many unanswered questions weigh on my mind. Unfortunately, I know it's time to go. We embrace, feeling content, knowing now the connection has been made and it won't be our last opportunity to experience our unusual relationship.

I'm excited about the encounter with Nadash, truly experiencing a genuine affinity, but my mind reels at the thought of possibly galavanting lifetime after lifetime in and out of various dimensions. Could this possibly be true? On one hand, I say why not, but I must admit it just doesn't coincide with my present understanding. So somehow I'm determined to obtain a broader understanding of how the seemingly endless dimensions interact. I figure since Aurora has led me into this confusion, it's up to him to straighten me out!

With these thoughts implanted, I set sail for another session with Aurora immediately. Unexpectedly, Aurora is right there, as if he were wondering when I would be curious enough to ask.

He promptly begins speaking, almost as if he had certain time constraints, wanting to be sure he fulfills his obligations.

"I would explain the dilemma for you in words, but I'm afraid you wouldn't grasp it. You function much better with pictorial analogies, so this is how we'll approach it! Picture a Mobius strip afloat out in space, constantly revolving. We'll call this simply a 'strip' and it will represent one dimension. Do you understand the metaphor?"

"Yes, I do."

"Now there are thousands and thousands of these strips rippling along in space moving like ribbons. Many of these strips are interlinked into chains; at times there may be four or five or even more strips linked together in the chain. If you visually pulled back further in space to observe all the strips linked together, they would appear to form a sphere or a hollow ball configured in space. Now, pulling back even further into space, looking from a wider vantage, there appear innumerable strip-linked balls floating throughout space, when seen together they look like an enormous geodesic sphere."

To assure him that I'm in sync and getting the gist, I interject, "So the strips that are linked to each other are each representing different dimensions whose proximity is relatively close—creating the high possibility that these two interlinked dimensions could experience occasional inter-exchanges."

Aurora nods in acknowledgement. "Yes, but let's zoom in a little closer to one of the strips. As we inspect up close, we notice that some strips occasionally have slits in their sides. If we were to take a rubber band and allow it to represent a strip for a moment, viewing it from its side, we now cut a slit in its side. Here we would have an approximate model with the slit illustrating an entry-portal by which you could slip through into another dimension. So the slit corresponds to the window that would take you from one dimension to the next—it acts as a transitional tunnel zone. This portal opening is the intersection you've been breaching to gain access to the other dimensions. In *Star Trek* vernacular it's the worm hole bridging two separate worlds. Of course, when these strips are in close proximity, it heightens the potential for dimensional shifting. So when two strips are linked, it makes it much easier to enter the interlocking dimensions. At times, some strips even slip through the entry slit in the side of another strip; obviously this creates even greater opportunities."

"I understand your model—it makes perfect sense as an analogy, but is it actually possible for a person to have one lifetime on one strip and then a succeeding lifetime on another?"

Aurora looks at me whimsically. "Let's see if we can stretch our analogy a bit further. Imagine one strip as the dimension we'll call planet Earth. This strip is revolving as it moves through space. When one incarnates he or she enters the dimensional strip at a certain point. One person's incarnation entry point on this strip could intersect Earth in 1995, another's might intersect Earth in 1212. Wherever you enter the strip is where you find yourself in relationship to the relative time on that particular strip. If one remained on the strip from that particular point of entry, time would transpire as a natural progression of the linear/spatial phenomena of that period of history. Now in terms of slipping into another dimension for several lifetimes—yes, it's very possible and happens naturally, quite often!

"Continuing with our visualization, imagine once again a slit in one of the strips. Remember now, another strip representing another dimension can intersect and actually slip through this slit-portal. These two dimensions intersecting at the slit are extremely interwoven and an incarnation entry occurring at this portal junction-point is more than just plausible. This, in fact, is what happened during your lifetime with Nadash! In that incarnation you entered right at a portal in the Earth's strip where Nadash's dimension slips through the slit in the Earth's strip. Shazam, you popped right into Nadash's dimension like an elegant parajumper. Although most of your incarnations have transported you into the chronological time continuum of Earth's historical drama, this particular time you entered Nadash's dimension because of the timing and location of your entry point. This might seem to be somewhat helter-skelter—but ultimately, where you enter is all controlled by the Lords of Karma. Do you understand?"

"I think your analogy is clear. I do understand, but the complexity in terms of the universal implications is a bit overwhelming. The possibilities seem endless! I'll have to spend more time mulling it over! Thanks for presenting the imagery in a way I can interpret rather than confusing me with complex abstractions."

As soon as I finish speaking, Aurora's eyes twinkle and he's gone—quickly hopping off to another dimension, skipping like a rock across a pond, touching down just long enough to bring his message through.

THREE

SHULAZ

mind-meld

I'M SITTING IN MEDITATION, VISUALIZING one of my drawings. Abruptly I find myself occupying a rough chair in some strange room. Then just as abruptly I'm back in the living room. I ricochet back and forth, unable to sustain myself in one location. Soon I find my attention rapidly cruising through clouds and I faintly hear Aurora's voice insisting, "If you want to go somewhere, think of it and focus."

I attempt to focus, but my mind is busy this morning. Wandering thoughts encroach—I try to focus again. Clouds form around me and quickly I'm zipping right along, lights zooming by. The clouds form a tunnel and surround me. I'm moving swiftly, straight through the tunnel. Then I stop. I close my eyes and am quiet—refocusing on the portrait I had visualized earlier. Wham, I'm back at the roughly crafted chair and wooden table; and now there are two strikingly brilliant cat-eyed women staring at me, face to face. Everything seems out of context, but I'm not jolted. The two beings are talking and nodding, seemingly enjoying themselves. My body is seeking solidity and again I hear Aurora being emphatic.

"Focus, focus! Feel the substance of the chair and table, connect emotionally and mentally with the physical!"

The table feels like wood. I sense the many associations I have with wood and I start keying physically into the dimension. I'm sitting on a bench, not a chair. A cool sensation brushes through my hair. The two women touch my hands, each laying both their hands together over one of mine. I'm solid. They smile, continuing to nod back and forth—projecting a sense of knowing. I feel their warmth and excitement over my arrival. But it seems they are not convinced I'm focused in the dimension yet. One puts a small rock into my hand—it's buzzing, vibrating a sensation through my body, around my ears, neck, shoulder, and finally up and down my entire spine. The intensity of the vibration firmly anchors me into my body. Finally, I've fully shifted dimensions.

"Welcome! My name is Shulaz. This is my friend Doopi," Shulaz beams.

Their cheery greeting instantly eases the tensions I'm still experiencing as a result of my rocky arrival—alerting me to my transparent attempt to overlook them. We're in a cave-like room, sitting at a table and bench resembling the rustic, well-worn national park furniture back home—minus the graffiti. The cave's surface is composed of beautiful natural stone with organic flows of silver-metallic material oozing through its grainy content. The metallic material is oxidized, exhibiting greenish patterns prominently etched into the surface. Its greenish color has a variegated patina which is extraordinary—I'm quite taken by its soft, sophisticated beauty. Animal furs are casually scattered around the room, giving the decor a peasant charm and ethnic warmth. The skins simulate our sheep skins, colored white, light brown, red, orange, and blue. Just as I think this, I am quickly impressed by Shulaz—these are not animal skins, but rugs woven from special plants. Amazing! I was easily deceived!

"You have dropped into our meditation cave," Shulaz offers. "This cave belongs to a cluster of five families. We comprise a small community amongst our people. I'm the leader of the group and Doopi is one of my students. We calculate years much differently from you, but if we were to estimate our ages in Earth years, I would be approximately thirty-five and Doopi about twenty-one."

It is obvious Shulaz is attempting to acclimate me and bring me up to speed, but just then I start to fade. Shulaz grabs my hand and motions Doopi to do the same. The contact helps me to solidify. Their actions draw my attention to their unusual fingers, which are similar to the look of their noses. Each finger displays a step-like layering of skin along the length of the finger. Shulaz then presses her thumbs down into my palms, pressing softly into my tissue. An energy begins buzzing around my ears. My heartbeat is pronounced. Shulaz's heart is beating so strong, I'm alarmed—so strong it almost feels like mine. It feels like we're merging into one. Suddenly, the energy is pulled away. Shulaz is noticeably disturbed.

"I'm so excited and eager about your visit I've gotten carried away. I sensed this would be acceptable with you, but it's our way to always ask permission before we enact a mind merge. I was remiss to proceed so quickly and I want to apologize. If we merge our minds, it's a way for you and me to experience what it's like to perceive through the other person's faculties. You will be able to feel my feelings, hear my thoughts, experience life through my sensory perceptions and I will be experiencing through yours. Do you understand the nature of the merge?"

"Yes, I do," I respond.

"Would you like to try this experiment?" she asks with anticipation.

"I think this would be fascinating, sure, I'd love to!"

Shulaz's eyes glitter and shine, "Then we can begin!"

Once again, I feel her energy buzzing, my heart starts slowing, pacing—eventually synchronizing with Shulaz's. Promptly my self-identity fades and merges into Shulaz's. Wow! It's a bit more disorienting than I suspected. I'm alternating back and forth from my personality to hers and I can't seem to anchor into one body. Shulaz is firm and succinct.

"Be patient, gradually let go of your fear, gently release your self-identification and allow my vibration in. You won't be harmed!"

I'm not afraid, so I do as Shulaz instructs. A tingling sensation encircles my skull, and slowly I phase fully into Shulaz's body and personality. I still seem to retain my own consciousness, but now I am perceiving through two distinctly separate fields of awareness, my own and Shulaz's. A rush of images assaults my consciousness. I'm randomly browsing her memory archives, indiscriminantly accessing her past. I can't believe it—it's like I'm resident right within her consciousness. I suppose she's dwelling within mine too—whew, that's a scary thought. Emotions and information just rise up like waves of alien data pouring from my alien mind. First, I gather that her father was the figurehead of a cluster like herself. He trained her and now she has assembled her own cluster. She is very young to be the overseer of a cluster. It's typical to remain single as a leader, and to this point she has no husband or children of her own. She interacts with the people and children of her group much like a mother; each is a special relationship which she nurtures and relishes, always looking out for their best interests. Even though the head of the cluster generally chooses not to marry, Shulaz has chosen a boyfriend, and being somewhat of a rebel like her father, she plans to marry someday—although it's unlikely she will have children. I detect a bit of a rascal—an inner twinkle, quietly proud that she's got the *hutzpah* to follow her heart. Already she's assuming so much responsibility that life is plenty challenging without her own children. She's a strong woman who is spiritually advanced for her age and sets an imposing example of accomplishments for her cluster to emulate. Her personal attributes are many and varied, and it seems her cluster mirrors many of her gifts, much to her delight.

As I register the rapidly flashing imagery, two scenes spring from her memory, the first of which is a cute illustration of her joy of teaching. She often carries the stone that she pushed into my palm. I see her strolling around a classroom fumbling the stone through her hands much like a rosary. A rambunctious child is being mischievous and she is having trouble keeping the child's attention, so she says, "Now watch this stone carefully, don't let it out of your sight!" She tosses the stone high up into the air, and when it comes down she bends back her head and quickly swallows the stone, like some reptilian critter from the rainforest nonchalantly snatching an insect. The child is astonished. She gleams a roguish glance, knowing her beguiling trickery has worked its magic in capturing the child's attention. She is serious about her teaching, but she interjects so much fun and daring into her delivery that everybody feels entertained as they learn.

The other snapshot is an image of free time she's spending alone. She loves to create abstract mosaic pictures of natural scenery. This allows her to sink deep into her creative juices, drifting off into meditative states. The pictures are comprised of thousands of tiny beads all glued together, rendering meticulous works of art. Up close you can't determine what the beads are depicting, but as you step away from the pictures there is a beautiful flow of energy and color, revealing the hint of nature. This activity gives her great pleasure and contentment, and she wishes there was more time for her indulgence.

While the images flash, all the associated feelings, flavors, and desires ebb and flow with each scenario. It's an amazing experience. If this isn't enough, I've become hyper-alert and attuned. My senses are incredibly keen, stretching way beyond my normal comprehension. I'm completely overloaded, feeling like every neuron is spinning cartwheels. Maybe it's what scientists having been talking about when they say we only use 10% of our brain. I feel the other 90% has been activated—turned-on. I have an acute new ability to perceive things unimaginable to my human sensibilities, the nature of which I imagine many Earth animals inherently possess. Not only have my senses been highly attuned, but my consciousness is acutely sharpened as well.

I'm hearing a cacophony of voices circling around my head, and I'm swamped in a confusing whirlwind of noise that immediately inundates me. Quickly I recognize that Shulaz's people communicate with a multitude of beings at once, some incarnate, some carnate. All seem to be vying for attention. It's like a chaotic symphony where each instrument is demanding to be featured. A quick transmission from Shulaz emphasizes one point. If I'm to decipher a single voice out of the crowd, I must focus on one source only, letting the extraneous voices trail off. If not, I will experience a bombardment by the sounding of insistent, persuasive voices.

Shulaz exclaims, "Focus your whole being onto one source, now concentrate! It might seem difficult at first—even though you have become a part of me, it doesn't make it effortless, because you still remain influenced to a small degree by your own personality. This is an ability we've evolved over time, so don't be frustrated if you don't immediately succeed. When we were young it was not so simple, but with practice we've become adept."

I attempt to get the hang of it, but I'm still overwhelmed by the myriad of voices seemingly insistent that I respond. I intuit that it would be good to devise a single approach if I'm going to be successful. I start to focus through my third eye. It is as though the third eye has become a trumpet, reaching out to amplify one voice in the crowd. As I do this, the surrounding voices recede and are gradually reduced to no more than extraneous sound. One voice is now distinct and clear. It's an exquisite woman's voice singing her song.

Shulaz interjects, "You've tuned into one of our ancient languages. The woman is singing a favorite devotional song of ours. How do you like it?"

The woman's trained operatic voice evokes so much emotion I don't require the knowledge of the language to easily grasp the meaning, but the telepathy does make it richer. She is praising her creator, lamenting her longing to feel the exquisite beauty of her creator's love. She sings of being a light, of her desire to unite her light with the great light of the creator; to feel the deep profound compassion of her creator. The song is so heartful—crooning her passionate yearning to infuse herself with light and love, to move towards the exultant light, drenching herself in the blissful intoxication of the vast ocean of the creator's indiscriminate, unfailing love.

I'm deeply feeling her song's soul-wrenching wail, how she so longs to be with her creator—her entire being, right down to the atoms, resonates her song. I've never felt such profound emotions and feelings. Oh, to feel so passionately, what a blessing! Her intoxication enthralls me—I can't help but drift and swoon into her haunting love.

As I stray, my consciousness slouches. Shulaz's body, ever alert, quickly recoils and straightens—bringing me back to focus. Centered and once again in her body, the first awareness confronting me is the acuity of her senses. Her eyes are extraordinary. My vision feels so alive, I possess a power that penetrates right through into the subject's core. As I look out, I intuit that if I focus deliberately on the wall, I'll see right through it. Sure enough! I see the wall, then like a laser I see the meaty cellulose substance of the wall, then I sear right through it, out to the rocky banks and beyond. It's so exhilarating! But I'm not finished. My vision continues racing through the rocks to the distant trees, and through the trees to the mountains miles and miles away. Incredible! Her eyes have x-ray, telephoto capabilities! Exercising my will almost effortlessly, I can see in detail nearly anything my attention desires. As my eyes start to shift back to the room, I feel heat around them and detect their color growing intense, changing to a deep orange. Intuitively I perceive that at night her eyes change to cool colors, but now as I return my vision to the room, my eyes—or should I say Shulaz's eyes—lose intensity, returning to normal once again. What a tremendous gift, but as I imagine these attributes biologically evolving into Earth's cultures, I'm left with the sense that too many have taken Charles Darwin's survival of the fittest hypothesis to heart. Such a gift would merely provide another way for some to dominate. It saddens me momentarily, but I know we're evolving and this will just take time.

"Long ago we didn't possess this quality," Shulaz explains, "But as our race evolved, we gradually acquired this attribute and now it lies latent within our gene pool. All anyone has to do is practice. Some are born with this ability, others like Doopi can develop it with some diligence. You don't think you have this ability, but you too can develop this talent, especially since you've experienced it through me. As you evolve morally on Earth, someday your peoples will possess this gift too."

Unconsciously, I look across and see my face smiling back at me. What a shock it is to see Shulaz looking out from my guise. I'm completely startled! I hadn't looked at my body until just now; it's so weird seeing someone else smiling at you from your own face. Through my body Shulaz is touching my hand. Strange, it's just strange, I can't get over it! She is focusing all her energy through my middle finger into her hand which I'm housing. I'm feeling a strong sensation through her hand.

She exclaims, "I want to demonstrate how we do healing. You can experience it through my body, which will give you an opportunity to feel the effects with heightened sensitivities. To accomplish healing we focus our entire being like a laser beam through one point of our body, such as a finger. When I say entire being, I mean all levels of our being, not just the physical, mental, and emotional aspects of our being; but all of our spiritual bodies as well! In this way the person receiving healing gets the full impact of our healing capabilities, creating the greatest opportunity for healing to occur."

I'm impressed with the power. Her ability to localize her energies in one spot is uncanny. Unmistakably, I feel an alignment throughout her consciousness, the focusing of what appears to be all her bodies of attention. Then healing light and intense heat physically energize my entire hand. If only I had the skill to magnify my focus like this, bringing all my levels of consciousness to bear on one single task. It seems obvious that anything would be possible.

When I withdraw my attention from my hand, the keenness of her senses fills my awareness and again overwhelms me. My usual consciousness is numb by comparison. Her senses are so sharp. I can easily detect when someone is about to enter the room long before they reach the room. She is completely anchored in her senses, readily picking up the slightest physical stimulus far beyond my usual band of awareness, and yet able to remain spiritually centered. It is a wonderful aliveness, such a multi-faceted attention. I have to admit I'm surprised at Shulaz's highly developed spiritual awareness, given she is so grounded in her senses. This seemingly disparate blending of spirit and body really opens my eyes. Previously, I suspected this capability would be impossible, with physical sensation being an insurmountable distraction to developing one's spiritual awareness. I see I was mistaken.

Shulaz breaks into my thought.

"I would like to give you something physical to take back, but the best I can do is to give you the gift of merging. You can see that you can be much more adept physically than you are! You can be both physical and spiritual simultaneously. Being physical doesn't jeopardize one's ability to experience the nature of the other, more subtle spiritual bodies. Desires don't necessarily run amok just because you are temporarily channeled through your physical body. They don't need to be avoided to advance spiritually. They can be channeled for good and enhance the experiences of the entire spectrum of being. You are encased in a physical body for a reason—enjoy it! Fully embody it, so you can learn to develop mastery of the physical realms of life. Don't be too quick to float off, not appreciating the tremendous attributes of the physical body. You as a race have just begun to develop the potentials of the physical body. Allow yourself to explore your senses at a deeper level and your highly focused attention will greatly expand the capabilities of the human body. You don't have to focus on it if you don't want to, but wouldn't it be good to experience the unique qualities of both worlds? Imbue the physical with the spiritual and the spiritual with the physical, allow their essences to intermingle.

It's similar to what you've been experiencing with the merging of our two beings!"

I now hear the buzzing back in my ears—I'm back in my own body. I look over and see that both Shulaz and Doopi have huge smiles spread across their faces, quite pleased with how our encounter transpired. Shulaz knows it's time for me to go and she exclaims, "I'm so happy you gave me permission to merge with you. I learned a lot, and from seeing your expression several times I know you did as well! You've been traveling—haven't you!"

I am fading fast. Doopi is touching my hand, insisting, "Next time we can merge," she spouts.

Our eyes lovingly connect one last time, then I'm gone.

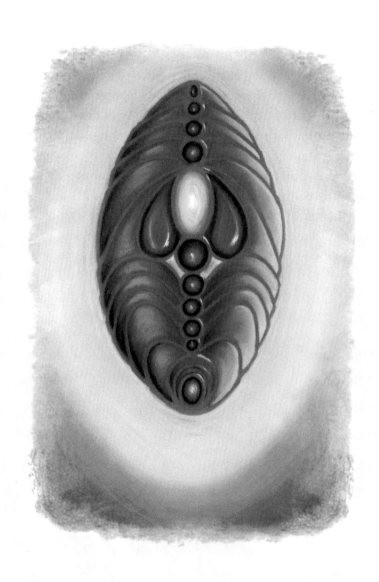

FOUR

YORU-YORU
healing cocoons

AGAIN, GARY AND I ARE SITTING side by side like two pilots ready for take-off, but we have no checklist to execute and the destination remains unknown. One glance at Gary and I'm gone.

Aurora is immediately here, guiding me towards a blinding light. It's flashing—flashing—flashing out towards me. I feel it touch my body; its brilliance envelops me. Lyrical cooing sounds waft out of the white light—I search, but I can't determine the source as of yet. Then the sounds seem to melt into the bright, bright light. Shortly I begin detecting a group of egg-shaped beings. They're suspended in mid-air, bobbing in a semi-circle configuration, shooting out light in my direction. It appears there's a welcoming contingency at hand, poised just for my arrival on blasts of white light. I feel like an ambassador arriving in a foreign land with an unexpected fanfare. Their unbridled chortling expresses their delight, making me feel at ease and planting warm goose bumps all over.

Looking about, I notice thousands upon thousands of these egg-shaped beings drifting in flotillas out in space and all around me. They are primarily indigo in color, but each emanates a slightly different color cast. I sense somewhat of, shall we say, a "let's-get-to-work" attitude—giving their presence a busy, industrious vibration. With such a reception, I recognize clearly they've been waiting for me, and immediately I know they feel my presence as a telepathic acknowledgment is imprinted on my mind. They are bubbly and happy I'm here to join them on one of their treks. I feel their love filling my heart chakra, then expanding throughout my being. First one sends its love, then another, still another and another, until each has transmitted its love. This chain-linked love ripples through me, proceeding from each one separately, yet it feels as though the love emanates from a single source—the feeling is overwhelming. I sense they're connected; they are all linked to some kind of unifying energy source, but I'm not sure what.

As we prepare to depart together, I notice some trepidation creeping into my emotional body. Everything feels so alien and bizarre. Telepathically they signal an assurance that the journey will be safe—not to be concerned. I'll be in good hands. I suppose that's what's bothering me—they have no hands. I notice my fear is a bit out of control with no real evidence to back it up, other than their unfamiliarity. I know their love is real, so I suspend my distrust and off we go!

On my left I feel a nudge. One of the indigo cocoons whose touch is surprisingly physical is guiding me along—supplying a source of comfort and attention. The cocoon's touch has a softness upon my skin, sending slight tingling sensations throughout my body. Although no smile is noticeable, I can sense its entire being smiling, feeling very excited that we're journeying together. Way off into the distance an aperture of bright light shines through to our location. We move through quadrants of blue space in the direction of the aperture. The opening comes quickly upon us, light glaring blindingly as we approach. The cocoons are flying just above me, forming makeshift visors to shield my eyes from the blinding brilliance. Right into the nucleus of the light we go, exploding into rays of purple, pink, yellow—WOW! Then we burst through the opening; daylight appears in a glorious land of lush trees, bushes, and flowers. It almost looks like Mt. Shasta, where Gary and I hiked and camped a few summers ago. After my eyes adjust to the glare, I survey the terrain. There are familiar landmarks—I know for sure we have somehow emerged from the other dimension into the Earthscape of Mt. Shasta—present time! But how can this be? I have no immediate answers and I'm completely disoriented!

My mind wanders back to last summer's trip to the Shasta area, where we had an interesting experience around a specific area referred to as "The Gate" by the locals. I had taken a moment to experience this particular area on an etheric level. As I did, fleets of flying saucers sped through the skyscape and disappeared into a mountainous cliff. As I followed, I found myself in the midst of a huge healing cave inside the mountain. Here I witnessed space beings administering healing treatments to numerous patients in different brightly colored rooms throughout the cave. It was an unusual experience, and I have wondered about it ever since. As these thoughts reemerge in my mind, the cocoons telepathically transmit information concerning this experience. They relate that what I perceived transpired long ago in the etheric realms of the mountain; I picked up the past etheric vibration when I psychically tuned into the physical landscape. How fascinating! It appears ancient etheric events are encapsulated in the physical matter that is in the closest proximity to the etheric plane. Then eons later the event may be retrieved psychically by a casual passerby. This is amazing—the entire Earth's history must be lodged in its molecular form, archived in the rock formations of the planet. It seems even the etheric history is somehow recorded into the physical matter.

Looking around, I see Panther and Squaw meadows in full bloom—it's Shasta at its best. Our past summer's vivid experiences begin to intermingle with present time; I become jostled and have to pause to refocus. It's a curious layering of present and past, a sort of dimensional sandwiching that becomes quite confusing. In refocusing, the immediate inter-dimensional experience of present time reappears and I carry on. I wonder as I see others walking about if they can see me; but then I realize I'm traveling in another dimension. I can see them but they can't see me. How strange!

My traveling partners are starting to fade into the light, their chrysalis forms barely apparent. They're sucked towards a dark hole off in the distant light. I too am drawn faster and faster towards the dark opening in the light. The pace is extremely rapid as we fly like tiny filings caught up in a magnetic current, frantically scurrying towards the central source. It's dark and paradoxically also light. We have been whooshed within the bowels of a mammoth creature so huge that it appears we've been propelled to the shores of a distant galaxy. But we are actually drifting within the inner sanctums of a mother cocoon! So this is the connecting force, the energy force that links and bonds them all together. Deep resonant sounds echo through the cavity, reverberating and soothing me like an exquisite Gregorian lullaby.

The cocoons with which I'm trekking float way back into the distant hollows of the mother being. The walls are immense, composed of translucent tissue, laced with red and blue vascular ribs arching through the translucent cellulose tissue. The little cocoons berth themselves in what appear to be some sort of docking grottos deep within the interior of the mother. I see flashing lights, a buzzing, a warm glow haloing around these little fellows as the mother being re-energizes them. It's a fascinating sight!

As I continue watching, a black liquid seeps and oozes out of their underside into a sac-like membrane. Geez, it's gross! Telepathically I now understand the cocoons are healers—this seepage material is what they've absorbed during the healing process. The sacs detach, then a hole appears in the middle of the mother being and the sacs are jettisoned into outer space. Out in space the sacs are magnetically attracted to each other, merging to form a single ball. A cocoon approaches the membrane sphere and roosts atop it, incubating its contents. As the cocoon pumps its energy into the ball, the liquid is osterized, eventually transforming into a transparent sphere. Soon the cocoon releases the ball—it drifts aimlessly, then explodes, spraying its contents into the far reaches of space. Thus, cleansed and replenished, the cocoons and I take flight; we swarm like bees through the cavernous innards of the mother, swirling upwards through her vast cavity and escaping through the vortex of her luminous third eye—out into space again. Thousands of us emerge in a bustling tornado cloud from the mother hive, all intent with a purposeful mission of which I am still in the dark.

We quickly descend, slipping into another dimension. A planet arises exhibiting an extremely dry, desert-like terrain. We scan the terra firma, hovering in search of a situation that demands healing. After a bit I see a man lying unconscious on the desert floor. From all indications, it appears he has recently been thrown from his horse. He is severely dehydrated and in urgent need of medical attention. The cocoons circle around him, fading like ghostly images, seemingly assessing the situation. I can feel their compassion and tender concern.

I get the impression that something is about to happen, but just what, I'm not sure. It seems to me the patient looks close to expiration and too bulky for the cocoons to heal.

Suddenly one of the cocoons swoops down upon the man, collapsing its body around him by inverting its accordion-like, ribbed body to form an envelope. It's an astonishing feat! The man now rests within the inverted cavity of the cocoon. The cocoon revs up its vibration, turning totally transparent during the healing transmission. Energy is pumping through the cocoon's third eye and its crown, encasing the man in a field of glowing light. The light pours out while the cocoon caressingly rocks the man in gentle loving movements. I am stunned by the intensity of the scene and the one-pointed attention each cocoon directs to the cocoon administering the healing. In the midst of the healing, other cocoons are scouring the landscape for a patch of shade to relocate the man. Eventually, they find some.

But how are the cocoons going to transport this massive body? To my amazement the man is easily levitated by the cocoon and transported to the shady location. Now the cocoon has fulfilled its mission and it's time to move on, but the cocoon is so empathically connected to the man it finds it difficult to release. After a few moments, the others beckon and the cocoon floats upwards, leaving the man unconscious—but now rejuvenated, renewed, and filled with vital sustenance. It's a marvelous sight to watch. The cocoons act completely out of love and dedication. They seek no recognition—in fact, total invisibility is their *modus operandi*. Healing is their purpose and their way of being and there's no pomp, just a sense of fulfillment. The cocoon who performed the healing is nearly depleted of its life force and is now en route back to the mother for rejuvenation. It is guided and supported by its fellow companions, who transfer their life energy so their comrade will reach the mother alive.

As I watch the entire operation, I am in awe of the cocoon's willingness to give of its life's energy, even to the point of complete exhaustion and death. Its total commitment to the task of healing is really an inspiration. I am so moved by the cocoons' life expression. They represent an entire life form demonstrating the grace of a St. Teresa of Avila, or Mother Teresa of India. I feel a sense of camaraderie, especially as a fellow healer, but I know my commitment falls way shy of the cocoons'. As I reach out to communicate my love and feelings, the cocoon who initially nudged me at the outset of our journey comes forward. I have felt some of the cocoons' presences during my healing work and now I feel one wants to communicate. My excitement rises, then I hear the telepathic impressions.

"We heal through our love and compassion. To love is to heal! To heal is to love! Love one another, support one another. Jealousy and envy have no place in your relations with one another, leave them behind. You all have the same ability to express divine intelligence. Allow it, encourage it, express it, and support it! TEAMWORK is our way and our message! Work endlessly to serve and bond with all of humanity. We have come to you many times during your work as a healer—you have attuned correctly to our vibration and presence during those particular sessions."

When one is totally devoted and focused on one aspect of life with one's total being, it is interesting how simple and precise one's understanding is. There is no confusion about one's truth. One just lives it moment to moment. I strain to think of some questions, but there really aren't any and I'm not inclined to ask for the sake of asking. So I simply inquire, "What do you call yourself?"

"We have no complicated names as you do. We each emit a musical sound and are known by it. Mine is YORU-YORU! Each of us has a slightly different variation on this basic sound. We shall see you again at one of your healing sessions. Good-bye till then."

True to the cocoon's nature, its message is brief—others are in need and the cocoon is quick to depart in search of its next mission.

FIVE

HAMAAZ

3-D thought creations

I'M IN A SPACE LIKE NO other I've visited. Everywhere I look are facets of varying shades of green crystal sheets, angling sharply around me. The space feels like a building, but because of the way it is formed I can't determine what is open space and what's solid crystal. If one imagines a crystal matrix as vast as the Earth, it's as though I'm walking through individual hollow crystal points — bound on all sides by translucent faceted sheets of green crystal, all lying within the confines of this intricate, planetary matrix. The space is bizarre, completely disorienting. When I reach out to touch a facet, sometimes it's there, sometimes it's not. I'm feeling lost in a perplexing, abstract, green-glassed arboretum — gorgeous, yet intimidating. At times the space appears to open up into a towering three-to four-story vaulted room, then within moments I'm cramped, nearly claustrophobic — mesmerized in a house of converging green glass mirrors.

While I'm pondering my dilemma, a green crystal being appears unexpectedly right next to me. He is anywhere from six and a half to seven feet tall, and if not a cyborg, I'd hypothesize a close cousin. I'm startled. He is scary-looking and from my quick scan devoid of any emotions I'm accustomed to — maybe even menacing. He gestures me to follow. I hesitate, then I think of Aurora and release my fear, following without trepidation. The cyborg guides me in and out of empty rooms, each fabricated from the green faceted crystal. My mind is experiencing unusual feelings and thoughts as we proceed. In some rooms, I experience absolutely no mind. I am blank, my mind feels squeaky clean, fresh and clear; my being is generating nary a thought—amazing, no thoughts! I find myself grappling to feel; my ability to experience appears nearly lost. But it's so effortless to just float, not feeling or seemingly even being.

While walking through the different spaces I gradually become more at ease and begin to notice subtle emotions that I hadn't perceived before. The normal self-chatter is gone, but a kind of personal smorgasbord of feelings arises. Each space engenders different responses. Then I hear him transmit. His communication is sterile; I sense he has eliminated all need to invent personal coloration for ego fulfillment. He says, "Each person experiences a space somewhat differently, based on who they are. An experience of a space could alter from day to day, depending on one's mood and how one interprets or characterizes themselves that day. In other words, some of the spaces are direct experiences of one's state of being at any given moment."

This strikes me as rather unsettling and possibly alarming, but it is admittedly phenomenal feedback, if one is willing to examine impartial reflections on their personal mindstates.

While we walk, thoughts travel back and forth between us effortlessly. We come to a glass wall—I'm looking for a clear passage to circumvent it, when out of the corner of my eye, I see him disappear right into the wall. I stop, wondering if I saw it right. Then shortly he reappears back through the wall, apologizing somewhat mechanically.

"I assumed you would follow and was so surprised when you were no longer with me. I forgot about your limitations at this point of your stay—I neglected to attend to this discernment."

"Don't worry," I remark, "We on Earth forget things like this frequently."

Suddenly I intuit that the entire spatial experience I'm encountering is actually an enormous being which is graciously accommodating us—a single consciousness, housing other intelligences such as myself.

The green being guiding me slows his pace and begins talking.

"I used to be from another dimension and I often traveled here to visit from time to time. Eventually, I found I liked it here and decided to stay; once I made the decision, I was gradually assimilated into the matrix being. But that was long ago. Before I came to this dimension I was flesh and blood, with all the normal organs, arms, and legs and similar appendages as yourself; but as I assimilated, I transformed into the crystallized being you see before you, just like the others. The merging into the walls begins the catalyzation of the body into the crystalline transformation process. Each being's crystalline form conforms along the contours of their past form, which is why I have a head, eyes, arms, and legs."

I think, boy, I better keep my distance from the walls—merging doesn't sound like my idea of an enjoyable Saturday morning. I could just see Gary's expression as he looks over at me when I return from my journey. That would certainly put an end to our little odyssey together! Crystal assimilation? Ugh, no thank you!

My imagination is rambling. I inquire, "If an egg-being assimilates, would its essential form still be egg-shaped, and what about me, what would I look like if I decided to stay?"

He explains, "Yes, the egg-shape would become crystalline and you would feature long beautiful crystal hair, a crystallized faceted face, along with appendages resembling an abstract simulation of your present self—crystal-morphed!"

"How long does the assimilation take?"

"It would take a while—it is hard to determine exactly in Earth years, but I would say approximately two to three years."

Whew! I can relax, I'm certainly relieved—I'm not in jeopardy of being assimilated after all!

"Is it a painful process?"

"No, not at all—it feels something akin to a focusing process, a clearing; you feel clear and lucid. The sluggishness characteristic of biological aging is gone. Cellular deterioration is erased—deleted from your chromosomal configuration, forever. But the process partially depends on who you are and where you come from; one never totally eradicates their personality. Personal residues still remain after the morphing process is complete. It is astonishingly easy to change in this environment. Remember when you first arrived in the empty room, you experienced just being; you had no thoughts and harbored no feelings. The crystal matrix fosters these types of experiences."

We continue walking through room after room. Nobody's in sight—I see different shapes, all made of the green crystal. Then, several beings pass, walking into the walls, disappearing like a wave into the ocean.

Suddenly there's a tear in the structure of the dimension, a sort of ripping through to another space—I'm seeing lightning strike in another dimension, one of the dimensions I visited some time ago. I don't understand why, but it's clear; I must be distracted and need to refocus.

Within moments I'm back in a huge room. The ceiling rises in shafts of green, glassy reflections, four stories high. In the center of the room is a round fountain. The base is crystalline, quite short in stature compared to the room; water is gently spouting forth, splashing over the base. I see many crystal beings milling around the fountain, a hodge-podge of varying sizes and shapes of translucent igneous creatures—moving like an animated Swarovski exhibition. Strange! Then several normal, organic humans capture my attention—they're walking as companions with the crystal people. Possibly they're travelers like myself. One is a woman with brown hair and a flowing long dress. We catch each other's eyes, signaling recognition. We exchange taciturn amusement—an unspoken acknowledgement of the fact that we're both dimensional shifters, coincidentally happening into the same space and time. I don't have time to analyze the surrealistic complications, but in a flash, I comprehend that I may recognize her one day on Earth. I sense she has the exact same thought. We pass like reflections, refracting through a crystalline labyrinth of time. After we pass, synchronistically we turn back for a final glance, as if to be sure we've indelibly registered each other into our cellular memories for that day, in the distant future, when space and time will once again collide and we'll relive this most bizarre, fractured moment. When I turn back, the entire room has disappeared. It's not large anymore and there's a huge wall right behind me where the woman was just walking. I'm miffed; everything appears scrambled and disjointed. I ask my acquaintance, "Where's the room I was just in?"

He responds matter of factly, "The rooms keep changing—haven't you noticed? Each room is created by thoughts. It could be your thought or several beings' thoughts grouped together. They form a sort of aggregate thought manifestation. In your case, it was the combination of your thought and the woman's thought which manifested the room in which you experienced the fountain. Everything you have seen so far is the sole manifestation of various beings' thought processes. When a being's thought is strong, the crystal captures the thought in form. So when someone subsequently passes through the room where the thought was registered, they experience the physical manifestation of the previous being's thoughts. If you travel back to a particular room you have experienced before, your ability to relocate it is dependent on whether that particular person maintained or retracted their thought. If they retracted it, the room has vanished. So when your thoughts are strong, the odds are someone within the crystal will experience your thought. When you release the thought, it's gone. At first, if and when one's thought is powerful, it forms live organic manifestations. Then as the thought-force wanes, the manifestations transform into crystal and eventually disappear. But all thoughts are stored within the crystal matrix somewhere; refocusing on the thought-forms generates the possibility of reaccessing and recreating the thought-creation in the future."

"Is it something like being able to access a past event from the akashic records?" I ask.

"Yes, something along those lines."

My mind is racing. I wonder if I can create something from our world inside the crystal matrix? I'm getting excited, this is really fascinating. I pose a question.

"Let's say I want to recreate the Botanical Gardens from Strawberry Canyon in Berkeley, California. Can I do that?"

He retorts in his usual mechanical way, "Yes, of course you can. Would you like to make an attempt?"

"Sure, I'd love to try!"

I attempt to project a lucid, powerful visualization of the Botanical Gardens; for fun, I decide to add a grand waterfall in between the cactuses, along with wild animals roaming through the gardens. A kind of Jesse Allen, high-chaparral fantasy painting, set into motion right in Berkeley. I close my eyes, feeling a mild sense of overwhelm—I could have chosen something more modest. What hubris! He patiently waits for my cognitive process to gel, then he adds, "Be sure to visualize it strongly, so it's exact; only then will all the details come into crisp manifestation!"

After a period of visual focus, I feel like I've got it.

"I'm ready!" I remark.

"Are you sure? The crystal energy is quite strong, everything you've seen so far was all formed out of crystal, except for the fountain water in the last room."

Impatient for the point, I break into his mechanical monologue, "Yes, I wondered why the water was actually moving and organic."

"When the visualization is powerful and fully formed, you can actually bring into full manifestation the material which you've visualized. Rock can be rock, cement can be cement, and so forth. So be sure your visualization is strong, then you will be surprised at your results. Let's walk some and see what you've created!"

We walk through several rooms, but I don't see anything. I think, shoot—maybe I wasn't able to create a powerful-enough visualization. It was strong, I thought, but now I'm no longer confident I understand the criteria necessary to produce the full manifestation. Inside I feel quite disappointed, uncertain. Boy, my ambition seemed to get the better of me!

"Be patient," he insists. "We'll find it somewhere!"

We're still walking in and out of rooms, seeing what I now assume are others' thought-forms, but no botanical gardens in sight. My success appears remote, so I decide to move on, shifting my focus slightly to engage in some casual conversation. I throw out, "What is your name?"

"I have no particular name since I arrived, but before the assimilation my name was Hamaaz. I was essentially humanoid like yourself, only the structure of my face was somewhat different than Earthlings; that's why my facial faceting is a bit strange and scary to you."

I introduce myself as we continue strolling through the rooms in search of my erstwhile creation.

"I'm Monica."

"Hello, Monica," he politely responds.

Everything is still pure green crystal, some rooms darker than others, but most are repetitively the same. Then my heart skips a beat—I hear water tumbling gently somewhere close by. My hopes rise dramatically. Clearly it sounds like we'll find my creation. Suddenly, presto—there it is! A full three-dimensional, vibrant technicolor manifestation of the Berkeley Botanical Gardens. Wow! Not virtual reality, but actual living plants completely terraced—exactly how I had visualized them! With one exception—all the wild animals are in green crystal. They're spectacular, yet not what I had visualized. I look at Hamaaz. He looks like he's smiling or at least I'm experiencing a sense of his inner smile. It's the first time I've detected any emotion, and I feel a bond beginning to draw us closer. I can tell he's thinking about the crystal animals, just like I am. Suddenly I have an insight; I reason that my fear of the wild animals overrode my ability to powerfully visualize them.

Hamaaz knowingly interjects, "When one is frightened or experiencing a degree of anxiety—inwardly in a state of mental or emotional distraction—it impairs one's cognitive clarity, destroying the ability to lucidly manifest one's visualizations. One's reality is a projection of their degree of lucidity."

Even so, as I look on at my creation, my feeling of accomplishment soars. I feel proud! Like I've just parented a creation. Some of the rocks and other small details remained crystal, but for the most part, everything's endowed with full living color, just like I visualized it, only alive! Even the crystal animals exhibit the breath of life, morphing about like incarnate ice sculptures. I can even smell the roses. Wow! Wow! Wow! This is fantastic! If I could only duplicate this on Earth! As we continue walking through my thought-creation, my mind turns to the element of fear which I was harboring. It seems so obvious to me from this vantage that each time I move through life holding on to fear while I'm in the midst of manifesting my desire, I will be sure to experience some degree of unfulfillment. Why do I fear, what do I fear? What is my distraction? But at this moment it seems to be merely a mild disability. I can only see grandeur.

Eventually my attention is back on the immediate and Hamaaz is talking.

"Most likely others have experienced your creation before we even arrived. Because your desire was so strong and you're still holding the thought powerfully, others will experience it after we leave. Then it will fade to crystal and disappear, eventually being stored away in the archives of the crystal's storage atoms."

I'm absolutely ecstatic—what a rush! This is such a wonderful experience, a clear window into the processes by which objects make their way into the physical universe. I imagine, at some level, all of creation is a demonstration of the power of divine visualization—manifesting through intentional will.

Our walk continues, but I'm aware my time is short. I thank Hamaaz for his patience and for shepherding me through his unique version of Silicon Valley. Then I remember the other crystal being I have drawn, and ask him if he knows of him.

"We are similar in nature, but I'm not aware of him; he must be part of a consciousness in another dimension."

I suppose I'll have to wait to receive any further information. I feel my attention disintegrating. I wedge in a quick goodbye, and whoosh, I melt through the crystal palace walls, returning to my living room.

SIX

FLAMES
pyrotechnic spirits of love

GARY AND I MEET EYES JUST before the session begins. Thoughts and feelings leap between us easily, and I feel the interconnection—I'm so glad he's here and we're experiencing these journeys together! I spout, "See ya," and my focus shifts inwards.

Sitting in silence I feel Aurora's strong presence beside me, a comforting reassurance builds, and I feel protected and safe. A familiar, brilliant white light arises off on the horizon; it flattens like an infinite number of vanishing lines hurtling themselves into the future. Effortlessly, I slip through the eye of the vanishing point like a jet disappearing into the whiteness of beyond. Although this was once a frightening occurrence, this sort of transitional zone is something I now feel rather comfortable with—soaring through the white cracks in space, a feat which often accompanies my journey.

Immediately, gleaming white pinlights dazzle and dart laser-like throughout the deep-blue space. I follow the pinlights back to their source, faintly making out facial features taking shape in patches of color. There are hundreds of these patches of color grouped together in floating colonies of inter-connectivity, all suspended in the richness of a vast indigo galaxy. Peering into the patches I detect that each patch within the separate groupings has a distinct flame-like face. Although comically alien, the faces have a unique individuality beaming out. Yet—it seems without question—each is linked to a group identity with an ultimate interdependence and inter-connectivity. I wonder as I gaze at them: "What's their purpose? Can I dialogue with these unusual beings and create some kind of relationship? What could we possibly have in common?"

Some appear to travel in groups of hundreds, while others move in groups of five to ten—all emitting flashing pinlights from their faces, signaling obvious communication back and forth as they drift their separate ways.

Gracefully they glide through their space, sailing…Then as I watch, the atmospheric background shifts, indigo giving way to green-orange, to bright white, with each flame's intensity paling in the shifting atmosphere. The sheer beauty of their nature is overwhelming. Attuning to their vibration I feel the awe and mystery of galactic light moving through my spirit. Then surprisingly I see flashes. Birthings are transpiring right before my eyes. Infant virgin flames emerge out into the naked night-blue, eyes dazzling all a-twinkle. Only one within the group gives birth and, as fate determines, the new being is an integral part of the grouping, taking its place as a fellow companion within the group consciousness.

There seems to be some commotion. Ah, a celebration breaks loose with each new birth! Hundreds of flame groupings come together with crescendos of flashing lights and sonorous, booming pipe organs. Flames rocket through stars, flickering and bursting gleefully about—just to beat the band; then their colors go, poof! Billows of hazy smoke spark and explode, then they idle admiringly, like spacey toads basking in their bliss. Deep down I feel like an intruder eavesdropping on intimate family affairs. But for some reason it appears they are deliberately revealing this aspect of their existence, providing me with an emotional bond, allowing me a glimpse of familiar emotional terrain which might link our two species.

No sooner have the birthing activities ended than like the touch of a remote control device, the channel switches. Suddenly, pastoral mountains and trees surround the immediate panorama. A lake nestles in the scenic mountain ranges before us, a veritable Lake Tahoe postcard. The day eclipses into dusk, into nighttime—the flame beings colorfully decorate the sky, diving in huge connected groupings straight down into the placid lake. They dive deep into the cool pristine waters, playing and frolicking together like mischievous comets, under the lake's surface. The whole event appears a bit ironic: the flames descend, *kama-kazi* style, submersing their inflamed bodies into their dreaded archrivals—water—but indeed, this is the scene. Surprising as it seems, from here it looks quite natural. When they re-emerge into the night sky it's a spectacular sight! A pyrotechnic frenzy of color and light surges out of the lake like a blazing phoenix taking flight, accompanied by the sound of ten thousand rainsticks, sizzling and tinkling in liquid staccatos. Hydrogen into oxygen—herds of prismatic nebulae steeds, lurching from black holes, ballistic to the stars—outrageous! To me there are events in which words have no place: this most certainly qualifies. Their joy and exhilaration are extraordinary, an orgasmic fireball gone nuclear.

Intuitively, I recognize that most of the time the flames dwell in outer space, but on occasion they swoop down through the trees of planetary forests, communing with the faeries and nature spirits, of similar ilk as themselves. We have once again jumped tracks, whisking and weaving a daring course through the forests. Stardust sprays in our wake as I strain to keep pace while the flame-beings continue showering the forests with their sparkle. Like cosmic crop-dusters they cleanse and purify, driving out the darkness and negativity shadowed within the nature realms. I'm happy to journey at their side, as now I realize their purpose—they're one of the custodians of nature, cleansing the vibrational realms of space, whether it be deep space or the dense, lush forests of planets.

We are off to another scene. In our sight is an enormous, optically clear, crystalline mountain, drifting among resplendent neighbors afloat in vacuous, bright light. The mountain majestically radiates vibrant, scintillating colors. I hear someone communicating, but which of the beings is it? I can't tell. For some reason they wish to remain a mystery. I grasp telepathically that a flame being has died. The grouping in which it symbiotically existed throughout its lifetime now makes the long sojourn carrying their beloved companion to rest. The grouping journeys with a melancholy spirit; emotions run strong and my bond deepens as I too experience their deep, compassionate feelings. Surprisingly, it's all too "human." A sorrow surrounds my heart and pulls at my being, but oddly the closer we move to the crystalline mountain, the more the mood transforms into heartfelt joy. When we reach the mountain they free the being; in a wisp, the flame merges into the mountain with an emphatic burst of colored light. Instantaneously, it dwarfs and dwindles, becoming just another color comprising the vast array of colors dwelling within the crystalline cosmic flame mountain. I feel a release; a calm tranquility courses through the grouping. Again I hear the makings of a voice. I sense a deeper connection—thought forms are arising. Then I hear, "On Earth you have a day called 'All Souls Day,' where you honor the dead. We also have such a day. On this particular day we return to the majestic, cosmic mountain, to the special spot within the mountain where we know our loved one vibrates on. Here we commune with our transfigured beloveds."

As we pay homage, the mountain begins to vibrate, pouring out beautiful Orpheus-like melodies, spreading love and joy throughout the grouping. The encounter is so compassionate, I am amazed at my empathy. I can relate! As I have these thoughts, I'm aware that the dominant orange flame in the grouping has come forward, moving right towards me. Ah, it's the orange flame who has been communicating all along. It's tethered to its group by a long thin thread of light. I sense it wants to communicate further. I'm receiving mental messages in rapid succession. I understand that usually one flame is the spokes-flame for the entire grouping, but other forms of communication also occur. At times each flame within the grouping will articulate one word; a sentence is constructed by each of them separately stringing words together in coherent rhythms of thought, moving from flame to flame to flame. At other times they all speak in unison, synchronizing perfectly, creating a powerful concert of thought and meaning. There is amazing cohesion and unity; yet an evident separate expression of individuality is present throughout the group entity—a wonderful sense of the evolution of the ego, unity through diversity. At this moment though, the orange being is in command and undertaking the role of the featured speaker stepping out from the pack. I feel its presence very strongly and I anticipate a direct and more personal communication. We acknowledge each other; then the flame begins to speak.

"Do you remember a particular evening a few months back, when you were feeling down and extremely tired? You slipped off to sleep quite early that evening. I came and cleansed the negative vibrations weighting down your spirit, filling you with love and light. Do you remember?"

The orange flame is so sweet and innocent of spirit, just how I imagined a nature spirit would be. I'm so delighted it came to me.

"Yes! Sure, I do remember! I was exhausted that evening and as I drifted off I had a vision of an orange flame-like color coming to me as I moved into the astral. I remember being filled with this vibrant, powerful energy. Shortly, I awoke filled with vim and vigor. Amazing! This was you!" Immediately I felt the flame was pleased—I had remembered. To my surprise there arises a sort of continuity to this journey. It actually ties into my past and points to the possibility of an ongoing relationship as well.

"It was indeed me, and we bring you our love once again. We ask you to remember, because this is our essence and purpose. Pure light and love will always cast out negativity. Fill yourself with light and love. When you do this, negativity might hover, but it will never enter. A person who directs negative thoughts towards you can alter your thinking and actions, but if you are full of light and love these negative thoughts will never influence or harm you! There's just no space for them to enter! When you fill yourself, you won't even have room for your own negative thoughts—how powerful this can be!"

The orange flame then adds, "If you use animated, emotional verbalizing of affirmations, it will be an extremely effective force in creating brilliant light and love shining forth from your being. If you do this over an extended period of time it will truly transform the quality of your life."

I am seeing a picture of myself projected by the flame. I'm saying affirmation after affirmation with immense conviction, just radiating pure light.

"It will be valuable to do exercises in the mirror each and every day, affirming and expressing to yourself, 'I am made of light and love, I AM a being of light.' Eventually this will create a similar effect to our shining out, paralleling our pinlights blazing throughout space. Then when your light shines out, it will not only be seen from Earth, but from all over the universe. Your light will attract beings of light from many other planets and dimensions. If you wish to commune with us, just send out your love and we will respond. Presently, you can only see us on the astral plane, but it is possible to enter our dimension physically. Admittedly, at this point of your development it seems rather unlikely. But when you become more adept in the astral, both when asleep and awake, it will certainly be possible to enter our dimension. Tonight we will come to you in the astral planes, so be alert! We bid a warm farewell to you and your beloved. See you tonight!"

(That night Gary was aroused in the middle of the night with a startling presence, so powerful it took on physical qualities to the point he thought I was hovering over him, only to notice it was one of the flames hovering near, sending its love.)

SEVEN

BYO-YUU

sultans of light

I'VE DECIDED TO FOCUS ON one of the drawings to start this session, attempting to master Aurora's unfolding curriculum. As I gaze into the portrait, many past dimensions simultaneously spring up—I see Nadash, Shulaz, and a kaleidoscope of colors. I hear Aurora's voice: "Focus on one place. Just visualize and isolate the original drawing's face."

A tunnel dips down through my vision, like an amusement park spillway.

Aurora insists, "One thought and you'll be there, that's all you require. Some people need a path, but if you just think it, you'll relocate, instantaneously!"

I abandon the tunnel, enticing as it looks, to pursue Aurora's coaching. I focus my thinking on this being's picture—wham, I'm at a gorgeous beach, with my visualization in living flesh-and-blood animation. I'm sitting in a circle with a group of unusual beings. It's immediate, there's no turning back; funny how there's never a script. Whatever arises is no improv class but a real-life drama, mid-scene—cameras rolling.

We're posed upon a huge carpet, designed with varying sizes of brightly colored triangles, afloat in a field of fire-red—*à la*

Kandinsky, the Russian painter. Off in the near distance the ocean is practically still. Slowly a scarcely-perceptible shift in the atmosphere occurs—yellow hues phase into an orangish tint. Just as I notice the shift, I receive an impression. I understand that as this home planet of theirs transits through the influence of different-colored suns, the proximity of the planet's orbit to each sun changes the atmospheric coloration, creating gel-like glazes in the sky.

Looking around the circle, I find twenty-five flamboyantly dressed beings all wrapped in vibrant, silky scarves, imaginatively concealing various parts of their bodies. Each sports a unique quasi-sultan headdress, which defines the direction and quality of the light blasting from their head. They each look like a mini solar-station pumping out magnificent light. Some have lights gleaming from their mouths and crowns; others their ears, cheeks, and third eyes. Still others beam from their eyes and the backs of their heads. It's a sort of peek-a-boo fashion, each presenting itself through the guise of inventive wrappings—creating a daring Islamic mystique. Wonderfully sacrilegious. Full of pomp and carnival! I seem to have landed amidst quite a spectacle—maybe the marriage of Busby Berkey Follies and the Sultan-Saints of the Future, but clearly this is no comic skit. And here I am, straight out of lackadaisical, casual, suburban America—my grungy sweats and all. They must think I'm a bit kitsch for the occasion! Surely the chic New York and Paris runways, with all their haughty sophistication, can't match this pow-wow for glamour and pageantry. I can't get over it—their entire heads are absolutely bursting with magnificent light. It's simply spectacular...unreal! Observing, I notice that the light glows softly as they listen, dimming substantially; but in the midst of expression, the light bursts out in lucid exclamations.

I'm sitting by the being I've illustrated. Information is impressed upon me. I'm swamped—they are all communicating at the same time. Whom do I listen to? I turn to the acquaintance next to me; apparently not understanding my predicament, he casually continues the chaos. Eventually, after numerous tourist gyrations, I get my message across.

He responds laconically, "Don't allow the jumble of noise to frustrate you. Just focus on one communication at a time." He then asks, "Would you like to participate in an activity we are about to start?"

Thinking I can't be much more confused than I already am, I agree to be involved. "OK. But will I be able to integrate myself into your energy—you know, will I fit in without disturbing your activity?"

With no answer, an energy field quickly builds around the circle. It feels like we're all being connected, becoming a single circuit of energy. If someone were to leave the linked circle, our connected integration would be broken, forcing us to regenerate the energy field to continue our process.

Now we are all connected, like bulbs in a string of Christmas tree lights—presto, unavoidably I'm glowing, just like the rest. I'm receiving their light, my inner mysterium leaks out, pushing beyond the exoskeleton, shouting its glory. Their energy has temporarily re-imaged me, turning me inside-out. It's remarkable. I experience an inner purity which ordinarily remains latent for fear of reproach, but now glowing uninhibitedly, a glorious light. I'm glowing like a delighted little Chinese lantern; not quite as phosphorous as my new associates—but nonetheless I am a fury of illumination.

All the communication transmissions are sent through their emission of light. It may come from their mouth, eyes, ears, or nose—it doesn't matter. Any location can transmit the thoughts which are instigated in their minds. All communication is obviously telepathic and seemingly incessant.

One of their joys is the ability to simulate musical sounds—directing virtuoso performances through the emanations of their bodies. The music is physically perceived, unlike their normal communications, and generates intense light. Similar to synthesizers, they imitate the sounds of various musical instruments simultaneously. The gifted can project the sounds of up to three instruments at a time from different parts of their bodies, harmonizing and orchestrating fabulous music. For instance, a person could play the harp from their ears, the piano from their mouth, and the flute from the back of their head—something like the old Rube Goldberg contraptions at the penny arcades of the fifties, five instruments jerry-rigged into one. Amazing! But here there are no rubberbands, tape, and bubblegum—just splendid, transcendent music.

The atmosphere has just shifted to a bluish tinge. I decide to ask my friend next to me how often this occurs. His response is somewhat complicated because of the difference in the way they calculate time. He responds rather thoughtfully, "One day, or cycle, equates to about four hours of your time. We have four different radiant cycles per day. So four suns come in and out of influence per day."

For me, these different color cycles seem strange, occurring in rapid succession like a rotating color wheel in the sky. But here time is different! If you remember how you once experienced time as a child and then think about how you relate to it as you grow up—there's no comparison. Time seemed to stretch into forever as a child, and as an adult it just evaporates in a flash. So they experience one of our days as approximately one month. This stretching of time also affects our night and day cycle, making the atmospheric changes barely perceptible to them.

Now that our energy bodies are completely linked, it is quite easy to pick up the others' thinking—it's almost as though we are one mind! Like an octopus, we are an intelligent, sentient being—with each individual acting as a tentacle, sensing and signaling vivid mental imaging to our group mind.

I can sense my friend tuning to me. Through our link he easily reads my interests. Gleaning my love of spiritual healing, he reaches out to relate.

"We as a people have little sickness—we have evolved beyond the need to experience illness. We are acutely aware of the ramification of thoughts, knowing that thoughts are things—perceptible radiations. When repeated over and over again they feed the generation of their imaging, bringing it into physical manifestation. Other races somewhat similar to us, without our knowledge or command, often come to us for healing. I'd like to share some of our experiences with you."

Just as he finishes his commentary, I see pictures of healing scenes lining my inner vision—I'm transported to a healing in progress. We are in a sparsely furnished room. The mood is heavy, as a person from another species is severely ill. One of the beings takes off his costume wrappings. Brilliant light pours through every cell of his body. I can barely distinguish the boundaries of his body—features just eclipse into light. He looks like a nuclear fusion plant going nova. The ill person is lying motionless in bed. The light being walks slowly and deliberately around the bed. His light lingers behind as he walks forward. Thus as he moves from point A to point B, his light remains present at point A when he arrives at point B. When he gets to point C the light at point A is just starting to fade. Now he begins walking faster and faster. Light starts to aggregate, building and building into a whirling tornado of pure light. With his mounting velocity, no light is dissipated; it just builds exponentially. Soon the light's radiance and force are magnificent. It naturally and spontaneously saturates the ailing person. Shortly, the being stops circling the bed and steps away. He puts back on his wrappings. The whirling force of light continues circling as if it had an intelligence all its own. The being sits in front of the bed extending his hands. Light shoots from his hands, uniting with the whirling force, augmenting its velocity. After a period, the light fades and the being retracts the residual light back into his body. The length of each treatment is gauged on the severity of the illness. The sick person is now charged with light. He rises from the bed fully healed and ready to resume an active life.

Immediately I am back in the circle. My friend instructs, "Through powerful visualization, you can achieve what you just witnessed. As a healer you have an immense amount of light around you. You can use this light to access an unlimited amount of light from the universe. There are many ways to heal—you have seen but one. Use your ability to visualize during your healing sessions. You will be surprised at your results!"

What could be accomplished with this sort of power seems unlimited. Instantaneous healings, in the mold of Jesus, maybe... Why not? I know it will take exploration and time to practice what I just witnessed, but it's wonderful to add such remarkable knowledge to my repertoire of healing techniques. I lock eyes with this being, and I radiate a great warmth towards him, appreciating his willingness to share his amazing abilities. Gratitude fills my heart and a rush of energy pours out.

I start to respond to him—it's so unusual...I'm witnessing myself as I talk. Light is pouring out of me, emanating from my heart. Tears unexpectedly well up. Strangely, I feel strong emotions vibrating from him. He is so attentive as he listens to me express my gratitude of his species for their healing gifts. He glows brightly from his heart and head. A message emanates from his third eye:

"It has been a long while since I've received an inter-exchange so powerfully direct from the heart," he genuinely exudes.

I am quite taken by his response. Light keeps pouring from my heart, he is overcome with emotions, the others are clearly taken by surprise. I feel the light growing stronger and stronger. It is dead silent—even the lapping of the ocean can't be heard. Suddenly deep feelings of love pour from him, inundating me. I'm overwhelmed. I look out to the others. Now they're all shining light from their hearts! I'm miffed—such a magnificent being, why is he taken by my strong feelings of emotion?

He sparkles, beaming at me.

"This is so wonderful! I am the teacher within our circle. We create the circle to communicate with other beings from different planets and dimensions. The circle constitutes a welcoming to travelers and an open exchange for learning. Your being here has been a key opening a door, allowing us to experience the value of communicating more from our hearts. It is not that we do not communicate from our hearts, but this particular group of students communicates more from their heads, and your love is genuine and pure—it's so beautiful. This experience has moved them, bringing new understanding of the power of the heart."

He holds my hand affectionately, saying, "Thank you, your gift is so valuable, not only to us, but the universe! I know you haven't captured my name in all the competing information, but now that you're focused I will articulate it again for you—it is Byo-Yuu."

The others continue shining from their hearts. I'm glowing all over, especially in my heart! I'm still a bit overwhelmed, feeling content in knowing I've contributed; I feel so joyous and happy. It is unbelievable to me. In some unforeseen way I've actually made an impact somewhere out in the inter-dimensional beyond. Wow!

So quickly the time has come for me to go, and I stand. Some are still shining, others begin to glow again. I step away—the light connection breaks. Instantly I'm with Aurora. Surprised, I'm so happy to see him. He hugs me, light emanating from his entire being as he holds me tight in his light body. I just soak up his love like a newly found puppy; then I gush, "Thank you, Aurora, for your love and dedication. I'm so happy you're with me!"

EIGHT

LOU-E-AH-NANA

*professor of
dimensional shifting*

WITHIN MOMENTS OF SITTING, I'M spiraling down the familiar tunnel. In no time I've popped out into a room. It exudes Old World charm, resembling someone's study. The walls are lined from floor to ceiling with leather-bound books. In the center of the room, a large elegantly carved Queen Anne table and chairs dominate the decor's mood. At the far end of the room an impressive set of elaborate wooden doors complements the table's period. This room feels so familiar, but why? It doesn't feel like another dimension, it feels just like Earth—I'm surprisingly comfortable. The furnishings are crafted out of a light reddish-brown walnut, in some way stimulating fond images of my past. Suddenly the room is wavering, fading back into the hinterlands. I grapple to hold on—I close my eyes, willing myself here.

When I reopen my eyes, everything is stable, the doors break open, and a distinguished, curious-looking being enters. Books tucked tenuously under his arms, he moves mindfully over to the table, cautiously releasing his treasures onto the shiny grained surface. Once unloaded of his burden, he seems to relax his concentration and immediately stretches out his hands in a gleeful welcome, speaking aloud and telepathically at once.

"It's so good to see you again!"

I attempt to respond but can't—I seem to be fading. Then once again, I will myself back.

"Oh good," he clamors, "Gee, I thought I was going to lose you!"

I'm glad he's transmitting telepathically, because I'd never understand his language without it. He is so friendly and happy to see me, and I'm wondering why he said it was good to see me again? I know I've never been here before, so he must know something I don't.

He picks up my thought and responds, "A few years back when you were drawing me, I attempted to communicate to you. You were experiencing difficulty drawing my eyes, stumbling on how to shade the lid area. I was never completely sure whether you received my communication or not, as you never put in the eye shading I indicated, but it's OK, because sometimes we exhibit shading and sometimes we don't, so your drawing is accurate."

As I think back, I remember this decision. "I did hear you! This is good verification for me. It helps me to confirm my process in doing the drawings. It was so difficult to achieve the shading the way you had indicated, so I opted to delete the shading for technical reasons. I'm glad to hear you accept my artistic decision."

"Good, good," he spouts, inviting me to sit down. We both pull up chairs to the table, then he inquires, "How are you doing being here? Are you feeling OK?"

"I feel fine," I say, reflecting on my attention. "I was a little distracted at first, because I was half here and half at home, but now I'm fully present and feel fine."

"Good! That is good," he says again. Then he reaches for one of his books. His hands are snow-white—tufts of white hair crest the back of his palms, and his fingernails are glacier-white. It appears the books he has brought are on dimensional shifting. I intuit that he has been studying the mechanics of shifting for some time and has developed an understanding of shifting using the vehicles of the vibrational, astral, and physical bodies. He's so delighted I'm here his energy is bursting. Anxiously he opens a book, eager to share his wisdom, first pointing out an illustration of a cone shape.

He states, "The use of triangles is one of the most popular methods to jump dimensions, but I like to use the cone shape. It helps me to pinpoint my landing. I direct myself through the narrowing declension of the cone and target a specific place in space and time. I'm always taken aback at how effective it is." He lifts his brows and looks up from the books, questioning, "Would you like to share with me some of the methods by which you travel?"

A quick scan of the illustrations and I'm amazed at the varied techniques used to jump dimensions. I don't really employ many. Actually, I'm hardly proficient at any of them and I'm embarrassed at my lack of knowledge, but I think it would be fun to swap techniques, so I say, "Sure, I will share what I know, but I sense I'm not quite the connoisseur that you are! Sometimes I use a flashing light—I see it as a wide band of white light setting into the horizon. Just before it slips past the horizon I slide into the last sliver of light, which shoots me out into the dimensional beyond. Another technique I employ is the tunnel of lights. A cyclone of lights spirals and spins before me; I step into the spirals, which gives me the velocity—propelling me through the interdimensional tunnelled gateway. And most recently I've been using the portraits—just like yours. They act as portals, so that when I gaze into them they guide me into the being's specific dimension."

His eyes peer intensely, then he asks, "When you visualize the portraits, do they always work?"

"At first it was difficult, but now they really work well as vibrational magnets, transporting me almost immediately. Of course, Aurora has assisted me, making the journey much easier and safer. When I focus on a picture, it assists me in pinpointing my destination—the picture acts like a magnet, drawing me quickly through Earth's gravitational fields, then the transitional zone, and into the being's dimension. But it has been primarily my trust in Aurora—his ability to teach and protect me—which has given me the confidence to journey. Some may think the universe is just an innocent playland, but I'm aware it's not just a benign fantasyland—one has to be cautious, protecting oneself from possible negativity."

"Good, good!" he dittos his usual response as he ponders and stores my comments.

"Lately, I just think of a particular being and will myself there."

"When you arrive, how do you sustain yourself in the dimension?"

"The best way I've found is to immerse myself at all levels of my being. By this I mean that I attempt to fully experience through as many of my senses as possible. This creates focus and concentration in the alien dimension. Aurora always says, 'Focus and concentrate.' I can't emphasize enough how this has helped me. The physical sensation of the dimension assists me, especially when someone is touching me or I'm physically engaged in activities. This awareness enables me to maintain my focus, sustaining me in solid form."

He's nodding his head, thoughtfully stroking his long, curvaceous beard.

"This is helpful. I like to accumulate diverse knowledge, adding to my study and understanding of this fantastic adventure. The truth is, the more I study, the more fascinated I become."

Then I ask, "How do you negotiate your journeys?"

"Well," he says, his excitement focused and engaging, "like yourself I've used the tunnel of light, which is a very common method of initiating the thrust needed to overcome one's inherent affinity towards their own dimension's gravity pull. Another of the techniques I like is to visualize myself stepping into a triangle—then spinning it and letting it take me willy-nilly where it may. It acts like a galactic boomerang, slicing me through hyperspace to my destination. Also, it's possible to direct the triangle to a more specific location, if one wants to be more exacting. But the technique I like the most, and which gives me the best results, is the cone. I start at the large end, imagining I'm walking down a tunnel that is getting incrementally smaller and smaller. As I proceed, I become more condensed—by the time I reach the end of the cone, I'm reduced to a tiny point of light. Then I can direct myself to wherever I want to go. I also have used other geometric shapes, but the triangles and cones are by far the most effective."

He then inquires, "How long can you generally stay in the dimension?"

"Oh, I'd say about an hour or a little longer, maximum! How about you?"

"At first it was rather short, like your experiences, but now I can stay six to eight hours, even longer in some instances."

I think, 'That's fantastic, how terrific! I wonder if I will ever be able to achieve that duration.' He picks up my thought, asserting, "Sure you will, you'll see—it will be easy after a while! I think we have spent enough time discussing our traveling episodes—now let me show you around."

We get up and start for the double doors. Halfway there he pauses, stroking his beard, lost in indecision—then remembering....

"Oh, now I know—I wanted to show you something in one of the books, but you're doing just fine. Let's forget it, maybe we can look later on."

I reflect, "Since you took the trouble to get all these books out, I don't mind looking through them quickly—it will be interesting. Let's go ahead and look."

With this license he can't help himself and opens to a marked page showing an illustration of a cone shape drawn in black ink on a white background. The next page illustrates another cone, this one drawn in blue; the following pages depict many cones all drawn in varying hues of blue. As I keep turning pages, the cone shapes keep repeating themselves over and over, but all in different colors.

Somewhat perplexed, I ask, "Why all the different colors for the cones?"

"If a being whom you are interested in visiting inhabits a red atmosphere or environment, a red cone can help direct you to that dimension. This assistance is especially good for those who may have difficulty in visualizing."

I keep flipping through the pages, and all kinds of geometric shapes—triangles, cubes, and rectangles—keep coming up. Many are drawn in three-dimensional renditions; some are even bubble-like, approximating spheres.

"The sphere creates a bubble of protection," he emphasizes. "It's good for giving one a more secure feeling—easing one into the journey with a gradual transition. It is a slower way to journey, and I like to travel much faster. I suppose you might say I'm an impetuous shifter. We must go now, or you won't have enough time to look around!"

We get up again and walk to the door, which he opens for me. Whoooa! I'm standing right on the edge of a threshold, looking straight down a drop of about ten floors. No elevator! My heart leaps. It is an open shaft—a sheer free-fall. He steps right out into the shaft without hesitation. I'm alarmed, but involuntarily my body follows like a fool. Somehow the space automatically shifts planes, like a revolving holographic box—we're now walking down a straight corridor. Relieved, yet confused, I'm reminded of a scene in a Fred Astaire movie where he dances up the walls and ceiling, defying all laws of gravity. The only difference here is, once you've stepped into the optical illusion, you've switched rooms as well. The illusion completely shifts—the previously illusory space is now concrete, and the space you've just left becomes the warped illusion.

What a strange hallway—now I know why I felt so at home when I first arrived. The entire corridor is decorated in the style of the Victorian era. Paintings, wallpaper, moldings, and furniture all exactly mimic Victorian styling. It's confounding. So weird finding all these Victorian antiques lining the halls of this dimensional mystery house!

He catches my disbelief, saying, "Years in the past, on one of my dimensional excursions, I turned up in your Victorian era. I liked it so much, I decided to imitate the design for my own house. That is why you feel so confused and at the same time, you're feeling right at home. Isn't it fantastic?"

I'm hoping his comment is rhetorical. As to thinking it's fantastic, I'm uncertain, but certainly amused.

We continue down the length of the hall; at the end we can turn either to the right or to the left. He gestures for me to go left, but when I turn there is a wall right in front of me. I stumble to an abrupt halt.

Nonchalantly he says, "OK, come along," and up he goes.

I look up and there's an entire room. We simply step onto the wall and we're in the room that I just saw on the ceiling of the hall. Yes, it's very strange, but somehow the house optically unfolds in the most unexpected ways. I'm completely disoriented—again the room's decor totally transforms. Now we're standing in a lush greenhouse environment. Positioned in the middle of the room is a relatively large glass sculpture shaped like a walnut. It's about nine feet wide, twelve feet long, and five feet high. He walks up to it and lifts the top section. The walnut's upper shell folds back into an open position. Inside are absolutely gorgeous, delicate plants, somewhat similar to orchids, but exhibiting more vibrant hues.

As he looks curiously in upon the plants, he radiates his enchantment, effusively musing, "This is one of my interests—growing these wonderful plants."

He bends down and points his ice-capped finger at one of the petals. It changes from one color to another, then to another, and on and on.

"Notice that when I talk to the plant, it sends out wave after wave of colors. I can tell if it is happy or sad by the way its colors glow."

He is really involved with these plants—talking away as though they were another being, cognizant of his every word. He pauses a moment, then gleefully introduces me to one of the plants. Subsequently, he introduces me to all the others, like we're at cocktail party meeting dignitaries for the first time. I strain to remember their names, unconsciously fearing embarrassment at the social pressure. I feel a bit goofy, trying to remember all these silly names. But he has given them all special identities, so I do my best to play along, knowing I can't disrespect such a wonderful man. Strangely, many of the flowers alter their glow just as he introduces them. Amazing! They certainly appear to be directing a color-pulsed hello my way. They're even moving slightly!

Then he winks. "Let's go back to the first one I introduced to you," he says excitedly. "See if you can talk to it for a bit with me. Don't be shy—just show them your love."

He pulls up two chairs to the glass walnut's opening. He begins discussing with the plant what he has learned from me—its colors keep pulsing as he talks. By the plant's color responses, it really seems like it's actually listening to him, but I find it hard to believe.

With the deepest sincerity he whispers to the plant, "Monica says that to sustain herself in another dimension, she needs to be fully engaged with the beings who are present—feeling the sense of a physical connection. I want you to help me prolong her stay with us by giving her your touch. Will you help me?"

He turns to me with an expectant, bright twinkle in his eye.

"Now put your hand out close to the plant, Monica."

I do as he requests—I look at him. His expression is focused while at the same time chiding me to be patient. Shortly, the plant begins to dip its appendage down—then I feel the tip of its petal touch me, eventually gently lying on my hand. My entire hand is tingling—it is transferring energy to me via its colored lights. I can feel the being resident within the plant. Its consciousness is so gentle and sweet. Feelings well up—I can't express how moving this is. What an amazing gesture! I know it takes a tremendous amount of effort to perform this gesture, so I bend down and express my enjoyment of its sweet charm—beaming my appreciation through an affectionate, loving guise. My host is sitting across from me conspicuously gleaming like a proud poppa. I feel so bonded with him in this moment—then I realize I still don't know what he calls himself.

Immediately he spouts, "My name is Lou-E-Ah-Nana. You have to pronounce it fast; it's an easy name once you get the rhythm of it. I know you have to go soon, but there is one more thing I want to show you before you do."

He closes the lid of the walnut's outer shell, then shuts off the lights so the greenhouse is quite dark. Inside I can see the plants' colored lights shining through the crystal casing. The room is filled with a multitude of sherbet pirouettes, dancing like mini searchlights upon the walls. It is so beautiful and soothing—their gentle energy transports me into a relaxing, dreamy atmosphere. I think about our plants back home; I want to spend more time with them, demonstrating my newfound respect. I feel now I can connect much deeper with the devic consciousness guiding them. As I do, I'm sure a more meaningful connection will develop with the plant kingdom. I'd love to take this plant home which touched me—it's so wonderful and I feel a special closeness—but I know it's a futile fantasy.

I turn to Lou-E-Ah-Nana, "I must go. I've stayed much longer than usual."

He acknowledges it's so, saying, "You have outdone yourself, but there's still so much to show you. You must come back soon!"

I assure him I most certainly will, and say my goodbye.

NINE

BLUE THUNDER
crystal-cluster culture

THIS IS THE FIRST SESSION after meeting Lou-E-Ah-Nana. I'm anxious to try out his suggestion of using the cone method to propel myself into the dimensional beyond. It's curious—I remember seeing a spiraling cone during the lead-in to episodes of "The Twilight Zone." Clearly they tuned into an aspect of inter-dimensional travel, possibly even utilizing this abstraction themselves.

I visualize myself walking through the inside of a cone, moving down its funneling corridor.... Whoom, I pop out somewhere in space, dropping gently down into a nightscape directly in front of a dark building. It is low visibility—no one is out and about. Nothing seems to be happening. This isn't what I'm looking for, so I decide to try again and perform another leap.

I think about one of the crystal beings I have drawn. I visualize a huge cone pointing its nose towards the image of the crystal being. As I walk through the cone's interior, it quickly transforms into crystal-clear walls, allowing exterior visibility. Color after color streaks by, moving me through nested dimensions. Some are cloud-like, others blue, then red atmospheres slip past. I move at a quickening pace—I'm almost running. Eventually I accelerate, condensing into a point of energy, hurtling at the speed of light. I explode into white.

Huge, mountainous, majestic crystal points rise from the landscape, all dusted with drifts of powdery white and blue snow. I feel dwarfed among these giant clusters which pierce the panorama; no plant or organic life is present, only a pure, eerie, crystalline heaven. Strangely, I don't feel cold. When I reach out and touch the towering crystal point to my side, it is oddly warm. Curiosity drives me to attempt investigating this warm, six storied crystal that "highrises" next to me. I peruse the facets, inspecting them for any obvious entry. With little effort, I locate an open doorway precisely machined into the glassy surface—it beckons.

Before entering, I turn to consume one last glance of the glorious view. If you have ever seen photographs of the polar regions, this beauty is comparable; only it captures an austerity without the uncompromising severity one finds at the poles. Looking closer, I notice the crystals emitting pale pastel lights, delicately softening the hardened forms. Each shines out to the adjacent crystals, twinkling prismatic colors—search-light-dancing through the icy atmosphere, bouncing off and through each other's subtle hues. Where the pastel rays hit the drifting snow, they silently absorb, disappearing. I feel as though I've stepped into a soft Japanese woodcut print. The subdued ink tones articulate the distant crystals, muting into the translucent fibers of the handcrafted rice paper, producing a haunting revelation of deep solitude. The beauty forbids description.

Reveling in the the scene, I loiter. Mild audible vibrations seem to seep out from the crystals, as if traveling from a distant star. The sound slowly begins to intensify, getting louder and louder, vibrating in my head, disrupting the serenity. It becomes so obscenely loud, I dash for the protection of the crystal's entrance, avoiding the overbearing intrusion. Whew! I thought I'd go mad! A hallway leads me into a large room. Everything is translucent—lucid-liquid crystal. The room vaults high, curving into a cupola-like igloo some six stories in height. Circular skylights open at the apex and aimless snowflakes breeze in, evaporating just before they reach my grasp. It is magical, a sort of Siberian sonata!

The room is huge and empty—full of anticipation, but at the moment I appear to be the only one here. In my mind's eye I begin to detect groups of crystal beings walking around. They are ephemeral—

nearly phantom images, like retinal after-images. They mill through a factory environment housing heavy machinery. Each is active, busily working the ghosted equipment.

Suddenly, it all disappears in a jiffy. I close my eyes, sounds come rushing in—it is the sounds of the people working. The room is lit in a dark red light. There are people working again, but with different machinery. Something is transpiring, but what? I can't seem to understand. There's a flash and the room goes dark. Now it's a different scene—I see more crystal beings gathering in the room. They are gazing through the ceiling's aperture. Stars dot the jet-black opening, comets trace their graceful trajectory across the hemisphere, while starships casually coast by. The scene shifts again. I'm seeing plants everywhere—they surround a pond-like habitat. A crystal being reaches out to touch a plant. As his hand grasps the foliage, the plant instantly metamorphoses into crystal at the point of contact, while the being's hand turns organic. When he lets go, they both regain their respective molecular structures. What's going on? Everything seems to be jumbled and disjointed. I don't seem to be getting the message.

The room has emptied once again. I am alone. Soon I notice a presence on my left. It is the crystal being I drew some time back—the one I focused on at the beginning of the session. Even so, I'm a bit startled. I suppose I shouldn't be by now. But I'm not sure how he got here, and since he is at least seven feet tall, I don't believe he could have snuck in on me, as there are only two obvious openings. I realize that he must have silently emerged out of one of the walls. I flash on Hamaaz, the other crystal being I visited. It appears these beings are similar, both having the ability to merge in and out of the crystalline material.

I say, "Hi," somewhat ill at ease, not knowing if I should shake his hand or just what the appropriate etiquette might be. Then I pause, lingering uncomfortably in the conversational void. Sounds pass through my head like planes muffled by overhead clouds. An energy passes right through me. Could this be his hello? He puts out his right hand above my head. Telepathically, he asks if he can touch my head. There are no fingers on his hand and it looks extremely heavy. I hesitate, not knowing his intent. I have no trouble remembering the plant I just saw touched by one of these beings, so I feel reasonably justified in my hesitation! I don't want to return home looking like a glamorous frozen polyhedron. Intuitively, I project my psychic antennae, and detecting no harm, I decide to indulge his request.

"You may go ahead; it is alright," I say somewhat cautiously.

His hand is so large it covers my entire head and then some. I feel a tingling sensation. Within moments he withdraws his hand.

As he begins to speak, an artificial rumbling echo bounces through my mind, *à la* Stephen Hawking's digitally enhanced voice.

"I have received information. I read that you previously visited another crystalline intelligence. There are aspects of our two worlds that are identical, but you will find many differences too. For example, you have just experienced a room here. The rooms in our domain are permanent, and not fleeting isotopes—existing as fading half-lives only to be conjured back through visualization, as you experienced in the crystalline rooms you visited in the past. The rooms here capture the transpiring events, recording them in holographic archives completely accessible in the leaves of time. They catalogue an infinite number of dimensions right within their walls, similar to a hard drive, allowing past realities to seep out to the visitors. Each dimension captured within these walls is originally generated by those who visit the room.

Right now you and I are engaged in a conversation. As a result, we are creating a new dimension within this room that will be molecularly archived. So if you leave and come back at a future time, you will reenter this dimension, because this is what you and I created. It will be quite easy for you to re-access this dimension, and you will perceive it as solid, not as the phantom images which you previously perceived. The phantoms were the images generated by other crystal beings and beings from other dimensions. That was their reality—this is yours and mine!"

I ask, "Is it possible for me to exist in the other scenes I saw earlier in my mind's eye?"

"Yes, it is! But you would not be able to sustain yourself for long. Your staying power is limited, as you are, shall we say, existing vicariously off the energies of others."

I'm intrigued. Further questions arise about the distinctions between the two crystal worlds I have now encountered.

"You say the rooms are all permanent. Do the other rooms in the crystal points have similar properties, yet different realities?"

He reverberates, "Yes. When you first walked into the room you didn't know what to expect. The room was empty with no one present. In your mind you came here to communicate with me and experience my world. Your thought forms were so strong they attracted me to this room like a magnet. This is the reality that you have generated! I am here because I wanted to relate and share this experience with you. Our energies and mutual intentions have created this particular reality—a reality completely separate and distinct unto itself, lodged forever within the walls of this room. Other rooms house different realities, each associated with the events once enacted within their walls."

I think that this isn't so different from the space created by two people who have been close friends over the years, sharing mutual experiences together. Immediately upon contact, they activate a special rapport known only to themselves, and a mutually created space arises out of their past shared realities. You might say they share their own idiosyncratic cyberspace.

"So there is layer after layer of realities sandwiched together within the walls of this room, molecules imbued with data, archiving specific episodes in the history of the room?" I ask somewhat rhetorically.

"This is correct. Some experiences are stronger than others, though. You perceived a reality where crystal beings are touching plants. If they continue coming to this room to re-enact that particular experience, the vibration will become more and more pronounced, generating an even more concrete image. Let us say these beings keep existing in this reality for a couple of Earth years, then they decide to leave, going on to another room for six to eight months. When they return to the room of their past experience, it will be extremely easy for them to access the past reality because they existed in that space and time for such an extended period—building a strong, stable vibration. Now if you stay here for one or two hours and come back tomorrow, access will be easy. But if you don't return for six months or so, it'll be difficult to re-access that particular reality."

"Oh, I see—the repetition of an enactment allows the scenario to be more easily accessed, much like the repetition of a movement generates its mastery." Then I ask, "Can I re-access the events I saw earlier when I first arrived?"

"Yes, you can. To do it though, you must first visualize them strongly, making the event real again, then they will reappear."

So anyone can access anything they want?"

"There are no restrictions on re-enacting the realities, no codes, no privacy, no censoring. You are welcome to go where you want, whenever you want, absolutely free. But of course you must possess the abilities that got you here in the first place and harbor no malicious intent. Any harmful actions towards others would be neutralized and not absorbed by the crystalline walls," his voice echo-rumbles through my mind.

Unexpectedly, I see another bleed-through of an event in my mind's eye, but it seems to be from an adjacent room. It is a small room, maybe a quarter the size of the one we are occupying. A group of forty to fifty Tibetan monks is meditating and chanting together, building up a powerful vibration. I inquire about what I'm seeing.

"Is this correct? Am I really seeing other humans in the adjacent room?"

"You are. Monks often travel here to do their meditation and chanting, but what you saw is somewhat deceptive. Actually, rather than the forty monks you thought you saw, there are only one or two monks who have visualized a group of monks to optimize the power of their chanting."

Wow! This is incredible. My thinking was so limiting. I imagined just visualizing inanimate objects, not fully appreciating the power and possibilities vested in such a reality. Gee, I could visualize Gary or my friends and family. This is fantastic! These monks are really on to something! This space deserves more time to explore. I would like to construct experiments to develop its full potential.

I sense that it's time to be moving on. My stability is wavering. I want to communicate my feelings and discover my guide's name, so I let him know I'm fading and must go soon. I ask, "What do you call yourself?"

"We don't have names; we are identified by a vibration," he retorts.

"Do you mind if I give you a name based on my experience of your vibration?"

"You can do that."

I contemplate for a moment then say, "You feel like thunder moving through my mind as you talk. There is a coolness and calm around you. How about if I call you Blue Thunder?"

"I like that—it feels good and seems to hit the mark."

"Oh, my name is Monica…if you like, you can use a little artistic license yourself if you feel it doesn't fit your experience of me. Let me know what you think it should be if that is the case."

"I will recognize you by your vibration. Come visit again—we can create something new together."

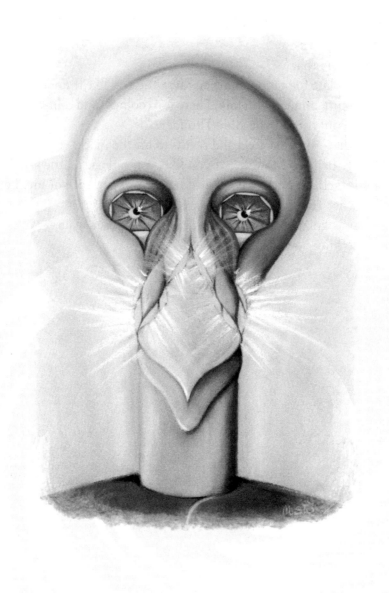

TEN

ANADRA

rapturous release in the opal cave

SHORTLY AFTER TURNING MY attention inward, I arrive at an enchanted natural setting near the entrance of a cave. A crystal-clear stream trickles by. Looking up from the stream I see a ledge jutting out from the mossy crags just to the right of the cave's entrance to the mountain. Upon the ledge rests a most exquisite creature. She is ten to eleven feet in height, clothed in ephemeral lavender chiffon, which gracefully layers around her elegant form. As I glance at her body, conspicuous openings appear around her nose, hands, and feet. They are actually slits in her flesh, shining out luminous light. She is one of the most unusual beings I've seen on my journeys.

 She hasn't yet noticed me and is idling the time away, dangling her long slender legs into the cool stream below. Nonchalantly, she aims one of her hands like a flashlight towards a shadowed area of the stream. Instantly, the bottom of the stream is illuminated, revealing all the little creatures zigzagging and flitting about. Now I see she has noticed me. Our eyes meet. Once they engage, I sense she had noticed me all along but elected to demonstrate the strange gifts of her biology.

 Her warmth is distinctly present—an inner glow physically radiates right through her clothing to me. Again she catches my eyes with her gaze, imprinting the name Anadra into my mind. Telepathically, she motions to me to follow as she descends from her perch and moves towards the cave. An excitement captures me when I think of her unusual nature and the opportunity to spend time with her.

Following her, I am immediately taken by her gliding gait. Her languid motion is captivating and leaves me stumbling along in her wake. How can I keep up? She glides so effortlessly. But she is quite attentive and together we move into the narrowing structure of the inner cave. The walls are made of a cold dark basalt and penetrate deep into the mountainside, much farther than I expected. After a bit of a hike, we arrive at our destination. The narrow cave opens into a spacious room, where both the ceiling and the floor are fashioned out of spectacular iridescent opal. It's really stunning! Brilliant flashes of green, blue, and pink swim through the opal's milky hues as I step onto the cave's floor. Never have I experienced such a vast expanse of gemstone. I'm sure the finest veins mined in Coober Pedy, Australia, are merely blah terrazzo by comparison! In contrast, the walls are rough-hewn charcoal basalt, which accentuates the glassy opalescent floors and ceiling to their height of beauty and mysticism. The crude and sublime are juxtaposed by the surprising quirkiness of ancient magma flows—a marriage far from the esthetic contrivances of the mind. Chartres couldn't be more beautiful.

At one moment the room appears quite small, then in the next it seems to stretch to infinity. My sense of spatial perception is completely whacked out; it just keeps shifting in and out and I can't get my bearings.

With a coy fondness Anadra remarks, "You'll adjust; it just takes a while to attune yourself to the space. I often sit here for meditation. Would you like to sit for meditation a while?" My mind whirls. I can't believe she isn't beset by the same disorientation.

"Are you sure?" I say, feeling hesitant and unsure, but still noticing my mind jumping at the rapture I sense impending. When I bend down to get into a meditative posture, my disorientation heightens—I'm sure I'm going to fall right on my face. As I attempt to sit, the floor proceeds to shape-shift like liquid mercury. It flows under my feet, vacuum-forming a rapid mold—leg, head, and arm supports all form perfect contours to the exact ergonomics of my body. After recapturing my balance I marvel at the accommodations—never have I sat in such comfort! It dawns on me the "nevers" are mounting fast. Other words come to mind, but none appear to be more suitable.

I look over to Anadra—she is completely vacuum-formed into place as well and appearing serenely content. Just before I close my eyes, I notice there are now eight seats molded into the opal floor. The others are occupied by wispy transparent spirit beings from Anadra's dimension. This is definitely promising to be an eventful meditation, far exceeding the billing. The spirits are Anadra's ancestors. Moving into spirit isn't a frightening event for Anadra's people, and often they interact as though there is no separation between the spirit and physical planes of existence. I suspect they'll be guides on our journey.

Anadra glances over and asks, "Are you ready? I want you to feel safe, and I assure you there is nothing to fear."

I nod to indicate I'm fine, even though I realize I've come to a very strange place and I don't know what to expect next. Given the events that have transpired, it seems clear this room could expand to accommodate nearly anyone and just possibly anything! So I think I should look up again, just to make sure it's still the eight of us sitting here!

I know there really isn't anything to fear, as all the events that have occurred are unusual, but not cause for alarm. Still I look up; I figure a little inter-dimensional caution can't hurt! I'm relieved. One by one the spirit beings reach out and join hands, gradually linking the circle. As I attempt to join hands with the spirit next to me, my hand passes right through its hand. A bit startled, I find myself disoriented and I scramble to regain my focus and quiet my emotions. Soon I detect a subtle energy build-up surrounding my hand. On the other side I find Anadra's hand—I feel her sure, supple fingers clasping mine. The warmth is remarkable. Finally, I'm calm!

"You can open or close your eyes; whichever you prefer is OK," Anadra whispers before she slips away.

With that, an energy begins to pervade the room. Surprisingly, it whirls up and out of the floor. The opalescent floor animates, bursting pink, blue, and green flames right into the room. The energy swirls in a clockwise direction, beginning to move up my feet and into my body. At first I can't really feel the energy—I just see it moving into my body. The entire room is alive with flowing, swirling energy. Then I feel a tingling on my cheeks and chin. I look down at my body. I'm stunned. It's no longer physical, but has merged with this sparkling flame energy. Only a faint outline of my body remains. Again disoriented, I glance over to Anadra. Her body looks similar, vibrating with scintillating colors, while the spirit beings' bodies can no longer be seen. Seeing Anadra puts me back at ease and I let myself go with the energy.

I feel extremely light—it's strange. I'm in the cave and at the same moment floating out through space. Anadra and I appear as stars of light, gliding through deep space. Looking out into its dark regions I see colored patterns taking form. One in particular is pulsating—it begins to breathe in and out, in and out. It's definitely alive or at least emulating biological functions and appears as though it has consciousness. It's altering its patterns at will, clearly aware I am watching—seemingly signaling a message. I've never seen a consciousness so immense—pure abstraction three-dimensionalized.

More and more complex 3-D patterns arise out in space. Absolutely exquisite. Each exhibits vibrant hues dashing here and there, for what I imagine to be solely entertainment. They just keep flying by, color after color exploding around me, shooting off streaking tracers of intense colors through lampblack skies. I feel like I am dwelling as a stationary point amidst the coordinates of a 3-D stellar canvas; colors are literally poured into the skies from buckets all around me. It's absolutely spectacular! Vast, galactic, liquid abstractions ooze into my holographic auditorium, spurting brilliant-colored dyes into gorgeous turbulent folds upon folds of endless fractal colors.

Far off, provocative orange clouds are moving towards us. As I focus my attention on them, image after image flashes out of the orange clouds in unpredictable fashion. Just how this occurs is puzzling, but the images are what one might depict as holograms floating in space, and they seem to be especially for me:

A hurricane comes roaring by, winds thrashing so violently that roofs are ripped right off their frames.

Next, Roman soldiers are rampaging through the countryside, pillaging and killing at will.

Then, marble buildings stand majestic in ancient time, unique archaic marvels.

Egyptians congregate, idly bathing in tranquil pools.

Water buffaloes are grazing through pastoral rice paddies.

A silver spaceship tracks through a solar system of beautiful planets.

A futuristic temple from a distant planet rises before me.

The images are fascinating and grab me on an emotional level; I know they have special meaning, but the rapid-fire succession is just too overwhelming. I try, but I can't integrate or decipher their import. I look to Anadra for an interpretation, but no response is forthcoming, so even though I'm more than curious I decide to move on, leaving the images behind for the time being.

With the fading images, a tunnel hangs in space right before us. Lights streak through it like speeding stars careening through a metallic chute. The colored lights just smear into the metallic surface, leaving fleeting traces of neon residue. Suddenly, Anadra and I are rushed through the tunnel, moving towards a flashing disco light at the end. I quickly capture Anadra's attention with an uneasy glance—she beams back a reassuring expression. As I watch her, she distorts and dwarfs, shrinking to only six feet tall. I could only be a midget by comparison. I suppose this transition zone has degenerated our star-light bodies—gone is the magical power and luster.

Soon we leave the metallic chute and emerge into a dark space. I adjust my eyes as we gently float down through what seems to be a sort of zero-gravity field. I have no idea what's happening and continue to feel uncomfortably disoriented. Anadra is laughing, fully enjoying the weightlessness and the strange body sensations. She exclaims, "Don't be afraid, just flow with the space, allowing yourself to be free. Relax! Release your tensions. You can do anything you want here! Nobody will ever know! Everything just melts into the void, leaving no trace. Here you can explore endless possibilities—freeing body and mind from cramping judgements. Soar and ride the light. Imagine yourself a stellar cowgirl, nimbly saddled to a bucking comet. Just feel the pulse of spontaneity—let yourself move to the rhythmic waves of the universe!"

I attempt to embrace her words. Relax! I thought I was relaxed! I respond somewhat bashfully, feeling extremely self-conscious and completely unaware that I looked so obviously uptight. I try to retrieve my composure. Gradually, I start to move my arms and feet around, tumbling much like an astronaut through space, rather than an agile buckin'-bronco rider. I'm still awkward, but the motion loosens my body. I start to limber up and let go—to play. Soon I'm laughing. A silly grin spreads across my face. I try, but I can't erase my smirk; I'm seemingly stuck in a state of goofydom. It doesn't take long and I'm fully into it. Snap! A full-tilt boogie uncoils and riotous coyote howls rip through stellar catacombs. Way down, deep within my soul, I feel frightening screams gurgling up from the depths of me, then they blast out daringly into the void, disappearing one after the other into oblivion. Long forgotten persecutions, wounds, and crimes lunge out of me like rampaging Brahma bulls.

Geez, it feels sooo good! I just let them rip, lifetimes of terrifying screams seems to release—some hysterical, some truly tormenting—all pour out an evaporate into the void. An exhilaration seizes my whole being. Rapturous moonlight exalts me. I glance over at Anadra and she's shrieking at the top of her lungs. I'm amazed at her childlike innocence, it's infectious. One look at each other and we burst out giggling. It's uncontrollable—volley after volley of goofy giggles babbles out. I know now for sure that we have regressed into adolescence—it doesn't stop. When we look at each other she begins imitating my stiff astronautic movements and the laughter escalates.

Unabashed zaniness seizes our imaginations. We stumble head over heels, bumbling-blathering through space with abandon. Our faces go through every possible contortion, mimicking every "goomba" to ever don a body. We shout out insanities, inanities, and profanities, as we spastically run through a charade of characters from Atilla the Hun to Humpty-Dumpty. I feel a pronounced sense of liberation—I've never felt so thoroughly free in all my life.

Anadra grabs me and looks me straight in the eye, exclaiming, "Whenever you are feeling self-conscious, rigid, uptight, or self-absorbed for any reason, remember this space. This experience is the unlimbering of the acrobatic spirit, where you give the poetic imagination free range of expression. It will always assist you in freeing yourself, allowing you to express your truth, love, and beauty. Do you sense what is happening for you?"

"I feel the release and freedom. Is there something else?"

"This type of release is an exercise in cleansing your cells from ancient bottled-up feelings and wounds which your soul has been clinging to for various reasons. But there is never any reason to restrict your self-expression. Past judgements of ourselves and events inhibit our ability to freely express, and when they're released our feelings flow like water, unrestrained and fluid. If you harbor them, they will limit and cramp your spirit, along with your ability to heal yourself and others." Then she smiles her demure, affectionate glow.

Strangely, we are back in the opal cave. I am feeling so much love, I can hardly contain myself. Anadra's love is immense and penetrating. She is looking at me with such compassionate eyes. I exude such feelings of gratitude—gushing, "I feel so grateful—you are wonderful. I am happy to be able to share this amazing experience with you!"

She reflects, "You have so much to give, there is so much love within you. You can now learn to let it out, expressing it freely. Let your light shine! I will assist you, but for now imagine you are one of us—just feel the light in the center of your being, and let it glow out from the very heart of you! Radiate your magnificence! If you focus on this long enough, this inner light will actually become physical. You can come back to the opal room whenever you want—use it to heal yourself! Goodbye for now. We will meet again."

After I had some time to think over the journey, I realized the sequence of events had a purpose. The barrage of fleeting images I saw in the orange clouds was tied to my past. The images activated unresolved emotions surrounding past events of my soul. I was at a loss and confused during the experience, but now I have some understanding. I've carried these emotional images from past and present lifetimes, lodged deep within my cellular memory. Visualizing the orange clouds was a way to conjure up past events, re-stimulating the emotions trapped in my cellular memory. This is why I first encountered the flashing images and then experienced the cathartic release that followed once the images had resurfaced. The traumatized cells were activated, and my experience of exhilarating joy at such a deep emotional level flushed and cleansed the trauma generated by the past events. It is literally like highlighting a paragraph in a computer program, then pasting in its place a different experience—one of unbounded joy. I know this is true, as I feel it throughout my entire body. I feel so free and renewed!

ELEVEN

RUUL

*mystery of the
phosphoric triangles*

I'M VISUALIZING THE FACE OF one of my psychic renderings. Lights flash. Sheets of light unfurl, flashing in and out and all around me like a turbulent magnetic storm. Somehow I'm cut free from the current…falling, falling, falling—down, down, down—free-wheeling through dark space. Thoughts tumble through my mind as I go. Will I fall into the rocks? A feathered bed? Water? Where will I land?

Abruptly and somewhat ironically I emerge in the flip-side—careening through brilliant, luminous light. Trees, mountains, and rivers rush in from below. I'm totally out of control, rapidly descending with no chute. I look up and the blackened void recoils like a diminishing twister and *swoosh*—the motion slows. I regain command of my extremities, straightening out my body, and I land feet first like a world-class gymnast into the lush, spongy, green grass—somewhere, somehow! It's so soft and inviting, I decide to cushion into it, relaxing casually up against a shady tree, running my fingers through the cushy interwoven ground covering.

The atmosphere here is unusual. Common microscopic particles appear to be magnified, riding through the currents of air as enlarged pastel-colored triangles. They drift in groups of floating colonies, moving through my outstretched fingers. A subtle sensation brushes against my skin as they make contact. They bob and drift like geometric flotsam through the wide-open skies. Watching, I detect that none seem to touch the ground. I put my face to the ground. There is a buffer zone between the air and the ground where no triangles exist. The "de-angle" zone. Then I notice one drift in here and there. When they touch the grass a vaporizing halo glows, then it's gone, magically evaporating with a wee bit of fanfare. What they are all about I haven't a notion.

I sit up, and waves of triangle flotillas glide towards me. Sometimes they move in thick batches, then thin. Glancing afar, I notice squadrons lining the horizon, readying for their approach. Unexpectedly, a presence lifts me from my fascination. A body is systematically materializing right next to me. It appears to be a light body—it's not quite solid yet, wavering in and out, slowly becoming more prominent. I reach to touch his shoulder, but my hand starts to fade as it moves into his auric body. I quickly retract it so as not to disturb him. The message that he is here to escort me back to his city pops into my mind. But, I say to myself, not before I solve the riddle of these mysterious triangles!

We are face to face. He has no mouth, but still I experience him presenting the expression of a smile. A warmth is transmitted to me, completely reflecting the emotional dynamics of a smile. It is bizarre, but that's what I perceive. He's transmitting through his third eye. Geez, it is so loud! Instinctively, I cover my third eye area with my hands, attempting to mute the blaring noise.

He reels in concern, apologizing for his oversight. "I didn't realize your body was so limited and incapable of processing our normal signals. Please excuse my error," he exclaims somewhat stiffly. "The times I have come to you during spiritual healing sessions, I saw your body as considerably larger, but now I recognize it was your light body I witnessed. Ahh...I realize what's going on. When you're healing there are many beings along your side, directing healing light. This influx of light expands and amplifies the nature of your body of light, making it glow so large and bright. Mistakenly, I neglected to account for the others' influence, assuming your body would be the same, but of course it changes when you move out of the healing modality. I will tone down my communication so it will not be so offensive. My name is Ruul and I am delighted you have come to visit me today," he says with an energized intonation.

During the pause in the conversation we look up. A wave of triangles approaches. Ruul motions for me to follow him away from the tree, out into the open grassy spaces.

"Reach out your hands and close your eyes. See if you can feel the triangles."

I do as Ruul suggests, and I feel the wave passing into my body. A subtle sensation comes over my skin; a ticklish, warm/cool feeling travels through me, then out my back. Wow! That's neat. I open my eyes—another wave is coming.

"Now see the triangles without opening your eyes," Ruul coaches. "Each wave carries a dominant color—try to detect its hue."

With my eyes closed I sense another wave coming, but I can't determine the colors.

"Visualize the colors now. Stretch out your vibrational tentacles, sense with your imagination...Feel the colors, will your imagination to perceive!"

I visualize them—they are baby-blue triangles with a slight tinge of misty green—and then I actually feel them! I sense them initiating a sparkling sensation through my cells, refreshing my tissue. It is phenomenal—I really can extend my perceptions beyond my ordinary senses. The triangles linger briefly then pass effortlessly through my body and back out into space.

Ruul continues, "The space you've dropped into is a special place. It is where we come to reenergize and rejuvenate ourselves. The triangles are unique energies; when lodged into the body they enhance psychic awareness and can assist in astral projection. They help to speed one towards a desired destination. We have schools like your mystery schools located around the country, where people learn to project to other dimensions and planets. At the classes students learn to utilize this triangle environment, gaining knowledge and practice in the process of storing the triangles in their bodies for added propulsion during astral travel experiences."

While Ruul is talking another wave approaches. I see pale peach-colored triangles becoming more and more intense as they near.

"Now, take this wave and store it in your third eye." Ruul talks so nonchalantly, as though it were a simple matter, but I'm uncertain and perplexed on how to proceed with such a directive.

"And just how do I accomplish this?" I inquire somewhat impatiently.

Oblivious to my annoyance, Ruul states, "Visualize the triangles congealing around your third eye—see them merge into it. Take them as though you were building with them, take them any way you can. But somehow visualize them mounting inside your third eye!"

I visually grab the triangles, pasting them inside my third eye. I imagine my third eye as a sort of tunnel, then I paste the triangles into the tunnel's walls, almost like a mosaic.

"Good, good—that is the way to do it," Ruul affirms.

The peach-orange wave passes and immediately I perceive another coming long before it nears. I seem to be attuning to their presence, increasing my sensitivity. It's a violet wave—no, actually light lavender. When it passes through, it becomes vibrant purple, filling my whole body. I feel somehow expanded. It's an extraordinary feeling—a sensory telescoping that extends my conscious awareness into a new domain. I'm wondering if these triangles are cousins to the phosphene images that shamans claim to see hovering in space just before they soar into non-ordinary reality.

Soon there is a break between the triangle waves. None can be seen on the immediate horizon, so we return to the tree. As we do, I can't stop thinking about the triangles. They're so unique—they seem to be a type of charging element, boosting one's psychic and astral powers, while refreshing biological tissue.

"Would you like to go to my classroom? I teach in a mystery school similar to that which we were previously speaking about," Ruul offers.

Since the mysteries of the triangles haven't been fully revealed, I'm inclined to investigate, so I say, "Sure, let's go. Maybe I can learn something!"

He requests that I close my eyes, asking me to put my hands on his shoulders as I attempted to do earlier when we met. I do… His body is fading—my hands melt along with it, the molecules releasing their form and fading into the ethers with the rest of my body. It is dark, still, and quiet.

"OK, we're here," he says.

I open my eyes and we're standing in a garden. It is situated within the confines of a glass building shaped like an ostrich egg. A Fabergé it's not, but still we're in a huge greenhouse, fabricated completely out of large glass membranes. I try to adjust myself in the space, but it keeps shifting configuration. I'm not sure what's happening. The seats in the room form triangular arrangements, then circles, then linear rows—talk about musical chairs. I seem to be losing my grasp. A voice inside insists that I be calm and still.

"Having come from the triangle environment, where you stored the triangles, you are now visually stimulating the reenactment of other times through your psychic center—times when the seating was arranged in different patterns. Your psychic centers are ultra-sensitive because of the accumulation of triangles within your third eye. Don't be alarmed—this is normal when your sensing has expanded like this." Ruul continues to settle me down, explaining, "You can control the incoming images with your will. Concentrate on not allowing them entry into your visual field of perception, and I will arrange the seats just for the two of us."

I become quiet, eventually opening my eyes. The room is dark, washed in soft moonlight. The seating is comfortable and we're sitting facing each other with several rows of empty classroom chairs filling the room.

"This is the classroom in which we meditate, study, and engage in special exercises that encourage the revelation of the mysteries of the universe."

Shoot! My body is weakening—I know it is time to go. Ruul has noticed my waning attention. He feels an inner disappointment mirroring my own and remarks, "There are many things to learn from each other—you must come again so we can continue. I'll meet you back in the triangle space when you are ready!"

I'm floating away—drifting back by the tree I first encountered. Ruul stays with me. I float up, up, up... into the dark space from where I entered, then I'm back.

Approximately a week later—feeling somewhat unfinished with my experience with Ruul—I decide to refocus on him, visualizing him strongly. The triangle landscape arises almost effortlessly. Ruul has not tuned into my presence yet. I decide to meditate. First I sit, then lie, attempting to avoid the triangles, so I might experience the dimension without their influence.

But my experiment runs short of time as soon Ruul arrives and we transport back to the classroom, where a group of his students awaits us. Today he has decided to approach the class a bit differently. A student has been chosen to run the class and he will remain an observer.

"This is Monica. She is a dimensional interloper, visiting from one of the dimensions associated with Earth," Ruul addresses the class, graciously introducing me.

Twelve students are present. One is in the front of the room, while the rest fill three rows of chairs. Ruul sits on a long bench off to the side and I'm standing close by. Suddenly I wonder what I am wearing for the occasion—feeling somewhat self-conscious. Oh my God, I've shown up in my sweats and sweater, looking extremely ratty—exactly how I look sitting on my living room floor. I'm aghast. How embarrassing! Intuitively, I realize I can imagine anything I want, so I visually whip myself into some jeans and a sweater. Voilà, there I am—looking rather appropriate—well-groomed, and even no glasses. Seeing perfectly, mind you. Amazing!

Rake, the student conducting, is speaking. Unknowingly his strong energy blasts my third eye, harshly jostling my vibrational body. Ooww! Immediately Ruul interrupts.

"Please be aware that Monica's third eye make-up is structurally different from ours. You must tone down your volume, Rake, so she can receive your communication. Your transmission is way too overwhelming at your present vibratory volume."

I flash on autistic children and what it must be like for them when their sensitivities are hyperactive—having no way of adjusting the input. After this auditory onslaught, it is easy to understand why they often learn to completely block out all input so as to control their environment in a manageable manner. I cannot imagine what would happen if this innocent but violent assault on my vibratory body continued. Rake acknowledges Ruul's communication but is somewhat at a loss about how to proceed, so he defaults into suggesting a meditation. Ruul jumps in.

"Rake, it is not often we have a guest like this. Why don't you seize the opportunity to run the class in your own fashion? Step beyond your confusion and lack of direction, and just make it up as you go," Ruul suggests.

Rake becomes excited, saying that first we will do a meditation, then have a discussion. It's quick—they close each of their five eyes, bowing their heads. After the abbreviated meditation, Rake asks if I would come to the front of the room. I go up. He puts his right hand on my shoulder in a welcoming gesture. I start to reciprocate, then pause—deciding to reach out my right hand in front of him. He looks confused, surprised that I didn't follow suit—not knowing quite what to do. So I take his hand, clasping it to mine, and begin shaking hands.

"This is our custom on Earth—it's our welcoming ritual for a casual acquaintance," I explain.

"Oh," he exclaims, feeling increasingly fascinated. Watching his excitement, I get a little playful, saying, "There are other ways to welcome people after you become more familiar; here, let me show you!" I walk up close to him.

"Now stoop forward a bit, Rake," I command. I bend to greet him, awkwardly hugging him as best I can. Not a simple task contending with his stiff, dangly arms—drooping uselessly by his side like the turn signals on some antiquated truck. It kind of looks like Auntie Gertrude, insisting on hugging her limp nephew, when all the kid really wants to do is go out and play. Stooped over Rake, I look around the class. The kids are amused and giggling at how strange we look all glued together in this crazy entanglement. I suppose for a people who are primarily psychic in nature, physical emotional enactments aren't commonplace and can look a tad strange.

"Rake, loosen up a bit, you're supposed to be enjoying this," I spout kiddingly, attempting to interject a little fun. The kids keep laughing, looking decidedly uncomfortable for Rake's sake. Now I sense an inner smile creep up through his rigid demeanor, but he's not outwardly letting on.

Then I ask, "Do you have other ways to greet each other?" He turns to the class, asking them to demonstrate. Two jump up and face each other. They shut their human-like eyes, then the uppermost eye activates—charging the eyes just below, while sending out an energetic connection between the two of them. Each emits a soft energy back and forth. Then the energy retracts and the human-like eyes reopen.

It was a charged exchange. Inwardly I wish I could participate.

"Too bad I can't join you—I'd love to experience this unique communion," I comment.

"You can do this if you really want," Ruul interjects. "Let's try!" Ruul walks up to the front of the class and sits down, inviting me to sit in front of him. Ruul is so tall our eyes don't meet, so he discards his chair for a couple of blocks, allowing our eyes to align. Then he turns to the class, sending out a rapid communication. He leaves me in the dust, but I catch a little—realizing he wants to explore this slowly because he is not sure it will work and doesn't want to put me in any danger or discomfort.

Then he turns to me. "Are you sure you want to try this? It will be an experiment." He is making sure I'm amenable.

"Sure! I'm game. Let's give it a try."

He closes his eyes, telling me to follow. He explains that this type of greeting is similar to one of my hugs—it's a type of energy exchange and I needn't be concerned.

"Now visualize sending energy from your third eye and I'll send it from my two upper eyes. The energy will be strong, but I will tone it down so you won't overload—just like I do when I talk, OK? If there is any discomfort let me know."

I close my eyes again, visualizing a pink ray of love going to Ruul from my third eye. A tingling sensation focuses around my third eye—I sense it must be the energy I am releasing to him. Then I feel the energy directed by Ruul. It's extremely clear and focused—penetrating my head. A liquid feeling ensues. Images of waterfalls download into my mind. It's a strong, strong energy—approaching overwhelming. Ruul detects the intensity and backs off substantially, ushering in a much softer experience. I realize, with the rush of energy, that I neglected to send while I was receiving. So I shift back into a mutual send/receivership mode, directing my love.

Ruul says, "Now blend our two energies together and you will experience a slight emotional merging—a sort of hybridization." After a bit he retracts his energy.

A female in the second row asks if she can try the experiment. Ruul gives her instructions—explaining to direct her energy slowly, releasing just a little at a time. She is quite tall as well, so when she sits on the blocks our eyes meet perfectly. We close our eyes and I begin to transmit the pink ray. I'm feeling her energy return, and a gentle inner giggle breaks our telepathic silence. Somehow I can sense her—she is very happy and excited, wanting to learn more about me and our planet. Her feelings and thoughts keep rushing in. She wants to travel to other dimensions and learn all about the various species throughout the inter-dimensional domains. In her excitement, her energy intensifies. Ruul has to remind her to settle down and soften her energy. She's really enjoying our interplay of energy. I hear a delighted sigh as we retract our connection.

Now others want to experiment, but Ruul steps in. "This is enough for now. There are many things to learn together." With that he instructs Rake to resume his leadership.

Rake turns to me, "How do you communicate with each other?"

"We speak through our mouths—verbally out loud, by structuring words into sentences." Then I say out loud, "Hi Rake, how are you?"

Everyone is shocked—it's shattering. For the first time they recognize the effect their powerful third eye communication has been having on me. Their third eye has been wide open and focused on my words. Because they are so unfamiliar with the spoken word, its vibration is so strong it takes them back. After bracing themselves, they ask if I can make additional sounds.

"How about if I sing you a song," I say—then I wonder what could I sing. Ruul delivers some instructions. I sense they have music, but most of it is telepathically imparted. Ruul begins explaining the nature of their domain to me.

"We don't have ears, so we hear only telepathically. If I were to hit this table, no one would hear it unless they had specifically focused their third eyes. Our hearing abilities parallel your sight in some ways. You see the physical world, and only the psychically gifted perceive the other realms. We hear telepathically, and only those gifted and trained can distinguish physical three-dimensional sound. Because this is a mystery school, many will be able to hear if you sing, but few in our dimension would hear you." I find this really strange—it seems we just continue exchanging mutually shocking information.

They are all leaning forward at attention, anticipating my song, anxiously waiting for Ruul to stop talking. After my initial stage fright, I decide to sing some verses from the song I wrote, *Come to Me*.

It is a song about the yearning for the beloved. They close their human eyes to better focus on the physical nature of my song. I sing a few verses and Ruul insists, "Sing some more, that is wonderful."

So I continue...some start stroking their heads to the rhythm and others look as though they're trying to hug themselves. They seem enthralled. I am so surprised at the reception; it makes me happy. When I finish, a gentle, soft sound comes to my head. One by one they all come up to me, putting their hands on my shoulder. It's amazing. I never expected it would be so moving. I'm touched and delighted by their display of affection.

Rake asks, "Are there other songs you can sing for us?"

I think for a moment.

"Sure, I suppose I could sing you some other songs from our world." I've been singing occasionally with some folks, so I guess it's a good opportunity to practice. I decide I would like to give them a little awakening; Big Mama Thorton's version of *You Ain't Nothin' But a Hound Dog* pops into mind. So I say what the heck, let's see how they like it. I start off with a bang, wailin' and a-howlin' just like Big Mama. Their facial expressions scrunch up, dramatically transforming. Once again they're caught off guard, but they can see I'm playing. Their telepathic attention turns to amusement then to out-and-out laughter—hilariously roaring, showing the kick they got out of it.

I explain, "There are so many types of music it is difficult to choose any single style and do justice to the vast number of recordings on Earth. There is Country, Jazz, Blues, Classical, Rock, Opera, Rap—there's just so much I'd like to share with you, but I'm at a loss as to how to represent it all."

How can I do this? I decide on a medley, singing a few lines from Gershwin's *Summertime*, then Patsy Cline's *I Fall To Pieces*, and humming a few bars from Beethoven's *Für Elise*. Finally, I tell them about one of the all-time inter-dimensional favorite groups, the Beatles—and I sing *I Want To Hold Your Hand*. They all put their hands on each others' shoulders and sway to my song. I'm amazed they're so receptive. The whole scene might appear kind of hokey to some, but not for them—they're immersed and really into it.

"If you practice these songs and come to our dimension, we can all sing together, out loud!" I exclaim in jest.

Rake is very excited and starts talking about a trip to the field of triangles, saying maybe that with lots of practice we can experience Monica's physical dimension. I'm starting to lose focus, telling them it's time to part. One by one they come up again, putting their hands on my shoulder. We all hug—it's so joyous. I feel I've made so many friends. It is wonderful, and I'm an inter-dimensional singing sensation to boot! Then I stand before Ruul to say goodbye. He stoops, opening his arms wide. We embrace for a long time. So much love—how wonderful. I kiss him on his cheek. Our eyes meet—energy sparks jump back and forth. Then I'm gone.

TWELVE

A-MEE-AL

bird-man and his canopy of friends

THE GLASS TUBE I'M MOVING through goes on and on. Outside I see weather patterns changing like accelerated newscasts—rain, fog, and bright sun whoosh by. In each condition, exotic colored feathers casually float down—adrift as if archangels were frolicking nearby. Suddenly, mountains are pressed into my focus and I can no longer see the changing patterns; through the glassy tunnel I slide—moving so quickly I close my eyes and feel the dimension reeling me in.

Anticipation and excitement leap, the pull is strong, stronger than I've ever experienced; someone or something surely awaits me. Hopefully, it is a welcoming! Wham, I drop out of the glass chute. *Kerplunk*, right on my butt—out into the bright shiny sun of another world. I look up—encircling me are vibrant, wild-colored costumes, with a whole flock of bird-like characters staring out from behind the tropical trappings. I'm plopped down, all sprawled out, right in the middle of their circle and their eyes are upon me.

Ohhh, Ahhhh, Ohhh, Ahhhh... sounds kind of whiffle in and out around the circle. I look around feeling a bit stoogey and thoroughly embarrassed; I stand up and brush the brownish dust off my smudged tush, looking as cool as possible, which isn't really very cool.

I intuit that I've landed in a sort of *soirée*, an intimate clan. Here their stories, problems, and ongoing experiences are shared. It is a gathering circle where they dance, enact dramas, and experience life initiations guided by their leader.

Walking towards me now, the leader is big, about six feet, six inches tall, and his eyes are intense. Then I recognize him. It's the being I drew some time ago—thank goodness, I was getting concerned. After he takes a couple of steps in my direction two others come in behind him. I keep hearing a flapping of wings, and the sound of the fluffing of feathers is pronounced as they near. When he gets within arm's reach the sound disappears.

During their approach, I notice a little guy on the right of the circle peeping out from behind two adults, waving his hands like crazy, trying his best to get my attention. I wave back to him. He squirms involuntarily—he's so excited I see him he is hardly able to contain himself. I stretch out my hand and gesture for him to come closer. He turns, looking pleadingly up to the surrounding adults. Once he has their approval, he tears out of the circle arms flapping, legs churning in every direction, leaping right in front of the others who have earlier approached me.

He earnestly stretches out his bright yellow hand, clasping mine in a friendly shake. It's so soft—he is as cute as can be, without a clue that he has just upstaged the leader. His face is similar to the others, only more yellow on the sides, which complements his bright turquoise crest plumage. A short-sleeved shirt covers part of his thoroughly yellow body. As he shakes my hand, I can tell he has retracted his claws beneath each of his four fingers so I won't be harmed. Holding his hand, I stoop down to greet him. His intense eyes soften when he smiles. The character of his eyes takes on his beaming smile, telegraphing his uncontrollable delight. We stare at each other eyeball to eyeball, glued in this whimsical moment.

"Hello, my name is Monica," I finally exclaim. He doesn't understand, so I point to myself and say, "Monica!" Now the being standing to the side says something to him. The little guy jumps up and down exuberantly, saying, "Monica, Monica," or nearly Monica—it is as close as he can get.

Now I say, "What's your name, little one?" He is so happy he can't stop jumping up and down. "Ai-You, Ai-You, Ai-You," he spouts gleefully.

"I'm happy to be here to see you!" I explain, trying to express my feelings, but he can't seem to understand or pick up my thoughts, so I dramatize them. I grab his hands and jump up and down holding the thought of how happy I am to see him. He gets so excited—like he's going to explode—just thrashing and bouncing about like nuclear silly-putty. A wave of sounds circles round the bird people—it feels like laughter but it seems as though they rarely express themselves in this fashion, so they must be finding the little fellow extremely humorous.

Now the parents call out to him. He lets go of one hand but will not drop the other hand—hanging on for dear life. Again the parents beckon and finally he acquiesces to their requests. We look into each other's eyes again and I say, "I will see you after a while!" Then he begrudgingly putters back to his place next to his parents. I turn to face the being that I've drawn. His arms are graciously outstretched and he exclaims, "Welcome!"

I'm not sure whether this is an invitation for a hug or just a welcoming gesture, so I too stretch out my arms, imitating him. This brings another volley of laughter running through the circle with accompanying fluffing. Then he steps closer and wraps his arms around me. Beautiful feathered wings stretch out with his arms and completely enfold me in his warm embrace. Fluttering sounds support the hug—when he releases I croon, "Thank you, that was wonderful. I am happy to be here!"

Then the two beings from behind him come forward—they are his wives and they stretch out their arm-wings and again I'm wrapped in glorious feathers. I feel like Horus has sent forth his dominions to give me his blessings. Thoughts arise. I understand the being of my drawing is the head of this council into which I've dropped. It is clear he has been waiting for me. He had tuned into the ceremony that Gary and I initiated before I started my journey. Once he knew our intent, he informed his tribe. They agreed to gather to send out unified thought forms in an attempt to attract me to their dimension. Ahhh. I hadn't thought of this. So this is why I felt the strong pull—they made it easy to make the shift. How powerful the group became by linking their thoughts, multiplying their energies synergistically and easily magnetizing me to their realm. Such a great reminder of the power of group thought! With all the arrival hurrah over, the others gradually go their ways and I'm left with the leader and his wives.

The four of us begin to walk aimlessly about, engaged in idle chatter. Looking around I see I'm actually walking on a slightly mounded area. Rocks are embedded around the perimeter of the circular mound. In the center of the circle lies a ceremonial phallus-like projection, embedded with rocks at the base of its shaft. Not far from the mound, primitive mud houses are sprinkled throughout the immediate vicinity. The primitive nature catches me by surprise. For some reason I expected a more advanced culture. Just as I have this thought, the leader picks it up.

"We are presently in the country—the city is quite a different experience." With that he projects a picture into my mind's eye. A futuristic skyline makes an impressive panorama—intertwining unusual metals in an amazing architectural weaving of geometric shapes and connecting buttresses. No individual buildings can be detected, as the structures leap over and under each other in a dynamic inter-connectivity of form and function. Their transportation systems are integrated seamlessly right into the flow of architecture, undulating through the forms like a graceful woof of a contemporary weaving. As beautiful as it looks, I get an emotional sense of congestion—the complexity brings on the feeling of claustrophobia. The intricate honey-combing of such a complex urban social organism as this must demand remarkable social advancements. I can only reflect on what immense challenges this structure would present for us Earthlings.

He retracts the image, explaining, "As you have theorized, many of us want to live much more simply than this type of advancement allows. If you enter our primitive homes out here in the open, you will see we still maintain our modern conveniences despite the primitive façade, but we choose to live mainly in a simple manner."

While he is speaking, his name just pops into my mind, A-Mee-Al. I stop him in mid-stream asking, "Is this right? Am I receiving your name? Is it A-Mee-Al?"

"Yes, it is close, close enough!"

I turn to his two wives, "And what are your names?"

The one on the right introduces herself as "Ou-Wee" and the other on his left announces she is "Ah-Hee-Ya." Both are extremely reserved and polite, but they have little to say. We have been walking a while through their simple grounds, casually absorbing the aura of their tranquil retreat. It is heaven compared to the mayhem of the burgeoning metropolis.

Out of nowhere I stop and abruptly ask, "Can you fly?" I'd been wondering this very question since the beginning, so I decided I might as well get my curiosity satisfied—there is no tomorrow here. I start walking again. A-Mee-Al is amused and not put off in the slightest by my rude manners—I am relieved, since I seem to have little control.

"We don't often fly, but we can," he reflects. I peek around his body attempting to get a picture of how he could fly with only wings attached to his arms. Immediately he puts his fingers to his waist saying, "We have tail feathers that are concealed by our cloth wrappings." He easily removes his sarong-style garment. From his waist down, feathers cover his entire legs, and right behind them are gorgeous tailfeathers fanned out for my benefit.

With his arm-wings expanded and tailfeathers spread, he is a marvelous creature, right out of the tales of yore. No minotaur, mermaid, or satyr could outshine his unique, mindbending splendor. I am in complete awe, he is absolutely outrageous. One can see in A-Mee-Al the ancient spirit of legendary beings. He is evidence enough for me to imagine that the old half-man, half-beast tales aren't purely founded on mythological hooey. Although seemingly ostentatious, he is quite modest and rewraps within a few moments. Clothing here is not so much a social custom as it is protection from environmental abuse. And clearly it certainly has nothing to do with sexual invitation, innuendo, or body embarrassment.

We keep walking, approaching an intriguing grove of trees. It forms a sort of faerie-ring, arching a canopy of variegated leaves while allowing occasional patches of sunlight to sneak through here and there—creating an enchanting enclosure. Inside it is an entirely different universe. Spectacular parrots, parakeets, lorikeets, toucans, eagles, and birds I have never seen before soar and flit through the exotic aviary. It is most bizarre, as many birds completely defy description. I feel I've entered the ingenious results generated by someone's use of a polyforming animation program. One bird has a poofed-up beehive hairdo, fanning out in a myriad of peacock colors—looking every bit the sixteenth-century version of Phyllis Diller on a particularly good hair day, glitter and all. A wee bit top-heavy, mind you! Another white parakeet-like bird sends up a wild ruby-red Florentine question mark for a crest, swirling into the air like an overly aroused flourish. Then there is a little mischievous bird with a yellow inverted triangular crest. It features two elfish horns on either side of the triangle—looking dead serious. He is an absolute howl—it seems he can't determine whether he is cupid's or Beezelbub's counterpart. I could go on and on—it's an extravaganza. A true feast of the birds of paradise—complete with a cacophony of tropical sounds.

No sooner are we a few yards within the cloistered canopy than birds swoop down upon us, like a scene out of Hitchcock's movie *The Birds*, landing all over our arms. Once they have landed they hop from shoulder to shoulder, up and down my arms and onto my head. They seem playful and I can tell they are as curious about me as I am about them. So I'm not freaked, but I must admit I was initially alarmed.

"Stretch out your arms," A-Mee-Al suggests enthusiastically. I do. Birds of every species imaginable are on my arms and shoulders. I look like a perch during the peak of migration. Most are relatively small, so it is not uncomfortable and really quite amazing. I am surprised their claws aren't hurting me, but they are gentle. I can't even detect their claws. The birds are so curious about me and many have cocked their heads with a perplexed look in their eyes—for god's sake, what is this? A-Mee-Al starts to explain to them that I'm from another dimension—a land where there are distant cousins of theirs, nearly identical in appearance to themselves. I'm surprised to see him talking to them—there is obviously a developed intelligence here that I am unfamiliar with, as they easily understand.

As he is relating to them I start seeing images of roast turkey dinner, holiday families all circled around the big juicy bird, stuffed and browned to perfection—faces salivating and wide-eyed, ready to devour. This is not good! Why must these flashes plague me now? Guilt starts to rise; I feel much the hypocrite.

Just as I have these thoughts A-Mee-Al jumps in, "Don't feel this way, this is your culture. We understand." He reassures me that they have no resentments. Whew! I feel better. I'm glad they understand; this could be unforgivingly embarrassing.

Suddenly I flash on a pet bird belonging to a friend of mine, Oliver. I recall all the cute, charming episodes she has related—the bird seems almost human. He gets jealous of others and seems to have *snitty*, emotional outbursts. I wonder if they might have a similar species. As I think about her bird I realize that most of the birds in this dimension have more advanced neocortexes than our animals. But even with the birds who don't have developed brains and are incapable of any genuine interaction, the inhabitants seem to treat them, even the least evolved, as young souls progressing along the winding switchbacks of becoming self-conscious beings. Here there is irrevocable honor and great respect for all, a world where they treat their animals like precious children, all trying to find their niche in the world. They do not keep pets. Not that pets are bad if they are truly loved and appreciated, but it seems that here all the animals are inherently close with one another and there is a certain intimacy experienced with the wild animals at large. It is obvious to see that they are far from treating their animals as we do on Earth: caging, harnessing, experimenting, and exploiting them for personal and social gratification. Their birds are part of the grand family, all sentient souls worthy of affection and respect. I get the sense that when a bird dies, they know its soul progresses and evolves into the more advanced forms of intelligence, moving evolutionarily toward beings like A-Mee-Al.

He nods his head, affirming my thinking, then he reflects, "You can see we all have different faces, but many quite similar to the variety of species you've seen under the canopy. Through our soul's journey, we carry specific patterning—evolving these imprints of the facial characteristics as we incarnate over and over again. You can see them quite easily in my face, right?"

"Yes, I can." I think, 'Perhaps if we displayed some of the animals' facial or bodily characteristics ourselves we may have a greater respect for them,' but I suppose this is idealistic given that we often don't even respect those humans of different racial and ethnic groups.

Time has come, I'm beginning to lose focus and my form is wavering.

He exclaims, "It is too bad you must leave, there is so much to show you." They all stretch out their wings. The dominant color is blue, but Ou-Wee is more green and A-Hee-Ya is more purple. They encircle me, fluffing me up in glorious colors and love—I beam out my affection and a fond thought returns for little Ai-You and I'm gone.

THIRTEEN

SOUL
confronting forgiveness

My mind is racing—I'm unsettled. At times my mind's stillness is as elusive as the blur of hummingbird wings. Aurora's voice echoes in my head, "Focus, try to focus." I hear him, but instantly my mind returns to scanning my precious past events.

Now Aurora is even more emphatic: "One way to focus is to open up and radiate pure love; announce your love to whomever is out there. Just fill them with love. This creates an immediate opening in which to flow—of course, this is attempted only after you have affirmed your intentions."

I follow Aurora's instructions, radiating out love. Quickly I project into space. Many beings enter my arena. Eventually, one area draws my attention. A slow-moving tornado of energy spirals into an opening. I gravitate towards the powerful force—I'm surrounded. A voice, seemingly at my side, signals me to close my eyes.

The powerful energy has vanished. I feel a warmth beating down. I open my eyes to another planet, which seems quite similar to Earth. Wisteria-like trees line the landscape, sending gorgeous lavender-pink blossoms lunging groundward in graceful cascades. Their fragrant bouquet lingers in the air. A small stream trickles through the grove of trees at a leisurely pace. The sun is so unrelenting—I head towards the trees to avoid the intense heat. Once I am in the grove, my attention is drawn to the stream. I bend down, hanging my head over the water—a marvelous miniature wonderland comes alive under the glassy rivulets. In a bed of blackish rocks, orange-hued, translucent pearls are nestled into rough pockets. Each pearl emanates a cosmic, dazzling fire, illuminating its immediate vicinity. Surprisingly, the rocks also transmit a glow, but not nearly as vibrant. Around the rocks rich, deep-blue grasses undulate and shimmer through the water, adding to the intrigue and aquatic charm.

I submerge my hand into the cool water—the grass is velvety to the touch. My hand roves through the miniature grottos, eventually seeking the cosmic pearls. Right as I pluck one from the stream, I feel a tapping on my shoulder. It jolts me out of my fantasyland. I look up. Astonished, I'm face to face with a stunningly beautiful woman. Vibrant orange hair "neons" her strong presence, resembling sirens of mythical proportions. She is adorned with the splendor of a fanciful cape, comprised of petite golden feathers. The feathers begin at the crown, sculpting a phoenix-like headdress, then sumptuously drape over her shoulders, beautifully defining her shapely bust and torso. She is a goddess stepping out from the corridors of time, possessing a beauty with which I'm completely unfamiliar, presenting a sexual purity that is alluring, yet not seductively arousing.

I'm transfixed. She gracefully bends down to sit beside me. Her hand reaches out, touching my hand. It is smooth, transmitting a gentle, loving vibration. Instinctively I understand that she would like me to give her the pearl. I place it in her hand. We both gaze at it intently. Slowly it magnifies its glow, melting from orange into pale green, to pale blue, to lavender. I determine that its color changes as she alters her thoughts; effortlessly she manipulates the form. The pearl is practically alive, absorbing her every thought and feeling! The pearl appears naturally to receive her intent, then to alter its internal chemistry. I intuit that the pearls are linked to the planet's nature spirits. When they are touched a connection is made with the devic realms of the planet. It is at this moment that they are activated and begin collaborating with the intent of a signaler.

She states, "The pearls act as messengers, passing on thoughts to the one who holds possession. Our culture's teenagers use them as love letters, secretly encoding their love in the pearl's molecular structure for their sweethearts to unlock. I refer to them as life forms, but in reality they are merely inert elements of the mineral kingdom, brought to life by the intention of a conscious signaler.

"There are much larger pearls than the one you were holding—spheres which possess the same qualities as these little pearls—but they are rare and difficult to find. We use the large spheres as healing vessels, directing healing energies and thoughts into the internal molecular structure of the sphere to assist a person in unfolding the secret to their healing. Wouldn't it be nice if we could transport these objects to Earth? What healings you could perform!" she says with delight.

With this she casually scoops up a handful of grass from the stream and swallows it. The velvety grass becomes a quick, nutritious snack. "We are non-meat eaters, subsisting primarily on fruits, vegetables, nuts, and underwater grasses. The grasses are quite similar to your kelps and other seaweeds—extremely rich in essential vitamins and minerals. Would you like to try some?"

"No, thanks," I say, not enticed in the slightest by the prospects of grass.

While enjoying the grass, she reaches into her pocket, finding a pouch. In the pouch there is a much larger sphere similar to the ones she just described. It is a three-inch-diameter glassy sphere with a portion of the globe sliced off, much like our paper-weights. Inside the sphere a mysterious orange substance appears to be breathing. It swells and subsides like the beating rhythm of a simple organism. She extends it towards my ear and asks me to listen. As I put my head next to the sphere's surface, a pronounced heartbeat pushes and pulses into my ear; then surprisingly it shifts, and the sounds of a synthesizer piano pound out a zippy melody. How fascinating—it appears it can capture the tonal quality of any sound. Now the sound comes to a rest, and absolute stillness ensues. In a split second there is another shift—the sound of the sea swells and rushes into my ear. It's so strong, as though the sea is actually surging through my ear. I pull back a bit startled—it feels as though the sea is sloshing right inside my head.

"See if you can let the sea wash through you—allow yourself to merge with its energy completely," she encourages. I close my eyes, with my knees pushed against my chest. Her hands are resting on my knees, holding the beautiful sphere against the side of my head. Wave after wave of energy comes over me—it is so strong the water seemingly rushes through my body, penetrating every cell, cleansing away the impurities and negativity. I acquiesce, collapsing my barriers, laying bare my soul. I feel so exposed. Somehow I sense deep emotional traumas loosening, unearthing; secrets long buried, not even privy to Gary, begin to break up. I'm feeling buoyant—an internal brightness intensifies, expanding and expanding to the point of bursting. Wow! I feel a release—a renewal. There is a stirring of the bottom of the pond taking place, events of the past are rising, but the clarity is still a bit abstract.

Suddenly I feel a hand touch my head. How can this be? Both of her hands are holding the sphere out in front of me—I'm perplexed! Again, I hear her voice gently massaging the inside of my head, "You are experiencing my other body of awareness. Don't be alarmed. Focus on the energy washing away the traumatic events of your childhood. Let go of the pain, the helplessness, the fear you felt and still feel. This energy can draw out the hurt and harm. Allow it to cleanse you—allow yourself to be vulnerable. Feel the love radiating from my hand, filling your body. Feel it replace the anguish with serenity; feel the love of all those who love you so deeply; let their love fill and overcome you." I see Aurora, my Mom and Dad, my brothers, Gary, and Jesus all beaming out their love to me. It is wonderful!

"Let go! Let go! It is not in your best interest to hold on, clinging to these past events. They inhibit your freedom and pure expression of light—let go, be free! You no longer need their story."

A beautiful blue emanates up and out of the sphere, surrounding and pouring into my soul. It is so blue, my skin radiates blue—bright blue. Her love penetrates deeply, soothing the unconsolable, accepting the unbearable—I'm overtaken. My shame loses its power, diluted in her bounty. I open my eyes and tears are streaming down her face, such love and compassion. Her eyes gently open, and a heart-warming smile spreads through her radiant beauty. My tears flow unrestricted, unashamedly. The unbearable has peeked out around my shadows, just momentarily, but now I know its form. I know she has tapped the very depths of my soul, revealing childhood wounds never fully acknowledged, opening festering emotions that have been casting menacing shadows unknowingly into the present. I, like many young girls, became the fixation of a demeaning tutor. I was so petrified at the time that even to this day I don't know exactly what happened when we were left alone. I experienced so much fear, powerlessness, and humiliation that I blocked out the actual encounters. But clearly I was sexually abused in some fashion and have struggled to break free from my inhibitions, shame, and pain.

This experience has reconnected me to my trauma—beginning the exorcism of my personal demons and the release of the sullied feelings that have tainted me. The love transmitted by this gracious being, who exudes such a pure and healthy sexuality, has provided me with the impetus to heal. I now feel opened and ready to face the process of healing. A feeling of gratitude and intimacy fills me, but I realize I don't even know her name. Instantly, the name "Soul" illuminates my inner screen. We lock in an eye-beaming embrace—diving deep, deep down through the canyons of our beings. The feelings...uncontrollably ecstatic; my spirit dances wildly, irresponsibly, like a bursting, mischievous sparkler—waving a glimpse of the mystery in the jubilant hand of a child. Shining for all it's worth. I feel so refreshed, elated—a fullness I haven't experienced since I was a child.

Now Soul asks, "Can you remember when you were drawing my portrait?" She reflects thoughtfully, returning the sphere to the pouch in the pocket of her gown, smiling at the memory. "Remember you had so much trouble getting the image of my headdress?" she laughs. "You kept asking Aurora out loud, 'Is it a snake, is it a bird? What is it? What is it?'" We laugh and laugh like two giddy kids, amused over some trivial secret. "Finally you got it. I was so excited I jumped and cheered right out loud! That was quite some time ago. I am so happy we have finally been given a chance to experience each other and commune. I know it is difficult for you to stay long—I would like to show you so much more, but it must be another time."

We both stand up. I don't want to leave—I'm so grateful. She puts her hands on my face and kisses me tenderly on the side of my forehead, saying, "You will heal, of that I am sure—Oway, oway, sweet one."

I float off, lifting back into space.

I decide to visit Soul a second time, wanting further clarity about the issues that seem to inhibit my sexuality and enjoying sex the way I'd like. After focusing my attention on Soul—whap, I'm inside a charming house. It's nighttime and I'm sitting by an expansive window. My attention moves casually around the room, taking in a Christmas tree and a Shaker-style easy chair resting close by. Out the window countless stars are adrift in the inky sky—a huge moon and gigantic planets hang like ornaments. It's incredibly magical—one can imagine how easy it must be to create a relationship with the heavens when the immediate solar system seems to be smack-dab in your living room. Astronomers would die to snatch a glimpse of this. When I return my attention to the room, Soul is sitting in the Shaker chair.

I am excited to see her and we exchange warm telepathic hellos, then I ask, a bit miffed, "Why is there a Christmas tree here? I thought only we on Earth celebrated Christmas."

"You have created this environment for your comfort and ease." A fire crackles in the cozy fireplace, sending a flickering orange glow into the room. Somehow the easy chair has stretched and we are both cuddled up in it with a warm blanket pulled snugly over us—it's just wonderful. It feels like my big sister has just come home for the holidays and we have months to catch up on. I'm so happy to see her. I notice the smells of Christmas scenting the air with cinnamon and savory herbs, wafting through the sweet scent of a Silver-tip Fir.

"You have created everything in the room, the objects and the feelings they emanate. This is what is safe for you—you feel comfortable and protected in this environment. You could stay in this space forever, couldn't you?"

"Yes, this really feels wonderful!"

Now her demeanor turns more intent. "There are many wonderful things out there waiting for you to discover and explore, some of which will enrich your life even more than you can imagine. You will not believe how aware and energized you can feel. But when you use past events to manipulate current emotions you keep alive the energy trapped in the past's painful events. In effect you are siphoning off a portion of your vital life energy to sustain the pain. When this happens it ensures that you remain a prisoner locked into the perception of the past event. Watch how you use these events to justify your present feelings of limitation, despair, or sadness. This retreat into the past bars you from your right to experience unbounded joy. As long as you experience a need to keep those perceptions alive, feeding them your life's energy, it will inhibit your freedom, stalling you from becoming the person you imagine you can be. Retrieve the perceptions, releasing your imprisoned life force from the perception's entrapment, and you set yourself free.

"I know you are reasonably content for someone living in your culture, but there are many possibilities ready for release, just waiting for you to heal, so you can experience these new realms. So many things you can't even imagine. Beings are waiting for you, things are being created just for your interaction. I know it is hard for you to believe or accept what I am saying, and inside you are saying this is not possible—this is not true. But just trust and go on from here.

"Right this moment you are feeling a kind of feeling which is foreign to you. You can see your mind and your being expanding. Your awareness inside your head is feeling as large as outer space—a space, shall we say, which knows no end. Stay in this space and just take what comes to you, try not to analyze it—just let these thoughts flow in without interruption." I attempt to follow Soul's suggestions.

"Now you are interpreting what I am transmitting to you. As I was saying, just let it flow, do not stop to think, stay in the space where you were before—where there is no beginning or end! Just allow yourself to keep expanding...continually expanding into the space that you are in right now. This is where you will receive clear communication from beyond your personalized self, from your essence. It is here that your mind is clear and sharp, and it is from here that you can understand anything that's being transmitted. Believe that you can maintain and sustain yourself in this space. Know you can hang on to this space for more and more extended durations of time, and if you practice, you can stay in this space indefinitely.

"Believe it when I tell you that there are beings out there waiting for you. You have already traveled to many dimensions and planets, so to some extent you already know this to be true, but there is much, much more. Before you reincarnated into this lifetime, there were certain events lined up; there are different courses that you can pursue, readied for your initiative. Many beings previously agreed to be waiting for you before you were even born. This might sound strange to you, and because of certain blockages in your life, you are not able to recognize and experience this yet. To project to specific places takes certain energies that you must be able to access and make available. If these energies are shut down, it eliminates the possibility. Vibrationally you simply will not be able to attune yourself to the experience or possess the vital energies necessary to project into these realms.

"As you know quite well, one of the blockages you are encountering is in the area of sexuality, and that is the reason you have come today. I am so happy that you returned to see me. I can help you, but it is up to you to overcome the blockages. I can tell you though, after you have let go of the past and overcome the events you will soon be re-experiencing, you will be so magnificent—you will be out of this world! And quite probably out of this universe! Yes, you are interpreting me correctly. You think I am just amusing you, but once you overcome, you will wish you had worked out this blockage problem long ago!"

She pauses. Now she is bringing out the large sphere she showed me last time. In the middle there is a cosmic color glowing golden dazzling flames. I focus my gaze into the sphere and the room seems to fade into the void. "Now, I want you to bring up your past, bring it up slowly," Soul instructs. "You have incidents that you have blocked, so they are lodged very deep within your subconscious. Be patient, bring them up slowly. The man in your childhood who was your father's English tutor…what was it that you loved about this man?"

I feel almost groggy as I attempt to access my memory banks. I tentatively respond, "I loved him because of the stories—it was the stories he told me. The way he told my brother James and me the stories was so gentle and loving. They always brought tears to my eyes. I could listen to his stories forever. I feel that his stories helped me to be kinder, to love others, and they brought me closer to God. That is why James and I always begged him to tell us the stories." As I talk I can't help but become emotional—tears well up and I'm crying and sobbing in gasps of breath. Shortly it subsides.

Then Soul asks, "What was it that you disliked about this man?"

Suddenly his face is right in front of me. It is so different from when he's telling the stories. There is absolutely no light in his face; it is dark and it frightens me so much. "I remember his eyes—he didn't have to say a thing, it was just the look he gave me. This look was so severe; this look says, 'I can hurt you, I can hurt you so badly that you will be lost in darkness forever.' I can see his hands. They are so dark and creepy, chills crawl through my skin. He is an East Indian man, and his skin is very dark, but when he tells the stories all I see is light and I would never notice the color of his skin. When he is threatening, his skin gets darker and darker—his hands are dirty and grimy. I smell a foul odor. I hated him for threatening me, I hated him for making me so helpless, and I hated him for giving me the feeling that when I was with him all alone I couldn't see the light. Everything around me would go dark—I was helplessly trapped.

"Although I feel the feelings and see the scenes, my memory still refuses to bring up exactly what happened. But I know I became so frightened that I always passed out. I felt so terrorized. What I am remembering right now and feel is true is this: I don't believe he raped me when I passed out, but I do remember being somehow molested and violated. I cried and cried, and then I believe he stopped hurting me because I made such a fuss crying."

Soul interjects, "What is the other feeling that you had? Say it out loud—it is something that you are just realizing right now!"

I am having a thought. I cannot believe I once thought this. So I say it out loud as Soul suggests. "Even though I didn't like or enjoy what he did to me, and I was frightfully afraid of his look and touch, this one thought crossed my mind. I thought I was special to him. In my mind I was thinking…if my brother asked him to tell us a story and he didn't feel like telling it, he would refuse. But if I asked, even though he didn't feel like doing it, he would tell us because I was special to him." Gosh, I am so shocked and ashamed that I ever had such a thought.

Again Soul jumps in, "What else are you realizing now? Just look at it and come to a conclusion. Feel into your past lives if you have to, but come to your own conclusion."

"Wow, it is coming into clarity… I had used my sexuality to manipulate the people around me, doing what was necessary to get exactly what I wanted in past incarnations. I had recognized that my actions backfired, causing me great pain. So I decided not to be sexual this lifetime or at the least minimally sexual, showing little interest and remaining for the most part aloof. I also see there is a fear that if I got too sexually involved I might lose control, becoming overly sexual and possibly losing my loving relationship. Since I have been so prudish this lifetime, this revelation is quite a surprise! In fact, I'm shocked! Now I understand for the first time that this man had actually unwittingly played into my fear around my sexuality, making sexual attraction dirty and dangerous—providing me with further reason to limit my sexual expression. And I suppose enacting karmic repercussions."

"There is something else I think you will want to look at—it is another person close to the family around whom you had a lot of fear. Is this so?"

"Yes." I go into another episode, revealing similar details, all of which I have worked hard to keep hidden within the confines of my private story—never realizing how damaging these episodes have been to my present life.

"Now that you are understanding the stories and witnessing what is orchestrating the blockage, how can you overcome the blocked energy and release the perceptions once and for all? Remember, the psyche continues holding the events as subjective images, completely separate from the actual event, solely based on your interpretation. You use them to support the beliefs for which you want to create support. In your case, it is your wanting to limit your sexual feelings.

"Can you re-image these events now that you see them from a fresh perspective? What role does the imagination play in holding these events in place, and in transforming them? These thoughts will take some time to be completely released, but in one session we have come a long way," she says with a happy lilt to her voice.

The room we are in is starting to fade into stardust. Soul says, "Keep working on your own and call on me whenever you wish, and I'll be there." She puts the sphere to my third eye area. I feel energy rushing into my head and down through the rest of my body—then I am gone.

Weeks have passed, and I am still not feeling resolved about the man who molested me. Again I decide to visit Soul. Immediately I find myself by the river I visited on my first journey, and there is Soul waiting beside the stream. We are chatty for a few moments, but we both know why I came. Shortly we delve into the matter at hand. Soul takes out one of her beautiful spheres and puts it up to my third eye. It is deep, deep blue. Instantly I'm lost, easily diving into its tranquil space.

In a wink I am at a metro transit station in San Francisco. This particular station is sunk down below street level about thirty stairs, where it expands into a large entrance-vestibule before one moves through stainless steel turnstiles to descend even further down to the trains.

In the vestibule plaza I see a man who looks somewhat familiar. Upon closer scrutiny, I see it is the man who molested me. He's run down, very unhappy, and sad-looking. He is walking towards me. I look unflinchingly straight at him, acknowledging him as a human being, but I can find no special feelings and really have nothing to say. Then I turn away and leave.

Immediately another scene flashes. The same man is now lying on the ground in the plaza at the metro entrance—completely down and out and destitute. I rush to him and start kicking. I kick and kick with all my might. He grunts and groans, clearly in pain. I feel no sorrow or remorse and keep on kicking, my anger raging into fury. Suddenly feelings of sorrow and pity arise unsuspectingly and I just walk away, unfulfilled.

Again another scene arises, as if three channels are simultaneously playing on separate tracks. The same man is walking towards me. I stop and embrace him; when I am holding him, I hear Soul's voice saying, "What are you feeling right now?"

I can't answer. I'm trying desperately to feel what is happening. But there is nothing. Again Soul inquires, "Of these three scenes you have just encountered, which would you pick if you actually had the opportunity to see this man again?"

"I definitely know I wouldn't kick or hurt him, and I know I wouldn't embrace him either; so I suppose my answer would be to simply acknowledge him as a human being."

Soul says, "This seems like the easiest path, the one of least resistance—does it not? But you are here to work, so let's look at the embracing scene for a moment. You are aware that he is no longer living in the physical, aren't you? He now resides in the spirit world. What if he were to come to you to ask for your forgiveness? Would you be willing to forgive him?"

I try to imagine forgiving him and to feel if I can. I simply can't feel it—it feels like such a sham to forgive him after all these years of feeling victimized. She states, "You know he is presently in substantial pain and Earthbound. Because of his mindset, he cannot forgive himself until he believes you have forgiven him. So for him to release from his pain, to get on with his soul's journey, he thinks he needs you to forgive him. He is trapped in his self-created belief system, which dictates this scenario. I am not saying that if you forgive him it will release him, only that this is what he thinks because of the way he has it wired, because of his guilt and self-loathing."

Soul's story is compelling. I know I would like to forgive, so I search my heart, but I just sink into this dead black hole. I can't feel it, I just can't feel anything! To forgive him seems so unfair. He has caused me so much pain for thirty-some years, taken away years of pleasure. How can I forgive him in a second? It seems so unfair and unjust. I keep thinking, though... I really want to forgive this man, but somehow even though my mind says it is the right thing and conceptually I know I am depleting my energy with my ill will, I just can't feel it—I can't let it go.

Then Soul comes forward saying, "Don't force yourself. You can only truly forgive when you genuinely want to forgive, not because you know it is the right thing to do, but because you know it no longer serves you!"

I am feeling bad that I am so small-minded that I can't forgive this disenfranchised man in pain. But this is how it truly is—decrepit, disempowered, abandoned or not, I cannot seem to forgive him—so what can I do?

"It is not good or bad," Soul emphasizes compassionately. "You are just being honest, and if you force yourself, there will be no value in doing something society or your spiritual path dictates you are supposed to do. Visualize the image of embracing him for the next few days and see what comes up for you! Then we will talk again."

Sometime later I experience a desire to review the three scenes I experienced with my departed tormentor. In the first scene where I acknowledge him as human and then walk away, I admit that my actions are clearly superficial and self-protecting. It seems easy to recognize I am fleeing something disquieting by taking a righteous stance. I know that the second scene, where I inflict punishment and pain, is not my way or desire—so it is obvious I don't want to pursue or feed this image. So again, it is the third scene in which I embrace him that at once has pull and repulsion. Each time I look at this scene I can't keep my mind focused. It just flies off, capriciously. I don't want to confront this option. But what I notice is that each time I go back to this scene, he has changed. He looks younger and younger—losing the decrepit urchin guise, while transforming to a young man who is now at ease, wearing a white pressed shirt.

So once again I ask myself: do I want to forgive him? Can I forgive him? But maybe the question is, do I feel I deserve to forgive him? Because isn't it I who is bound every bit as much as he? He through his need for my forgiveness and me through my perceived need for retribution? Do I still want to bind myself to this man? It is clear that I do not want to be bound. I do not want to keep hanging on and on to these painful images—images that tie me to these ancient events, which have no meaning in my present life other than to ensure that he gets his due. It becomes so vividly clear that this unforgiving stance leaves me strung up—completely wound in his past web—bound in pain and wanting.

I want to face my sexuality in a healthy way, not using negativity to move me away from feared desires. I want release—for myself and for him, the suffering is enough, enough, enough. When I think about how unfair it has been that I have suffered all these years, and that when I forgive him, he is just freed in a second, it seems so unfair... I despair.

But now I see the truth is how unfair I've been to myself, maintaining this binding hatred, extending my suffering for fear that he might not adequately suffer. What a foolish pursuit, keeping myself in fear—bound to the man I want most to be rid of. I now see how my need for retribution has sapped my vital energies. Realizing this, I embrace him, embracing my future, embracing the notion that we have both been entranced by illusions—each doing the best we could under our hypnotic perceptions, he thinking some little girl could bring him happiness against her will, and I thinking retribution will bring me happiness and safety. Both confusions. In forgiving him I forgive myself for all the transgressions I've enacted, all the illusions I thought I needed, and I release our souls from this wretched misery, allowing God's love to heal us.

With this I realize instantaneously that I have forgiven my parents as well, as I had blamed them for not protecting me, for not perceiving my vulnerability, for not being my confidants, and for letting this incident happen to me in the first place. Then I realize I have also forgiven myself for being so weak, for being so afraid to tell my parents, and for feeling so very, very helpless and ashamed. Even though the event happened when I was quite young, I had continued to blame myself for being so stupid as to ever allow this to happen. I am amazed to see that forgiveness goes so deep, uprooting so many layers of contempt—forgiveness, how could I be so blind? With this purging—it is like an exoskeleton of emotional cladding falls away—I am buoyant and enspirited. I am free. I am light and I am happy!

FOURTEEN

AAH-NUK

*scouring the universe
for signs of life*

THIS MORNING I'M ATTRACTED to one of the beings in particular, so I'm visualizing the drawing of him as I drop into the journey. Immediately I'm transported to a city. I stand in front of two abstractly embossed silver doors, swung wide open, beckoning me into a unique triangular building. The building is clad in a metallic silver and golden skin. Glancing around, I see many similarly shaped buildings interspersed with futuristic gold spheres. The globe-shaped buildings are quite unique. Their exteriors integrate a thin silver-welted spiral bead, seamlessly stitched into the golden surface, gracefully winding its way up and around the façade, finally culminating at the sphere's cap. It's a fascinating and spectacular city, incorporating flashy metallic and glass surfaces—right out of the best and glitziest of sci-fi. But as I turn there is no time to soak in the esthetics. A gigantic lizard is heading my way, sending me scrambling. It is at least as tall as I am and twenty-five feet long. I scamper, quickly lunging behind the opened doors—sliding behind them just in time to save my hide.

I watch the lizard approach from the crack between the hinges. Its forked tongue flits, snapping and hissing—erratically knifing in and out. My heart races like crazy. God, I'm terrified. What am I doing here with this humongous lizard? This is not a casual rendezvous! My mind is completely torched. I can't figure out why this prehistoric beast is roaming around at will amidst this beautiful futuristic city. Things just don't add up, something is amiss here, what has Aurora gotten me into?

Now the lizard nonchalantly heads into the open entrance, but its enormous girth wedges into the door frame, where it's stymied. God, I'm freaking out, my mind is not fielding the paradox. Here I am trapped by this Jurassic creature, pinned behind a door, sweating torrents and feeling quite paralyzed! Just about the time my tolerance short-circuits, several colorfully dressed beings rush the lizard, wielding long silver prods, shooing it backwards. The lizard looks nonplused and I can see it's actually quite docile as it moves defensively, attempting to avoid the waving prods. Its legs awkwardly struggle, eventually reversing direction, claws scratching away—attempting to gain traction on the slick surface. Slowly it backs itself out of its predicament and wanders off like some insect who has just had its path rebuffed, completely unconcerned and directionless. Whew! I can't say how happy I am to see the delightful fellow go! My emotions begin to subside now that my safety appears evident. One of the beings who just rescued me motions me in, closing the door behind me.

"Follow us. Don't worry—you're safe," he asserts in a friendly manner, "for the most part they are harmless."

Abruptly, I have a realization—Wow! These beings who are welcoming me are just two inches in height. I can't believe it! All I can think is that my vibrational body must have shrunk—if I'm not their size, I'm extremely close. Strange, how strange! I have apparently landed amongst a civilization of Lilliputians. Everything is in miniature, so that's why that lizard was so huge. Somehow they don't seem to be affected. I haven't returned to the Jurassic Epoch after all—that's certainly comforting. My mind runs and leaps, flashing back on childhood...to Gulliver and then all the cartoons I loved so much. How fascinating, this is really incredible! Then I think of Gulliver's ordeal. Thank God I'm not his size—that would be really surreal.

Once we move further inside, I see two rows of columns leading inward towards the center. They alternate in pairs about ten feet apart. The first pair is soft and rounded, turned beautifully in a pronounced veined marble. The next pair is shiny-silver and to say there is a contrast would be an understatement. They are triangulated, hard and rigid with a shallow groove routed into the flashy silver cladding. The groove rises up like a thermometer of golden mercury. Around the perimeter, gold walls gradually slant inward, forming an apex of clear glass, centered like a crowning jewel atop a futurist's symbol of royal sovereignty. It's quite regal, yet the building's vast spatial proportion gives it a bit of a municipal atmosphere.

My new acquaintances lead me meandering towards the central arena. Many people are milling about, all in brightly colored outfits—chartreuse, fuchsia, orange, cobalt blue—each sporting funny baggy pantaloon trousers. The dress is somewhat akin to ancient Persia, but each garment is shimmering like metallic chiffon, giving its design a distinct futuristic feel. They each wear a festive turban headdress, all displaying colored gemstones mounted on a finial, festooning the crest of the turban. And the jewelry, it is everywhere! They are adorned with sleek ornamentation around their faces, heads, and bodies, most of which is cast out of polished gold and silver, in varying triangular motifs. I've never seen anything like it, and although it's certainly sleek and decorative, I sense the jewelry has a functional purpose.

We proceed. I notice activities happening around me, and I pause. Just when I'm about to investigate further I see my guides motioning me forward, indicating that someone is waiting to see me. They insist I can come back later if I am still interested, so I continue on. The center of the building is coming into view—a mammoth silver and gold metal lotus blossom is positioned under huge overhead skylights. It appears to be something like a massive radio-telescope or an elaborately sculpted micro-dish. It is not necessarily esthetic in nature but primarily a scientific apparatus. If I am correct I suspect SETI would be quite envious! On the inside of each thin metal petal are thousands and thousands of small metal antennae, each alert and awaiting an incoming signal.

Circling the base, complex operating panels are housed in control modules. Each control station is manned by a technician busily manipulating the operations. The technicians have their right hands on the controls and their left hands moving rapidly, almost in a slapping fashion. Their hand slaps from one piece of jewelry to the next, in random sequencing patterns, so rapidly their movements are just a blur. They move from their third eye piece, to their throat, to their nose piece, back to their third eye, to their mouth, and so on continuously.

If I didn't know better I would say it looks like they are victims of a habitual tic, uncontrollably moving their hands from place to place. But I can tell their movements have something to do with the operation of the apparatus. I intuit that they can operate the controls without the jewelry, but in order to increase the speed of the complex calculations and theorizing, the galvanic skin response created by touching their jewelry seems to optimize their performance. The neck jewelry facilitates more precise verbal skills involved in communication; the third eye jewelry stimulates rapid cognition; and the nose jewelry increases the intake of energy from the atmosphere, replenishing these beings as they raise their operating speed. Each piece of jewelry's placement has a specific function—making the technician more efficient at the various tasks. It is an amazing sight to watch. They fly through their operations like someone locked in a flurry of Hail Marys, systematically focused on salvation; then periodically their finial gemstone sparks, bolting out an impressive flash of light. Ah, the epiphany!

Oh, there is the being I have drawn! He is seated at one of the terminals. He turns and gestures for me to wait a few moments and he will be right there. Shortly he motions someone over to take the controls. When he climbs out of the station, his movements are stiff and deliberate, almost robotic. Then he puts his hands on the jewelry surrounding his waist, he exhales with a big sigh, and the robotic motion disappears.

Now he gives me a slight bow. I intuit that he would like me to give him my hand. I reach out, and he takes my right hand with his right hand and bows down. He presses my hand to the jewelry embellishing his third eye, then to the egg-shaped gemstone atop his turban. We connect eye to eye—he sparkles and lets go of my hand. I'm moved to repeat his ritual. Imitating his actions, I take his right hand in mine, touching it to my third eye, then to the rosary around my neck. Something seems to complete itself and we are at ease.

He begins talking. His speech is so rapid I can't understand a word. He stops and seems to recalculate by touching his hand to the jewelry around his neck. Immediately I begin to understand. Even though his movements are no longer robotic, there is still a certain precision to his actions—very staccato-like. He is not about small talk or pleasantries, and he launches into his interests immediately with no segue.

"The gesturing I enacted is our way of welcoming! I know you are interested in the apparatus so let me explain. It is an ancient technology developed long ago by our ancestors. We have continued upgrading the technology. Each of the antennae is tuned to frequencies of different planets and dimensions. They are constantly receiving messages. There are innumerable planets and dimensions throughout our universe—we continue discovering new sources all the time. Our operators are continually adjusting the reception so we receive the clearest possible signals. This is an operation that goes on around the clock. Different shifts come and go to ensure no transmission is lost. We have the computer technology to be fully automated, but we are able to upgrade and fine-tune the programming more readily by manning the stations ourselves. The computer can do all the recordings and attune to the various planets and dimensions, but at critical moments that determine whether or not we record a signal, it does not adjust to an unknown emission in mid-process like we do. The jewelry allows us to work as fast as the machine, making us more effective overall.

"You can see we are quite an advanced civilization in many respects, then on the other hand, we have situations like the lizards, which have become a real nuisance. We just have not spent enough time addressing and solving this problem. They are harmless, so we have not tried to eliminate them. Many can be tamed and made useful. In some parts of our world farmers have trained them, utilizing them successfully in our crop production. I apologize for the episode which transpired just after your arrival. It happens sometimes. I find it quite disconcerting and would like to do something about it in the near future.

"We, like your culture, enjoy many different types of work; we like art, music, and dance…in fact, we live much like you except there is the difference of our size."

As he is talking my mind wanders, remembering how as a child I used to enjoy imagining little people as my friends. I've always liked little things like small teapots, or anything that is in miniature. A big smile stretches across his face, as I see he picked up my thoughts.

"Looks like your dream has come true," he delights.

"Yes, though not quite—since I'm the same size as you! But I'm glad, because this way there's no separation between us. Being the same size allows us to genuinely interact on an equal basis."

"We tuned our antennae to your dimension long ago. There are many on your planet who have an awareness of us without actually knowing it. Some have written tales alluding to their inner knowing, not knowing they have tuned to our dimension. Our imaginations really act as lenses—focusing our consciousnesses into other realities. As we shift the focus of our consciousness, we shift our reality. It is just like you are experiencing now—no one could tell you what you are experiencing is falsehood or fantasy. It is an experience as valid and real as any that you will encounter. You are left with images in your mind just as you are with any encounter which people call real. When others read your book they will discover they have attuned correctly, especially when they were children like you."

I'm fading and he recognizes it. I wish I could stay longer, as the conversation is just getting interesting, but I know the signs—it is time to go.

"Looks like this is it for now—you are welcome to come again anytime. Before you go I must tell you my name. I am Aah-Nuk!"

FIFTEEN

SHAFUNA

energetics of placement

It is late evening or very early morning. A striking atmosphere illuminates the landscape like dawn. I have arrived at a circular temple. A small gong hangs on a simple wooden fixture close to the entrance. There is a perfect, peaceful silence. It is that kind of silence you experience in the dead of the night when the city's psychic chatter has ceased. It seems apparent I have dropped into a village sound asleep.

After a while someone saunters out the entrance door and heads for the gong. The being picks up a mallet and performs a short respectful ritual, then proceeds to beat out a series of blasts on the gong. A deep metallic resonance seeps through every hovel of the village.

The sound is powerful, so much so that its reverberations provoke unusual sensations moving through my biology. My pores feel alert and refreshed. In Buddhist terms you might say they seem extraordinarily mindful. Shortly, one by one, beings start exiting their homes. They each have mallets and enact the identical scene I just witnessed, but on a smaller version of the temple's gong. The entire village is engulfed in a deep resonant bellow, rising up like the soul-stirring sounds emanating from the remote halls of a Tibetan monastery. What a glorious sound! The heart of the planet is pulsing—singing out its passionate song.

As I listen closely, I detect each of the individual gongs separately chiming their drone, generating this marvelous tympanic roar. By my calculations it is around three in the morning, quite an unusual time to be carrying on in such a manner. I think, what a strange affair! Then I have an intuition—the sound is meant to facilitate mystical states of consciousness for those who are sleeping. Once a week a different family member carries out the duty, so each may experience this special state.

Soon the harmonic roar stops. The being at the temple places the mallet next to the gong, performs another respectful bow, and walks back towards the entrance. Suddenly he jerks as if startled, realizing I've been leaning against one of the columns watching all this time. Immediately he veers in my direction, quickening his pace. As he approaches, a distinct flower scent precedes him, wafting up through the air like a sweet, subtle incense. When we meet, he puts his hands together and bows respectfully—I return the gesture as graciously as I can. He is about five feet tall, just a little shorter than me.

Without warning, I'm hearing a cacophony of sounds booming in my head. First they come quickly, then the rapid succession slows down markedly. I can't detect any words, just feelings; my head is extremely expansive, like the sensation I've often experienced during meditation. It is clear he is responsible for what I'm experiencing—the rampant racing of a multitude of feelings dancing and slaloming through my mind. Quite strange…it's an extremely empathic sensing.

Then I hear a succinct telepathic communication: "These are some of the feelings we experience during this most auspicious time in which you have arrived. I thought this would give you some insight into who we are as a people. Now let us move to the courtyard, where we can talk more at ease."

He gives me his hand. It has four fingers and a thumb. Three of the fingers are the same length. They are so soft, comprised of thousands and thousands of tiny hairs, similar to the minute hairs of a bat wing—sensuous and velvety. He clasps his other hand over the hand which he is holding. His touch feels so good—yet it is odd, as another wave of unusual feelings spreads through my body. They seem to be a flurry of welcoming, joyous waves, then he gleefully says, "I'm so glad you are here!" It's remarkable—each time he speaks I pick up his emotional content before I receive his actual communication.

As we walk towards the entrance gate, he releases my hand and affectionately puts his arm around my shoulder. At the gate, he jumps out in front to open an intricately woven door. His manner is gracious, almost chivalrous. I suspect he has cultivated his ways through years of some type of spiritual practice—it seems so natural and effortless for him.

It is dark inside, but as we enter, a light automatically illuminates the foyer. When we pass through the door at the foyer's opposite end, the light goes off, and a light in the larger room we are entering comes on. I scan the room for fixtures, but the soft light glows onto a domed ceiling and reflects down into the room without a fixture in sight. The room's walls are entirely fabricated out of glass, opening into a small, beautiful garden courtyard. In the courtyard are several stone benches. We take a seat. His pleasant scent pervades the space—then his face lights, flashing that he has struck on an idea. He indicates that I should wait a moment and he will be right back. He quickly disappears through a set of tall rectangular glass doors off to our left. Momentarily, he reappears holding a tray with two cups, a plate and some paraphernalia; a number of scrolls are tucked loosely under his arm.

On the plate are greenish squares, something similar to seaweed compacted into green bouillon cubes. He puts one of the cubes into a cup, pours hot liquid over it from a small vessel, and hands it to me. It slowly dissolves. Then profuse puffs of steam spurt out of my cup. I instantly start blowing my little heart out, for I fear I will be expected to ingest this scalding, frothing concoction.

"Don't be afraid of getting burned," he insists. "The plant will adjust its temperature. You will see, it will be perfectly fine!"

"Are you sure?" I blurt, somewhat skeptically.

I look into his eyes. They are so kind, I feel completely embarrassed about my distrust. I take a gulp. It is smooth, not hot—not cold. A different, unusual sensation bordering on comfort fills me. I feel the drink oozing through my whole body, purging and cleansing every cell. I start to take another sip when he intercepts me midway.

"Wait," he admonishes, "let the first sip settle and assimilate."

I start feeling the drink, and a biochemical reaction ensues. The oozing becomes more pronounced. Starting at the base of my spine, it spreads up through my body, eventually slipping out through my crown. I feel more relaxed—a clearing seems to be taking place within my mind. Of course he knows....

"Now, take another sip."

Within moments the identical perceptions reenact themselves.

"Take another sip, only this time hold the liquid in your mouth without swallowing," he instructs.

I follow his cue. My eyes close. Wave after wave of green appears on my inner screen. I can hear him inside my head—it is as if he is nodding in agreement with what I'm sensing. Then wisps of pink edge into the fields of green. Then nothing.

"Now, take your next sip and attempt to hear the sound of the colors as you taste and feel the drink."

In my mind I think, 'It isn't too difficult to see the colors, but to hear them—I doubt I can do this!' Immediately he asserts, "This is not true. You are hearing what I am saying—isn't that proof enough! Utilize your visual perception to assist you in hearing the sound—hold the intent to hear. Watch your thoughts. Align them with your intended results, so they will not prevent the results you are wanting to achieve!"

Of course he is right. I take another sip. I hold it in my mouth—it feels so smooth. I see the green and I hear nothing.

"Don't try quite so hard—just be, and relax! Feel deeply. Feel from a different part of you—allow yourself to feel in a completely new way. You will hear!"

My mind is jumping all around—trying to feel it, see it, and hear it all at once. I am starting to get anxious. I decide to swallow. The clearing feeling oozes up, again catalyzing this amazing lucidity. My mind is at ease, completely open and fresh. Gosh, I am beginning to hear a sound. It's like a single note played on a synthesizer, but it is not like my normal hearing. It's fuzzy, almost like a pleasing static vibrating through my body. I am not hearing this sound with my ears; but experiencing it with my entire body. So this is what he wants me to experience. It's extraordinary—I'm experiencing as though all my cellular tissue has ears, each neuron has expanded its capabilities. At this moment I imagine I can smell with my eyes, feel with my ears, and taste with my nose. I feel excited and can't wait to try this type of perception when I return. I notice he now drinks his tea with a slightly new attitude, like someone who has just accomplished a feat. Mind you, he's not gloating, but he glows a tad, and I can see he is quite satisfied with my results.

I ask him with my mind about his scrolls. He twitches somewhat involuntarily, snapping out of his mini-swoon. Then I hear a pensive, "Oh—yes, yes, yes."

He takes out one of the scrolls, spreading it out on a nearby bench. It is a map of the layout of his city, drawn with a deft hand—presenting an artistic feel like the wonderful architectural drawings dating from Renaissance times. Great love and dedication were put into every detail of these drawings—they are absolutely beautiful. He is pointing to an area at the city's center. I look closely—there is his temple, right where he's pointing. As I look around I see that moats of water encompass the entire city. Little by little I take in the complete drawing—I intuit that he is the one who designed the city. I'm impressed. How surprising to have the opportunity to spend time with the master planner. And he is a terrific architect, artist, and mystical prompter all wrapped into one!

Glancing over the plans, I see there is still much open space in which to expand. I understand he is in the process of working with the elders to compose further developments. Looking at the various city layouts, I see that the main temple is always centered, with satellite temples sprinkled symmetrically around—each contributing their support to the main focus. He speaks to me of the nature of placement and the symbology of the designs. He is in the process of devising innovative new schemes.

"I am contemplating designing the next cities with a new concept. You see, each layout generates a vibrational energy that surrounds and pervades the city based primarily on the placement of the various elements of design. I am now thinking of creating a city with four large main temples situated around the city's perimeter, rather than one centered at the city's hub. It might be three or four—I must spend some time exploring the different vibratory relationships before I make my final decision," he reflects.

I'm still thinking about the nature of the vibration when the temple is placed in the center, so I ask if he would explain.

"OK, close your eyes," he prompts. "Visualize a city with the temple at the center and with smaller temples encircling it. Now, hold that visualization and I will transmit the feeling this type of configuration engenders. Let us see what you perceive!"

I see a light blazing up from the central temple. At the temple's crest the light is brilliant—it sprays out its nurturing light equally to the entire city, much like a lighthouse. The feeling it projects creates a balanced, solid foundation at the core. It is a vibration which radiates out that all are welcome at the city's heart, where they derive their main sustenance. The beings who live in the surrounding vicinity feel they are spokes of an integrated unit, all connected to the vital core. They remain individual components, yet feel they are instrumentally part of the whole—operating together for the common good. It could be compared to a beacon standing for a common goal. The temple's central placement gives it solidity, exemplifying a truth, shining its essence for outlying community members to model in their own way.

We have been talking quite a while; I realize the daylight is beginning to dawn. People are finding their way to the temple one by one. It's not quite time to worship, but many are coming early to do their *seva*—gardening and other odd jobs around the temple's grounds. As I watch, several tend the plants in the garden courtyard. I think, 'Gee, the courtyard is so well kept, what can they possibly do? Everything has its place. Their culture is incredibly meticulous, with no exceptions that I have noticed.'

He responds, "These activities are done every day. As you have discerned, we are meticulous. Everything has an order to it, even the garden. We believe everything has a spiritual energy linked to its form. We put our total love and energy into that which we do, endeavoring to understand the unique energies inherent in each object. Our intention is to enhance each object with our love as we work. This can only be achieved by forming an intimate relationship with each object, completely grasping its nature on all levels. Once a genuine communion is achieved, then we can better harmonize with the natural order of things."

My focus is wearing thin—I know it is time to go.

I wonder to myself…who is this being I have been enjoying so much this morning?

"My name is Shafuna!"

The light above his nose shines brightly as he speaks his name. His love beams out to me. The intensity of his emotions shines bright through the light emanating from his third eye. I see that love, compassion, and friendship trigger his lights to burst forth.

As we exchange our affectionate goodbyes, he says, "Perhaps when you come again, I will have completed the four-temple configuration, and we can discuss what I have learned about the nature of the vibrations."

As he closes, I slip away into the late dawn.

About a year later I decide to visit Shafuna again because I am becoming more interested in the dynamics of space and the energetics behind the art of placement. I drop right down by the temple entrance once again, but this time it seems much darker. Even in the dark I can tell there is something different—ah, it's the gong. It is now hanging on the wall of the temple and is much larger than I remember it. A new gong has replaced the old one, and it's much more ornate. All around a centered embossed area, braille-like bumps project from the metal surface at varying heights. Just as I am brushing my hand over the raised metallic surface, the door opens and out comes Shafuna. His face is gleaming and he chirps endearingly, "I thought it was you!"

I'm so happy to see him—it's like seeing a long-lost buddy I've been missing. "Hi Shafuna, I'm back again!" He puts his hands together and bows to me in his gracious manner. I follow, but my imitation sorely lacks his grace.

"I was in the study working and I felt your vibration. It just got stronger and stronger, so I decided to come out—sure enough, here you are!"

"Don't you ever sleep?" I quip. "It's the middle of your night, What are you doing up at this hour?"

"I don't actually require much sleep, and when there is so much to do, sleep is not of much interest to me. I see you have spotted the new gong," he says with delight.

"Yes, I have, and it's quite different from the one I saw before."

"This gong is specially designed to further enhance the sleep experience. It extends way beyond the previous gong's abilities. The small bumps vibrate different tones depending on their height, creating a more dynamic experience. I start by hitting the central embossed area of the gong and then move to the smaller bumps. It's quite amazing how the tones from the smaller bumps begin to move and take on a life of their own. The movement generates a powerful force, breaking the inertia of the sleeper and catapulting him or her into other realities. Each person picks up different tones, which shoots them off into different dimensional locales. The striking moment is getting near, so you should stand back, as this is much different than before. The intensity of the sound may be too much for your vibrational body. But if you stand at a distance it will be fine. See what you can experience."

I stand back as Shafuna suggests. First it's behind the column close to the temple, then I decide I am still too close and retreat to a bench much farther away. Watching, I see Shafuna in the shadowy dawn, mallet in hand. His brightly lit forehead mystically gleams, reflecting off the bumpy, ornate surface of the gong. Somehow I drift into an ancient mythical civilization for a moment. Then he turns towards me to be sure I am at a safe distance. I nod—he nods back his acknowledgement and prepares to strike the surface. It is so quiet here—a quiet like I've never experienced on Earth. It's nearly tangible, like an all-pervasive liquid in which I could suspend pristine 3-D imaginings.

I close my eyes. A deep-space quiet fills me—the gong resonates. It sounds close by. Then the sound gets bigger and bigger—so loud it's sounding only one omniscient boom. I feel as though it is pouring like an ocean directly out of the temple. The tone is so loud and powerful it is like a liquid on my skin. It passes through me like a physical wave, vibrating through the membranes of my every cell.

Now I hear another sound and another and another rippling through my body. I sense he has hit the bumps. The sound zips and moves, as scintillating exhilaration surges into the neurons of my cellular structure. I am trying to feel it and at the same time listen attentively to the nuances. It is similar to Tibetan bowls. But this is more intense, with softer and sharper tones all resonating within the magnificent sound of the central, mother drone. It is so magically mystical—it goes on and on, with each tone drowning in the deep drone of the central sound.

But for some reason, maybe because I came to glean Shafuna's wisdom about the energetics of space, I can't seem to completely shift into a journeying mode. Then a rapid acceleration of striking tones booms into my soul—with that the sound recedes and trails into the ethers. I notice, somewhat surprised, that even though I didn't shift locales I've become stronger. My vibrational integrity within this dimension has been strengthened substantially—but no mystical tripping.

I look over to Shafuna and he's standing by the gong looking my way. I head towards him as telepathic impulses flash on my inner screen. He's inviting me to follow him to the temple. We join and walk together through the same doors as last time—all the lights automatically illuminating our way. But this time instead of going out into the courtyard, we walk down the corridors into a room which is obviously his study. I pull up a metal seat to his over-crowded desk and we exchange pleasantries for a while, catching up on each other's recent activities. It is so wonderful being with him.

Then I ask, "Have you finished the drawings you were doing during my last visit?"

"They are close to being finalized," he responds as he turns to locate the drawings. "Would you like to see the new scrolls?" Without waiting for my response, he spreads the scrolls across the table where I can view the ongoing project. He has situated the largest temple in the center of the city and has located three smaller temples in a triangular pattern spoking out equal distances from the hub temple.

"Last time I was here you were not sure whether you were going to use three or four temples in conjunction with the main temple or even use a central temple at all. So you have chosen a pyramid pattern."

"Yes, I was playing with the idea of four to eight supporting temples, but this is what I have finally arrived at. Each shape generates a different urban vibration, and I feel the pyramid configuration will create powerful energetics."

As he is explaining the dynamics of the energy distribution, I start seeing scenes and realize he is simultaneously projecting telepathic images. I see lights shooting out from the three temples, converging towards the light shooting straight up from the main temple. Looking closer, I see the light emitted from each of the temples forms actual planes of light, creating a three-dimensional light pyramid hovering above the city. It simulates a geometric shield of light—protecting and surrounding the entire city. Seen from this vantage, it's obvious the temples' placement is strategic and demands some precision. The shield operates on both vibrational and physical levels, bouncing away any negative energies.

"This is really neat, Shafuna. Recently I realized I want to do *Feng Shui*, and now I can visualize how the dynamics of placement form patterns of light, building up vibrational forces which function energetically to enhance positive forces!"

Shafuna reflects, "You will be good at the art of placement, because you have the gift of psychic sight and will be able to perceive the flow of light. You must be able to perceive the spiritual forces at work or you are merely reduced to the observance of physical and psychological components at play. When you stand in a room, close your eyes. See and feel how the energy is moving. See the light as it moves through the space. Does it move quickly? Is it congested? Does it move in a smooth, balanced way through the space? Are there dark areas—blockages inhibiting the natural flow of energy? Are there holes in the room's membrane, allowing vital energies to seep away? Is there an intrusion of negative energies inundating the space? Each room will feel and transmit energy differently. Tune in and then make adjustments based on your psychic, energetic findings. This might not be so apparent immediately, but as you practice sensing this way, attuning to each room you enter, your innate abilities will be enhanced. So do not let this talent go to waste—practice and you will see! It will be a bit different for you than me, primarily because you will be working with existing buildings, whereas I am most often working with newly created structures and cities.

"When I work, I am aware of the entire biosphere—you might say the corresponding vibrational spheres of the environment. First, I tune into the energy that the environment is generating. What is it speaking to me—what is the nature of its expression? Then I design a strategy to best accommodate and enhance the natural energetics inherent in the local ecology. It will also be good for you to be aware of this aspect. To a certain degree you are stuck with the structure's placement. But if you tune into the flow of light and darkness surrounding a structure you can improve the quality and force of life energy moving in and around the structure. So always pay attention to the exterior of a building, attuning to the environmental vibrations surrounding the building you're addressing."

"When I returned from the journey last time I thought of you as an inter-dimensional *Feng Shui* master. I was so impressed with your drawings and how you approached the project from so many different levels of existence. I'm wondering, Shafuna—would you be willing to assist me at first, if I reach out to you when I am doing a project? It would really bolster my confidence," I ask, somewhat reluctantly.

"I would be happy to," he spouts immediately. Then I wonder if he can come when I send out the call. Suddenly I remember one night when I was doing my healing work. I saw him working alongside me healing—how happy I was to see him! Oh, of course he can come. I so easily forget about the nature of the inter-dimensional highway of the mind. Then I hear, "Yes, I was there that evening."

"Are you often involved with physical healing as a discipline?" I ask.

"What I do in my work with the art of pattern and placement regarding a structure is connected to spiritual healing. Creating the most beneficial flow of light through a city or a structure allows the inhabitants to live a more harmonious, healthy life. It is very similar to manipulating the flow of energy through the body. So I see myself as a healer—I am just focused on a different area from what people generally interpret as healing."

I'm beginning to fade and I thank Shafuna for all his support and willingness to assist me on my venture into *Feng Shui*. Then I'm gone.

SIXTEEN

TIBETAN EGGS

*theaters of the absurd
on the fringe of oblivion*

OUR MODEST LIVING ROOM environment has receded into the background of my consciousness along with Gary, and I am floating effortlessly through a vast space. All around me are eggs ranging from five to ten feet high. They are idling in mid-space like surreal mirages from a Magritte painting. Odd—it appears I have just arrived at an Easter Day UFO convention. But the eggs aren't your normal, everyday henhouse variety. They are brightly colored, all sporting Tibetan mask guises, and they seem to be housing some quite lively, goofy characters. Their movement is efficient, yet exceedingly comical. When they direct their pointed head forward, they begin to rock back and forth, creating the momentum to propel themselves through space. The more exaggeratedly they dip their pointed forehead, the more rapidly they "motate" through space.

    Within moments, I find myself queued up, floating in line with a group of zany-looking characters, waiting for who knows what? The mood is light, almost as if we are gathering for the latest MGM release. Looking up to the front of the queue, I notice an egg's mouth stretched wide open, harboring a subtle inner grin and a rascal's twinkle in its eye. Its expression seems to capture the essence of some divine paradox which I must be missing, but apparently am soon to experience. One by one in an amusement park procession, each of the eggs positions itself at the lip's edge, then leaps deep into the awaiting egg's gaping mouth. As they disappear into the mouth's chasm, raucous belly laughs reverberate out like jolly ghetto blasters, bellowing strange signals into my wondering mind. Amazingly, I feel only mild trepidation—you know, that antsy anticipation which can creep in while waiting for a rather hairy carnival ride. From what I can tell from this vantage, these eggs mysteriously vanish into the wily rascal's munching cavity. My mind spins and runs, skipping a few beats, but the slapstick quality of the egg's temperament overrides any rampant fear, and I prepare myself for what's sure to be an exhilarating rush.

As I approach the leap, the mouth keeps expanding wider and wider into a cavernous pit. I look inside from the lip's edge and suddenly I am aware that the eggs who have previously leapt are nowhere to be found. Gulp! Well, maybe this is some sort of cosmic joke—the divine paradox starting to reveal itself, like, where do you go when you jump from somewhere into nowhere? My mind flashes on a wise old roshi cackling away over this seemingly all-too-real koan, his crazed eyes alluding to that which still remains a mystery.

My heart races, pushes up into my throat, and then—involuntarily—I breathe in one of those "Oh my God" breaths and off I go, diving head first into the reddish-orange infinity. Falling head over heels through space, I catch a glimpse of an opening way back in the furthest reaches of the egg's cavity. I'm being pulled towards this opening and I decide not to fight it, not that I have much choice, but it seems prudent at this point to pretend; so I release all resistance, allowing myself to tumble into the opening. Whooorsh...POP! I'm jettisoned into another space, enveloped in a dark-blue, then reddish-orange, white, yellow, and finally a dark-blue cosmic field.

Huge mountainous asteroids hang suspended in space everywhere. One directly before me appears to have a comfortable ledge, and several eggs are perched upon it. Telepathically, they grab my attention; I feel them motioning me to join them. In my curiosity I welcome the invitation and take a place on their cozy perch, situated perfectly, facing the galactic panorama.

What a sight—gorgeous, yet so outrageously comical I have to laugh out loud at the absurdity! Here, out in the middle of some inter-dimensional galaxy, I am couched on an asteroid in between two cosmic eggs, both wearing the most ludicrous expressions you could imagine. If I only had my Polaroid! Then I wonder, 'Where in God's creation is Aurora guiding me?' Looking over the asteroid's ledge is like a view into forever; stars and planets peep out and around the other asteroid mountains that hover throughout the galactic majesty. It really is breath-taking! Glancing around, I see that all the other eggs who leapt before me have taken up similar positions on neighboring asteroids. We are all sitting expectantly in unconventional theater fashion doing—I don't know what!

Funny as it seems, cricket-like sounds emanate out of the dark-blue universe and for a moment I slip into the past. It is almost as if it were early evening and I'm sitting on the veranda at a rural house in the Midwest, whiling away the evening. But as my hand happens to touch some strange spherical forms in the damp moss, I'm immediately reminded that the Midwest is quite a way off. In between the mossy fibers, thousands of pearly beads glow pale translucent hues from their tiny nests, all threaded haphazardly together in a plant that is completely alien to me.

Watching for clues as to what's going on, I get the impression the eggs are fascinated with a brilliant moon coming into focus off to our left. They all seem to be waiting, as if in anticipation of an event about to transpire. Soon the moon begins to release sheets of colors, and transparent filmy gels wave and ripple into the pristine skies. In moments the entire skyscape transforms to pink—then layers of green undulate out of the lunar form, sweeping the pink. The pink blends perfectly into the green overlying gels, while sprinkles of multi-colored stars twinkle through the layers, as layer after layer of jello-like colors flows out of the moon. Symphonies of sounds glide through the distance, co-mingling with the crickets, and the galactic auditorium swells, heightening its phantasmagoria. The colors animate languidly, deftly evolving into elegant, ornate, Brunchwig and Fils' floral patterns—each swooning to the rhythm of the cosmic choreography.

The visuals are impressive beyond description, vividly delicious—but as I continue to wonder why the eggs were so eager, the real hit comes. Each egg leans forward in eager anticipation. The colors seem to be loaded with a vibrational charge and when it hits, from the looks of things it doesn't disappoint. As I look around, the eggs are actually physically bent back from the blast. You would think there were howling hurricane winds storming past, yet the skies are perfectly calm.

I feel the eggs on either side begin to brace themselves. I think it not a bad idea to ready myself for something—just what, I am not exactly sure. Sheets of pale yellow then magenta overwhelm us. My whole body is tingling; it is as though I'm screaming down the descent of a roller-coaster ride, shrieking out of my mind. Such an incredible exhilaration—body, mind, and soul are raging on fire. Wow, unbelievable! So this is what it's all about, and it's drug-free—if they only knew, they would outlaw my living room! A soft massaging sensation oozes through me cell by cell, atom by atom. My body bends back—I'm lifting, almost up and out of my body. Unusual sensations are rampaging through me and suddenly I start to feel myself hanging on. I don't know if I can withstand much more, as who knows where this episode might turn next? My body is delirious with ecstasy. Right in the midst of it all, one of the eggs looks over to me with this corny, foolish grin and asks, "How do you like it?"

I think, is it serious? How can you talk or even function at a time like this, much less engage in idle conversation? Is this just a rhetorical, inane, telepathic expression? I'm bewildered. Completely unable to respond, I don't bother trying. How do you narrate an orgasm at its climax—impossible! I figure my blown-away, ecstatic expression pretty much tells the story!

After an extended bask in the orgiastic after-glow, one of the eggs angles over in my direction and asks, "How would you like to try another egg?"

My mind, thoroughly blitzed, thinks, 'Sunny-side up or scrambled?' but I quickly edit and say, "Sure, why not?"

So we leave the spectacular light show and head towards the wild-masked guise of another egg-theater of the absurd. Once again our leap carries us into yet another dimension and I experience nearly the identical sensations as before. I conclude that each eggs acts as a portal leading to a separate dimensional experience unique onto them. If their mouths are open, they are entertaining travelers; if not, they're closed for the day. Each egg seems to concoct its own realm of unique fascination—a sensual garden of delights. Here each of the senses is sprung wide open, stimulating the ultimate sensory gratification—a sort of cosmic mushroom, beckoning consumption. Although erotically Bacchanalian and gloriously hedonistic, each egg seems to innocently offer itself as a gift, candidly presenting its revelatory version of cosmic ecstasy—a veritable pleasure palace for those who happen by. Why? Just because! It looks like every galaxy isn't necessarily a collision course with karma, educating one on the heavy responsibilities of free will. It seems obvious here that pure happiness and pleasure exist for the taking; free from guilt, free from shame—if one so chooses to take the leap.

Pop…swooop, I've dived into another amphitheater. A deep bluish-green aurora borealis sky opens with huge, spectacular lotus pads floating in every direction. My travelling mates are now couched upon one of the lotuses. Once again I join in, sitting between them like old-time pals, all curled up together ready to watch the late-night movies. I decide it might be fun to partake in some harmless chit-chat, so I ask them what their names are while we await the next phenomenon. They quip, "We don't have any names, but how about John and Bill!" Then they start laughing like crazy, completely lost in their existential buffoonery. Now the one on the left says, "I'm I," and the other says, "I'm M."

Then they start roaring again, ablaze with zany laughter—absolutely amused and pleased with their self-absorption. I have to admit the whole scene is hilarious, as here I sit between two eggs sailing through space on a lotus pad, in God knows what dimension, and these two goofy eggs are playing metaphysical name games with me. So I think to myself, I'm sitting between I and M—I suppose they're trying to tell me something. Perhaps we're some type of cosmic anagram. Together if we composed a word we'd spell I'M or I AM. Just possibly I'm losing it, but that's all I can come up with, so I'll have to go with it—or maybe I might lose it! But quite possibly they don't have any names and they're just having fun with me! Could it be? I guess they recognize each other by their essences, what better way? And out in the middle of all this insanity I'm still insisting on my ordered, logical, familiar world.

Maybe what they're trying to say is, "Loosen up a bit, Monica—many of the greatest joys in life involve just being a goof."

When I look up from my comic companions, I see an enormous pointed star stretched across our path. The middle opens up, pale-colored petals unfurling in organic fashion; soon a chrysanthemum-like blossom eclipses the shining star. Now the petals draw back through the flower's seeded ovaries into the star's nucleus. The star gradually starts to whirl, then begins whipping towards a neighboring lotus pad, filling the entire lotus with its auric radiation. As it moves away, the eggs glow in phosphorescent radiance.

Our turn is coming, so like little kids we bounce with giddy excitement, awaiting the flower-star's arrival. The star keeps spinning, whirling its way towards us. As it descends, it's as if my head opens and beaming, brilliant, white light lasers in. A ticklish sensation ensues, not uncomfortable—just a feeling that all my senses are racing like a team of wild horses, insistent upon jamming into my head at once. Everything explodes into bright light; nebulae colors glow and dance through my head. The eggs on both sides are glowing so brightly I can't even look at them. They've gone nuclear! M bobs his head in my direction and spouts, "Psychedelic, eh?" and laughs that absurd chuckle.

But for me, it's pure oneness and bliss—dazzling lights spraying luminous abstractions in every direction, silhouetting archipelagos of distant asteroids. The difference is, now I have a grin on my face rather than a furrow between my brows.

It is interesting to note that the picture depicting the character of this journey ["I"] has a stunning resemblance to an Eskimo shaman's mask from the Lower Yukon River. This mask features deeply carved, rib-like concentric circles, and it is believed by anthropologists that they represent the tunnel the shaman enters before encountering the visionary experience. It is by entering the void at the center of the tunnel that the shaman penetrates the Underworld or Sky and transcends the bounds of the physical universe.

SEVENTEEN

MAYTA

chieftainess creating unity through diversity

I AM FOCUSED ON one of my illustrations of a dimensional being, but I keep floating away. After several attempts, I find myself standing in front of a huge pair of cast-iron doors, set under a large Gothic transom window. Shallow bas-relief embellishes the door's cold surface, and somehow the flowery, ornate design belies my inner caution. Ordinarily, my instincts would shout, 'get the heck out of here!' but at the moment I feel rather calm. Aurora said he would always be with me, so I trust, take a deep breath, and open the door.

It is dark. A hall leads to another set of identical cast-iron doors. Again, I open the door and brazenly trespass. Another set of huge doors forbids my vision and barricades my progress. Maybe I was floating away for a reason! What's going on? Have I stumbled upon some sort of Transylvanian airlock system, Catherine de Medici's dreaded dungeon, or an alien's idea of a mammoth Neolithic cheese maze? My nagging questions won't subside. But the main question eating at me is—what are these chambers buffering anyway? It certainly isn't a patch of primroses! Once I'm through the doors, another set arises. Again and again I pass through these medieval gates, until finally I've passed through five sets of doors; my unwavering trust in Aurora pushes me on, but I must admit, not without some hesitation.

As the last set of doors swings open into a fairly large, apexed medieval chamber, I find myself standing before a stone, Gothic-style throne resting atop six rough-hewn stone steps at the far wall. A spartan woman with an intense demeanor sits on the throne. This is not a casual setting or mood. Set directly behind her massive throne, a beautiful Gothic stained-glass window provides a fleeting escape from the severe psychological rigor weighing heavily within the chamber. Working their way towards the throne, stark stone columns stand like frozen sentinels, precisely stationed and readied for the least sign of deception. There appears to be no break from the oppressive austerity underlying the architectural ambiance. I feel cast back in time, and my senses are taking in images as rapidly as possible while my arms' hairs stand at attention.

My sudden unexpected appearance startles the occupants, and in an instant eight female attendants spring up out of thin air like Nintendo commandos—weapons pulled and charging. I am completely at their mercy and quickly assess I shouldn't pretend otherwise. I simply have no choice, so I continue my course down the sentinel colonnade, totally relying on trust or possibly sheer naiveté. Just before her bodyguards are about to assault me, a shout bellows out from the throne.

"Stop! It is OK. I have been expecting her," the chieftainess insists.

The attendants warily peel back. Thank God. I am happy to be able to say that my persistent trust wasn't rewarded by being skewered in some back-alley dimension, lost forever in obscurity—but I must admit my confidence has never been more thoroughly challenged. Relieved, I gingerly continue until I arrive at the first step of the throne. The chieftainess is sitting in a stiff, high-backed stone chair, intricately carved with flowery designs similar to the cast-iron doors with which I became so acquainted earlier.

A strong, clear voice declares, "I've been expecting you for quite some time and finally you are here." She nods her head, as if saying, 'I am generally not accustomed to waiting this long.' Her look is so stern, but as she nods, a quick smile surfaces from her steely mask. The charm is clearly uncharacteristic of her usual demeanor, and I feel welcomed in a strange way. She has clearly revealed a reserved but deep respect, again knocking me off balance. I wonder about her candor. I awkwardly nod back, attempting to demonstrate my mutual respect. I fumble for the appropriate words, finally uttering, "I'm glad I eventually reached your destination—I was experiencing difficulty at first."

She motions me to come closer. I'm hesitant, but I walk up the six steps, getting within touching distance. She asks one of the women to bring me a chair. A female attendant responds promptly, effortlessly lifting a massive stone chair and placing it down right next to the chieftainess. I sit down. Boy, it's freezing cold, but my body quickly adjusts and I'm fine. This is most different—I have to wonder what circumstances have congealed to escort me into this steely-cold, Carolingian-like era. I see the attendants are extremely curious about me, seemingly musing, 'What is this scrawny little strange girl doing here in our high court!' Again I catch them snatching disguised glances my way, in what I can only assume is an attempt to conceal their runaway intrigue. But maybe I'm just paranoid—feeling so out of place sitting here in this humongous chair looking like Thumbalina—not knowing what to say or do.

Beside the chieftainess stands a nine-inch round stone table with water filling a shallow depression in the table's top surface. She dips her third finger into the small water trough, while motioning me to move even closer. I attempt to pull my chair up, but there is no way I can budge it, so I casually opt to lean over, attempting to look as graceful as possible. She reaches out and touches me on my third eye with the moist finger. Then she dips three fingers from both hands into the liquid and swabs my cheeks. And finally she immerses all five fingers.

"Give me your hands," she politely demands.

I reach out my hands—she embraces them gently, then leans back in her chair. I begin to ponder the ritual's significance. As I'm thinking, she transmits a message. "This ritual when enacted with my people signifies an event similar to knighting in your culture. When it is done with someone like yourself, from another dimension, it represents a friendly gesture of peace and greetings, indicating a willingness to exchange our culture in a seal of peace and friendship."

Then she begins to reflect aloud, "There are many similarities between our worlds. As you can see, our architecture resembles the period associated with your Middle Ages. Our planet has been through an extremely difficult transition, moving away from a violent, warring culture into a time of establishing peace which closely approximates your current situation. We have not fully completed the transition. This is why you were met with some alarm upon your arrival. Tensions and fears are endemic here. They have molded and dominated our lives for many centuries. I apologize for the reception, but we are still a paranoid culture; even unthreatening strangers such as yourself still unleash fear, provoking our guard. Given our past, I am sure you can understand.

"Initially we fought among our own peoples. We are a planet of many different pigmentations. Your planet has mild skin variations by comparison. It has been difficult for the people of your planet to overcome their skin-based prejudices, and still today you confront much racism. Ingrained, rampant, and incessant prejudice tore us apart. We have races with blue skin like my own, purple, white, and orange throughout every sector of our population. The races have inter-bred, creating offspring of a multitude of color variation. You can imagine the hatred and bigotry!

"Briefly let me describe the diverse conglomeration of races that exist in our world. Our white-skinned peoples have dark hair; they have been the slaves of our culture for many centuries. They are the peaceful ones, being our greatest healers. The orange-skinned follow next in rank, having bright orange hair to complement their skin. They are the imaginative peoples, creating wonderful art, music, drama, and clothing. The purple-skinned people are next in caste; their hair is colored an exotic white or fuchsia. These peoples' gift is their attunement to the plant kingdom. They are the gardeners, bringing us food and magical gardens. Finally, there are the blue-skinned people, who have held the highest rank and would be considered the ruling caste. We have governed over the planet, implementing social structures to provide a force of law and justice.

"At this time the caste system has become outmoded, slavery has been abolished, and the races live in relative harmony. There are still outlying, troubled areas, but with these few exceptions, we have established peace on our home planet. In the past we were not only beset by inter-racial warring, but we endured inter-planetary conflicts as well. Our striving for peace has been a brutal, arduous, evolutionary process. The divisive inter-planetary wars have been temporarily overcome; we have approached the negotiating table, but still without complete resolution. So there is cautious optimism, yet constant vigilance. I feel we are within reach of a lasting inter-planetary peace treaty quite soon.

"Occasionally inter-dimensional travelers have dropped by uninvited, so we are somewhat wary."

This comment piques my interest, bringing up questions that I have often thought of but never actually pursued with my previous hosts. Now is my chance to find out. I exclaim, "Was I invited?"

"Yes, of course. When my picture was projected to your page it constituted an invitation. I have wanted to communicate with you for some time now. Even yesterday, when you held your session, I was trying to get your attention. Gary tuned in, picking up my vibration correctly and receiving my communication, but you were focused elsewhere on another dimension. And I think you were a bit concerned about my nature, seeing me visually as somewhat frightening, and as a result you were not overly receptive to my vibration."

I am so impressed with her ability to focus. Her impeccable discipline enables her to focus in two dimensions at once—fully capable of operating effectively in each domain simultaneously. Many impressions of her rush my mind. Without question she has served in many wars, battling heroically and becoming a living legend. As one of the planet's primary leaders, she has made irreversible decisions, causing the loss of many, many lives. But she has always earnestly fought to reconcile her actions based on the greater good of all, no matter how pivotal the decision. She has walked an emotional tightrope with unwavering courage. An unenviable position for most, but a role in which she has thrived, mostly because of her immense commitment and unhesitant will, which she has aligned solely with peace. Through her actions she has created many adversaries, but none who withholds respect. She is a powerful female amongst a strong, willful female power base. Females have held the position of authority for centuries here, and now the gender dominance is gradually changing. Our Feminist movement would find this culture rewarding and disconcerting at the same time. Women's power is obviously flourishing, yet clearly feminine nurturing qualities were sacrificed when they endured a period where violence and dominance wielded an upper hand, completely eclipsing many of women's inherent attributes.

I leave my inner thoughts and refocus on her conversation.

"I feel we can learn from each other. Our worlds are faced with nearly identical crises. We are both in the midst of transforming past patterns of violence and domination. On our planet, peoples are learning to coexist, gleaning from each other the healthy assets each race demonstrates. We found that each race has certain inherent predispositions—traits which enhance the harmony of the whole and traits which have a more disruptive effect. Of course this is a generalization and not a truth, but it facilitates looking to that which is positive. We are now orchestrating these attributes in ways which accentuate the contribution each race makes to an integrative whole, rather than isolating our ethnicity and insisting on defining narrow restrictive boundaries based on our differences. No one attribute is touted as superior, all complement each other, acting as integral components in the harmonization of our culture and peoples. We have learned from each other and are now synthesizing our divergent sensitivities. Unity through diversity is the way—a passageway that each planet must pass through, to initiate and achieve a stable, lasting peace with mutual respect for all. No one ethnic group or race is laying sole claim to their gifts, but looking to see how they might instill them into the population at large in the most beneficial way. It is the maturing and broadening of the group soul."

She becomes very quiet and meditative. Her eyes close. I decide to close mine and join her. As soon as I do, I begin to fade. I realize I must get her attention. I don't know whether to touch her or speak out, and as my inner struggle escalates, she opens her eyes.

"I sense you have to go. My name is Mayta. I am pleased we have finally spent some time together. There is much, much more to discuss. But briefly I picked up your concerns about the strife of your planet. The violence, ethnic cleansings, wars, inequalities, etc. We too have been through this. We have come a long way. You must know the solution starts with one person's thought of peace, one person's thought of love! Keep visualizing, keep affirming and sending out peace. You must be disciplined and focused—it will happen, you will do it! We are still working, struggling—but I affirm it will happen very soon for my planet, because of my will, discipline, and focus! I see myself as the cause at the center of the transformation—this is how each person must learn to hold themselves if transformation is to take root throughout a society. In this way one is in action, always moving towards social resolution. I seek to be of the highest service I can possibly enact. Through determining how one can best serve, one realizes their unity with all peoples. This is my message for you."

cause at the center of the transformation—this is how each person must learn to hold themselves if transformation is to take root throughout a society. In this way one is in action, always moving towards social resolution. I seek to be of the highest service I can possibly enact. Through determining how one can best serve, one realizes their unity with all peoples. This is my message for you."

EIGHTEEN

ARRION

*retrieving
heartfelt communion*

THE NATURE OF THE IMAGINATION has been on my mind—lingering like white sound, persistently nagging. I know my journeying is not a product of fantasy, and at the same time I know I exercise my imagination throughout the journey experience. I interpret the imagination as a sort of sense organ which I employ to negotiate and propel myself through dimensional realities. I am wanting Aurora to elaborate further on my understanding, so I might fill in the gaps of my awareness. Some say that in *devashan* and other levels of reality, entire worlds spring from the imagination. I'm wondering to what extent this is true of my experiences.

Not knowing where I want to journey today, I decide to visualize a tunnel and let it take me where it will. Immediately I hear Aurora's voice asserting, "You are using your will, willing yourself through the tunnel."

"But is it my imagination making up the tunnel?" I inquire.

"There are endless tunnels which exist—you are employing the imagination to grab a tunnel which already exists. The imagination directs your experience to an extent—one might say it organizes the experience, but it does not create that which does not already exist! It could be called an organizational magnet, drawing all the elements into a cohesive experience." True to form, Aurora is succinct, and like Federal Express, off to his next delivery before I can formulate my next question.

Right on the heels of Aurora's commentary, about fourteen different tunnels appear, floating in a circular pattern. They move out from a hub like spiraling spokes on a wheel, each representing the entrance to a different dimensional corridor. I'm questioning which tunnel I should take—none seem to have any particular interest at the moment nor do they display distinct features to tip off my final destination. Finally, unable to detect any obvious clues (like maybe an embossed Air Alaska logo strategically placed), I get frustrated and capriciously jump towards a tunnel, willing through my imagination.

Immediately I drop into a space where there are vapor-like pastel colors floating through the atmosphere. Some condense into soft lines then intensify into brighter colors. They pass like wispy smoke formations lost in space, drifting aimlessly. This scene is familiar—I remember being here once before. I stayed briefly once, meeting a young woman—then just couldn't stabilize so I returned home.

It appears to have rained recently. The ground is moist and the air fresh and alive. I find myself in a small city in the vicinity of what looks to be a gathering place around a fountain. Smooth cobblestones surround the fountain, giving the area a quaint, Old World ambiance. I'm alone, but I have a strong hunch someone will be here shortly, so I relax by the fountain, enjoying the soothing sounds and watching magical vapors passing by.

A short distance away, a huge mass of color moves towards me. Nothing like the vaporous colors, it's a light orange-peach, a huge amorphous form. So large, as it gets closer, I expect it will surely fill my entire visual field. I start to walk away to avoid it, but there is no place to hide. Then I intuit that it's not harmful and I stop my mental running. The color arrives and passes into my immediate surroundings. The entire space turns orangy-peach—the buildings, the fountain, cobblestones—everything! The feeling is subtle. I can detect a vibrational difference, but it's not overwhelming. What does capture my attention is the way the block freezes me in space and time, totally incapacitating my body's movement for maybe ten seconds. It's not uncomfortable—then again, perhaps it is a touch unsettling, as I experienced a mild lapse in my neuro-motor functioning for its duration. The cloud moved much more slowly than the vapors, not causing any claustrophobia *per se*, yet still it dominated my entire experience for ten seconds. Very strange. What an inexplicable phenomenon!

Then I have an intuitive cognition—of course! The blocks of color provide a sort of mechanism to stop one in their tracks, prompting conscious reflection, catching one at times off guard. You could well imagine in what provocative mindframes and positions this might occur. I wonder how these people interact with this unusual phenomenon?

Someone is walking towards me carrying a basket. It's the young lady I met before, she's anxious, hardly able to restrain herself from running. A big warm smile and bubbling laughter push my stray thoughts away, emotions surge—the kind of emotions one knows are tied to intimate knowings. My sensing is uncanny; I feel the nuances of our greeting even though she is still quite a distance away. As she approaches closer, I see others moving into the plaza—the entire gathering place is gradually coming alive. Shops imperceptibly unfold. Suddenly vivacious banners bark out gay solicitations, pungent smells entice breakfastless strollers, and chimes and bells lure the undecided. The entire scene miraculously activates as if this lady's presence cues the backstage crew to roll the set. It's a festive atmosphere—the early morning dawning to the scurry of a medieval marketplace.

I stand to greet the young lady approaching. I know something more than just a casual acquaintance awaits. She reaches out her hand, telepathically welcoming me.

"It is so good to see you again. It has been a while since you left so quickly on your last visit. I have been waiting for you—I'm so happy you're back!"

"Yes, I know, I wasn't able to stabilize last time. I have wanted to come back since I felt a closeness, but it wasn't happening. Perhaps the timing wasn't right. I will be able to stay longer this time; I'm much more adept now." Right in mid-sentence a mass of light-blue color drifts in. Shortly everything freeze-frames, again for maybe ten seconds—then it passes through the plaza. The color's vibration turns my focus inward for the ten-second duration. During this brief sequence, thoughts rush in. 'What am I doing here? What is my purpose here? What is the nature of our relationship?' I become acutely aware of my thoughts and feelings—then the cloud passes.

She asserts, "The masses of colors aid us in centering on the present moment. They often drift in—if you want to take advantage of their influence you can learn much about yourself and how you interact with your world."

"How do they operate?" I ask.

"When the color appeared, didn't it stop you from continuing what you were doing for a moment, almost forcing you inward in reflection?" she queries.

"Yes, I noticed that—yet it's quite fleeting."

"It is, but it's a long enough pause to capture one's attention, allowing the entrance of reflective thought. One can choose to engage the reflections or ignore them. So often we get swept away with triviality, falling prey to pettiness, sentimentalities, useless anxieties, or short-sightedness. The color masses provide the opportunity to constantly re-attune to spirit, purpose, and the concrete finite activity. They freeze one in the emotion and passion of the moment—candidly revealing the now. One instantly knows if one is conscious or lost in the mindless repetitive drift of unconsciousness. The color masses induce a sort of meditative state, injecting contemplation—frozen in the immediacy of the moment. Most attempt to take advantage of the colors. Of course, some are more adept than others, but all who earnestly interact with the colors receive value. There are different methods by which to employ the colors. Some of us use the blocks to connect our thoughts; let me see if I can explain this in a little more detail.

"Let's say I am a visitor here experiencing a blue block of color and a thought comes to me: 'What is my mission while I'm visiting this dimension?' Then the color passes. I continue doing whatever I was doing before the color arrived, but now this thought, 'What is my mission?,' becomes part of my thought process, likely triggering an answer or at the very least provoking additional thought on the subject. While this thought lingers in the background of my mind another mass of color arrives. This color will again refocus me on the question, providing a connection to the earlier thought while further clarifying related questions which may have arisen in the meantime. In this way, insight and direction spontaneously open, helping me to better understand my mission while I am in this particular dimension. So on and on it goes—this process is especially useful when one is in the midst of personal difficulties or issues where there is a tightness of emotions. The prompting can really assist one in getting to the core of the blockage, nudging one to stay present with their unfoldment by continuing to reflect upon spirit while not settling for partial or no resolution. So do you see how the colors foster new connections between thoughts, encouraging conscious internal dialogue, prompted by the inner planes of spirit?"

"Yes, I do, this is fascinating! Are the colors a form of intelligence?" I ask.

"They are an energy, which ultimately has intelligence, but the colors themselves have no inherent intelligence—they act as emissaries of spirit or one's higher self," she responds. "Their energy is something we can choose to interact with or not. They are simply present to foster refocusing, assisting us to achieve our highest potential. This is essentially everyone's goal, but it is up to each person to take the initiative. If one does not want to receive insights, then they will not. Insights only occur through intention. The colors reveal tendencies, inclinations, providing mind leaps, but they are not panaceas, just promptings. Often when people are wrapped up in the routine activities of the day, the colors keep them focused on what's really important to them, redirecting them inward, pointing them to who they really are. Do you get the idea?"

"Yes, I do!"

"There are many ways to use the colors—they can also enhance one's spiritual gifts and talents. Someone who likes to sing could use the color masses to enhance their voice, capturing themselves in mid-performance, to assess the quality of their voice or performance. There are many other applications which I am sure you can imagine."

"Do the color masses drift in and out all over the planet?"

"Yes, but in some locations they are very infrequent and in other locations they tend to be more intense."

"Do they pass into buildings?"

"No, but if there are unsealed openings, they enter."

Just out of curiosity I ask, "Could one enhance negative thoughts as well as positive?"

"No," she says incredulously. "Negative thoughts are never enhanced by the blocks. Possibly long ago there were those who used the blocks to become more powerful in negative ways, but now our peoples are attuned to higher principle and peaceful ways. We are a loving race—even though we may have difficulties, our attitudes are positive. Our culture is no longer enmeshed in disruptive, destructive tendencies. We have transformed ourselves over the millennia into a self-actualizing civilization, intent on expressing harmony rather than discord. When the majority of any race engages in life-affirming activities it has a transforming influence, gradually redirecting others in a similar direction."

"I wonder, with the manifestation of such energies, do you still experience disease on the planet?"

"We do, but it is not prevalent and becoming less so all the time. I know within a short period disease will be a footnote from the past. I feel as this evolves we will begin to lose our physical bodies and merge with the colors. I don't know when this will occur, but I suspect rather soon. Many disagree, but many others feel strongly that this will be the case—so I suspect those who think they will evolve beyond the need for bodies will! For those who don't, the transformation will transpire sometime later."

During our talk a vibrant mass of color, much more intense than any I have seen, moves in. I see an excitement building in her.

"It is unusual for the color to be so brilliant—let's engage it," she suggests.

The color is violet. As it arrives, I easily shift to an inner mode of reflection. I feel extremely still; my entire awareness is focused on being, as if I have become pure thought. Then this thought spontaneously arises—GOD, CHRIST, INNER TEACHER, ME, THE WORLD—and passes. The words are not new to me, but they were certainly unexpected given my present surroundings. I will have to give this phrase more thought. What is the essence of its meaning? Does it tie in with the prompting I received earlier?

"What thought arose? Did you have a revelation?" she asks curiously.

I relate the phrase.

"These words have importance to you—that is why they have

come to you at this particular time. It is never without reason. The colors always focus you on what has meaning for you. Isn't it wonderful how the colors keep us open to a larger picture of who we are?"

I think back to the first prompting, 'What's my purpose?' then to 'God, Christ, Inner Teacher, me, the world.' What is the message? Then it occurs to me that when I am journeying I become so engrossed in the environment and personalities, I forget that everything I am encountering is part of God's majestic mansion—even that which seems at first strange and bizarrely alien. And I am part of all the glory, an instrumental element in divine creation. The divine impulse steps down through energetic patterns until it finally expresses itself as me. The paradox of how the entire play is an expression of Infinite Being and my individual focus simultaneously. The thought allows me to see the intimacy of the universe, the interconnectivity, the holographic nature of how we are all expressions of God, simply expressing from different reference points, but instrumentally part of the whole. So I suppose my purpose is to understand and be aware of this distinction as I travel through what seem to be completely separate realities.

She pauses for a moment reflecting, as if acknowledging my thoughts, then replies. "I want to show you something." She brings out a pouch. She fishes out a piece of shiny rose quartz which has been fashioned into a delicate alien head. A look of surprise fills my face. What an unusual object! One might even say morbid and clearly alien to their dimension. But in my sensing it vibrationally I know the object contains a delightful presence.

"I knew you would be surprised—do you want to touch it? Put it up to your ear, see if you can hear what she is saying."

"She talks?" I say skeptically.

"Indeed, you will see."

I hold it in my hand, still disbelieving. It's vibrating rapidly. I put it up to my ear, feeling a wee bit foolish thinking this piece of quartz might talk to me. I am astonished. I detect a singing sound—something like "Aruu Aruu" moving through a melody. I look at my friend perplexed.

"I heard something similar to this word in another dimension—it was 'Asaru.'

Later I composed a song using this word. Could this be the same word coming from the lips of the quartz carving? Am I hearing it right?"

"Basically, but it is a little different—it means everything and anything!"

Amazing, the interconectivity is astounding! For a few seconds I dip into thoughts of Anadra, who sang these words to me—thinking of how much I enjoyed her. Soon I flip back to the present. I am wondering what my new friend's name might be. Immediately she attunes to my thought.

"My name is Arrion!"

Suddenly my energy is waning and I feel it is time to go.

"Oh, I wish you could stay longer—there is so much we have to learn from each other. Will you promise to come again?"

"I will come, really I will—you have my promise!"

"I will tell you something." She's reflecting, not sure if the timing is just right for her revelation. "This is something you will probably tune into on your own at some point. But I want to ensure we have a chance to share in more depth, so I will tell you now. Many lifetimes ago I had an incarnation on Earth when we were sisters. Remember the strong feeling you felt when you first arrived? Well, this is why! You vibrationally understood but just have not had time to put it all together!" Even though I recognized something unusual about our connection, I am stunned.

"You shouldn't be surprised. Can't you feel the closeness when you gaze into my picture?"

Tears are welling up in her eyes and she's unable to hold back the unexpected emotions any longer. Immense feelings pour out.

"I can't express how happy I am to see you. I have been waiting and waiting. Last time you came you kept losing your focus and couldn't stay—I tried to assist you but I just couldn't stabilize you. Now that I have told you our secret, I know you will begin remembering our past times together. And if you can't recall them—come and visit and I will reawaken our memories."

We are holding hands. I feel so good—there's an electricity in the air, a deep knowing and an anticipation. She hugs me—it's one of those cellular hugs you could melt into forever and ever.

With much emotional confusion and yearning I know I must go, so I turn to Arrion and affectionately say, "Goodbye for now, Arrion."

Since our meeting, I have spent some time tuning into our past life together on Earth. It brought up many astonishing emotions. Now I am set to return to confirm my recollection. I direct a visualization of a tunnel to Arrion's picture. In a jiffy I am standing in front of the fountain where I last met Arrion nearly a year ago. She is sitting at the fountain with her eyes closed in reflection. A pale, pale yellow color block has just arrived and it appears she is lost in its revelry. It's similar to a citrine in color.

I decide to pause a moment and allow the energy to sweep me up. A clear, pristine feeling springs into my mind. It dawns on me—I can use these huge blocks of colors I have discovered here at work or in other places. When I'm upset with someone or something, I can stop for a moment and visualize blocks of light blue passing through the situation or myself. I sense it will help me transform my upset while initiating insights into my unhappiness. When I open my eyes from my momentary interlude, there is Arrion, looking right at me with such affection.

"Welcome back," she says effusively. Then we give each other big hugs and I kiss her on the cheek. I am so excited about my discoveries about our past together, I waste no time.

"I remember you," I exude. "You were my little sister sometime around the sixteenth century in England. Oh, I loved you so much, but the time we had together was quite short—I didn't even get to say goodbye!"

"I waited as long as I could," she insists longingly. "I wanted desperately to see you one last time, but it was in vain. Did you know I came to your bedside while you were giving birth to your little girl? I think you knew—didn't you?"

"Yes, but it was vague. I saw you standing by, so radiant and dreamlike—I was still waffling in and out of exhaustion, so I wasn't sure what I was seeing. But I knew I felt your vibration. You were in your astral body looking over me, weren't you? How did you have the strength to project when you were so sick? You looked happy and healthy—you were holding my hand, beaming out so much love from your compassionate eyes. I was so comforted knowing you were there." Tears well up now—we are both overwhelmed with love...stirring, brewing, inchoate emotions.

"Did you know I named my baby Arrion?" I ask with my heart yearning nearly audibly, pounding in anticipation. Then the feelings ravage my heart, erupting. There is no more control—the longings, the wailings, and bereavements burst into wild gasps and fervent outbreaks.

"Yes, yes, I knew, and I knew even though the name was slightly different than my name during that time, you were honoring me," she laments. "It elated and thrilled me." The tears flood our souls.

Then I say, "How strange that you now call yourself Arrion. I really wanted you to know my baby—it saddened me you never had each other's communion. You would have enjoyed her so, you were both unbelievably alike. As I reflect, I see I had tuned into your soul's vibration and named baby Arrion after you."

"Yes, you did, but I'm not surprised—at some level we both knew the name would keep us together in a mystical way! After I was with you when you were giving birth, I returned home to my physical body and waited for you. I waited and waited, trying desperately to stay in my body for our one last visit." Tears stream down both our cheeks again, as we know this is the visit we so dearly wanted. "I fought tenaciously, but I just couldn't hang on. I knew it would be difficult for you to come after having just given birth. You came anyway, weak as you were, as soon as you were strong enough to get upright. Your husband protested, but you insisted, since he had won out before, keeping you at home just before the birth for fear it would be too traumatic for both you and the baby. So this time he acquiesced. I knew you were coming, but my will collapsed. It was no use—I just wasn't strong enough to endure any longer. I guess I found consolation in the fact that at least I made it to your baby's birth and that would have to be my goodbye."

We can't stop crying. Centuries of sorrow and grieving pour out—it feels so good, like some unseen reservoir breaking open as long-forgotten parts of my soul spill out. The sorrow is odd—its expression fills me, somehow giving me great pleasure and fulfillment. I'm grateful.

"I want to tell you of the other flashes I saw during our time together," I spout enthusiastically. "We were extremely close to each other. One of the main reasons was that we shared in our ability to see the spirit world, the faeries, and nature kingdoms. We would tell our parents about how our past grandma was dancing through the house in gay attire. They would get so distraught, telling us to stop talking about it as though it were something we could just turn off and on like a spigot. When we told our friends they would soon stop playing with us. I was the obedient daughter, so I stopped talking about our gifts, because I saw it causing so much turmoil. But you—it was who you were, you couldn't stop. It might as well have been a lobotomy as far as you were concerned. We still talked together, but you didn't want to be forced to control your experiences of life—forced to express them in secret like some sort of untouchable pariah. It made you feel dishonest and dirty, distancing you from the world."

"Yes, I remember—why in the world would you try to control your God-given nature? I felt I might as well be dead; how could I live being so inauthentic? Oh, I remember talking about these matters in front of our parents. Father got so furious, waving his hands in disgust. You would always get stuck in the middle trying to protect me, attempting to keep Father from getting so angry. Gradually it became just our secret. I finally dropped talking about it with our parents and we were happy and content with the delight we took in discussing our sight among ourselves," she reflects.

"Then we grew up," I say regretfully. "When I was eighteen I fell in love and got married. Even though this was a happy event, we both felt some sadness because this brought to an end our frequent intimate sharings. Once, just before I left home, we traipsed out to the woods a short distance beyond the manicured grounds of our estate. We had stopped for a while to dally and chat, sitting on an old mossy snag which had fallen many seasons ago. At one point you moved away, across a small clearing. We fell into watching the faeries frolic in the glen, as was our habit. Suddenly, I caught a glimpse of you that froze me; you had become absolutely ethereal, fading into the realms of the faeries. You were so faerie-like to begin with, at first I wasn't startled, but then I knew this was different. You had shifted into the kingdom of the faeries and I knew without any doubt it was a sign. You were going to die soon. I was astounded and became so disturbed I insisted we leave the glen and start back for the house. I never told you about the vision, because I couldn't deal with the immense sorrow I felt. I just didn't have the ability to make peace with the thought of losing you. That moment is still perfectly vivid for me. I couldn't rid it from my mind.

"After the marriage I moved away. The distance was great enough that it became difficult to see each other anymore. We did occasionally, but not often enough for our likes. You tried to be brave dealing with the loss, but it wasn't the same. You felt lonely, isolated, with no immediate communion of love. Soon you got sick. Your health suffered and gradually it permanently deteriorated. Shortly after I became pregnant our visits were limited even further. Then you became gravely ill. After I gave birth, I rushed to see you as soon as I could, but I was too late. I arrived to the wails of our mother—I needed no explanation."

We look at each other again. Our love beams strong as ever, tears flush our faces. Momentarily, I brush away the tears and say, "Now, how come I am stuck on Earth and you are gliding through this wonderful advanced dimension?"

She doesn't say anything and just smiles, gleaming at me! Then after a long pause, long enough to let me know there really is no need to answer this question, she articulates the obvious.

"It doesn't matter what things seem like—the advanced technologies, the glamorous dimensions, the unlimited fascination, or dismal, wretched politics. It is that which is in your mind, that which is in your heart, that which is in your consciousness which determines how you're experiencing your dimension. It matters not what is on the outside, it's solely how we perceive things that matters. Do not compare yourself or your dimension with others—as long as you are happy and doing what is important to you, you are creating the world of your liking. Wherever you are is the most perfect place. It always affords you that which supports your fulfillment. You can create it as a heaven or a hell, it is your choice." We keep walking as she continues expounding on her wisdom. Arrion's insights are helpful—terrific reminders about how life is always presenting us with nuggets, but often mossy and in disguise. I am really fading now, and my curiosity to find out more of Arrion's present life is bending my thoughts.

I inquire, "We have talked a lot of the past, but what of the present—are you married, do you have any children?"

"No, and for now I'm happy being alone. I have lots of friends and I am content."

Time is out for me, my focus is completely fractured. We hug each other—big, warm, loving hugs. I am so happy to have another part of my soul connected, and I can feel the same is true for Arrion. I exclaim, "I always wanted a younger sister while growing up—three brothers in a row, no sisters! But now I know you will always be my younger sister!"

NINETEEN

ELIOSATH

*fugitive healers
ride the winds*

AFTER SITTING I AM QUICKLY ENGAGED. Images project in rapid sequencing of frightening events. I watch as beings run pell-mell, scattering like jack-rabbits as doom and terror rain from the skies. The foreboding gray sky empties arsenals of ballistics down onto an unsuspecting civilization. Hordes of beings funnel into small black saucer-shaped ships, while others remain behind to assist the maimed and trapped. The evacuation process is hampered by each ship's limited passenger capacity, creating even further panic. A large ship awaits in the background, but at the moment it is a mystery why it's not being loaded, as circumstances couldn't demand more urgency.

A huge temple complex exhibiting an open central altar stands abandoned nearby. Around the outer circumference of the central opening, groupings of colonnades gracefully dovetail into numerous understated buildings. With swift precision, elaborately sculpted praying-mantis ships swoop down on the complex, firing at will—mounting horrific terror and significant collateral damage to the temple and adjacent buildings. Havoc and chaos run rampant, in what I can only imagine to be an unprecedented attack. While the strategic weaponry pounds the planet's surface, the temple's altar silently retracts into a subterranean silo, shielding itself from the alien hostility. Then a hatch-like door effortlessly glides back over the escape route, providing a seal of protection. It seems there are similar hatches throughout the area, as beings seem to appear and disappear intermittently through these secret passages, without which they would have surely faced immediate genocide.

I am shocked as I view helplessly the outrageous onslaught and devastation of a seemingly peaceful world. In a flash I catch a glimpse of a dark face, presumably one of the beings who are attacking. They are wolf-like and menacing. In a rapid viewing of their home planet, I see dark statues of venerated wolf-beings occupying stations of honor throughout the interiors of a temple. It's eerie. I perceive a dark, negative, threatening vibration. These beings are especially violent, aggressive even amongst members of their own race and obviously systematically ruthless when it comes to distant peoples. I shudder to think of what the likes of Hitler, Pol Pot, Mao, and other contemporaries would do with such technologies at their command.

But against uncommon odds, some of the wolf people have transcended the violence and hatred to practice peace and tolerance. Many of the converted have migrated to the peaceful planet that is now enduring the assault. After the successful integration of the wolf-beings upon this planet, ambassadors were sent back to the militant home planet in hopes of generating a more nonviolent, peaceful atmosphere. This action has backfired, provoking the dark malevolent force to retaliate in the events I am now witnessing. The destruction has assumed cataclysmic proportions, forcing refugees to scour the immediate star system for suitable accommodations.

I now segue into a past event from the peaceful world. A group of priests and priestesses encircles a central altar. The audience congregates in expanding circles around the nucleus of spiritual leaders. The leaders extend their arms with the congregation following their movements. Healing rays of light shine from the priests' hands, exemplifying each person's power and healing force. The members' hands also emit light, but it's substantially less powerful. The priests' energy gradually builds, amplifying the congregation's healing energy. The energy is so intense it actually becomes tangible, crackling like lightning upwards into the planet's surrounding atmosphere—creating a veritable shield of protection. To ensure protection, many rituals like this are linked synergistically, at different locales around the planet, bolstering the solidity of the protective light web. But in the incident I'm witnessing, the surprise attack tragically caught the planet with its vigil relaxed. It is difficult to understand how this could occur, but that's how the events unfold.

I am now feeling one of the planet's inhabitants reaching out to me. She is singing this haunting melody—

"We–travel in the wind–
We–travel in colors–
Through the light our colors do shine
Light—Light—Light—Light
    Iridescent purple, emerald green
    and soft pastels
    Effervescent rainbows, fiery crimsons
    and midnight blue
We–travel through dimensions
We–blend with other healers
Healing is our only purpose
Light—Light—Light—Light
    Iridescent purple, emerald green
    and soft pastels
    Effervescent rainbows, fiery crimsons
    and midnight blue
Feel our love—feel our touch—
Healing with thought and with light
Know that you are light beings
Light—Light—Light—Light

Al——le——lù——ia
Al——le—–lu——ia
Al–le–lu–ia, Al–le–lu–ia
Al—le-lu——ia——"

The song is filled with melancholy and longing, reactivating the feelings of their bygone eons, alluding to a people who possess a great spiritual heritage. It offers hope and healing to those who aspire to their vibration. These beings sing of those in the race who are advanced, of those who seek enjoyment and fulfillment whisking through the endless dimensions—riding upon the rays of color, bringing their healing. I am flooded with emotion as I hear their song.

A glorious past, but now they are a people whose home planet is dying under the continuing terror of negative forces. As a result their race has splintered, dispersing to the outer corners of their star system, where they have been rekindling their culture to minimum levels of survival. Only a few survivors remain on the home planet, doing their best to fan the embers of the past. Their planet is responsive to love and healing, so the refugees attempt to reenliven their beloved planet by sending powerful healing vibrations. Even though their efforts are great, it is a remote chance that they will ever be able to return.

Way off on a distant mountainside I join a small group. Three beings, each about four and a half feet tall, climb an outcropping of rocks, fighting their way through a fierce rainstorm. They are harvesting varieties of wild plants and grasses for their subsistence. Even though their circumstances are dire, they are a happy, loving people—laughing and hugging joyfully as they gather food. I am moved by their demonstration of such deep respect for each other. Even though they are considered accomplished healers, they are constantly endeavoring to find greater insights into the healing process. Through greater understanding, they believe their collective powers might well provide them with the solutions they need to return home.

Their unusual physiology has led them to develop unique methods of healing. We have come in out of the storm and I have been invited to join them while they demonstrate one of their healing techniques. As I watch, I see healing sounds visibly emanating from their third eyes, harmonizing with sounds coming from their mouths. This is quite fascinating. I often feel a sense of sound while I heal, but I refrain from articulating it. Perhaps this is a part of the healing vibration, and expressing the sound could accentuate it. When they touch their third eyes, they aggregate the vibrations, building up the healing energies in their hands until they actually glow. They then direct the accumulated vibrations, transmitting them through their touch.

Over at the side of the room, I am watching a couple sitting opposite each other with a glass container positioned on a table between them. Smoky-colored layers pour out from their hands, depositing sedimentary-like layered bands into the glass container. Layer after layer of colors compacts tightly into the container, until just the right mixture is formulated. Then the container is taken by a person requiring healing. The person lies down in a prone position. The colors slowly seep out of the container and surround the person, then hone into the exact location where healing is needed and merge into the body. A remarkable sight!

Now the lovely troubadour who earlier aroused my spirit comes forward from the healing session to establish a deeper rapport. My attention leaps and I am unexpectedly emotional, feeling such a deep love for her spirit and courage. I have felt this one who has come forward many times. Ever since I drew her picture, I have felt her presence, especially during healing sessions. I never realized though what she and her people have had to endure, and it saddens me so.

"My name is Eliosath. I am one of the more advanced of my race and an adept healer. I frequently travel from dimension to dimension and have often joined you during your healing sessions. I feel so joyous when healing manifests. I am aware you have been cognizant of me and I am so happy you have allowed me to interact with you. You are a good channel for me to transmit healing through.

"If you believe healing will manifest, it will—you must have no doubt. See that healing has already transpired! Do you believe you can heal? Do you have no doubt? Just keep working and really believe! I know you have questions surrounding the manifestation of physical healings. Healing will become physical when you heal with absolute love and a pure heart. There must be no intention of being glorified. Use your whole being. You can heal—know you are a channel for Light and God. Love yourself more, love yourself unconditionally—for this promotes loving others; and have complete unwavering confidence that you can heal!"

TWENTY

JUULES

awakening the full sensory palette

I HAVE SLIPPED INTO AN idyllic scene, standing in the vicinity of a majestic temple. At first I thought I had transported back in time, but upon closer scrutiny it is easy to see that the temple is unusually crafted, much different from anything I have ever seen rummaging through the pages of Earth's history. The rectangular temple is granite, and each side angles upward, pyramid-style. From the smaller sides, immense beatific faces protrude through the outer skin of the temple, pushing out from the tranquil inner sanctum. They are spectacular images adorned in full ceremonial regalia, headdress complete with ornamentation. Each depicts an unwavering serenity, as though momentarily caught drinking the inner revelation, absolutely free from temporal distractions. I have never seen a sculptor capture such rapturous transcendence.

Surveying the site I see many parents accompanied by their children, each with an eager spring to his or her walk. I sense their happiness at being on a family outing, enjoying a place of beauty and cultural meaning. The people have pointed oval heads with colorful plumage rising up the backs of their necks towards their ears—they are very refined and distinctive-looking. Many questions about the site are running through my mind, but no one seems available to answer them.

Since for the moment I seem to be on my own I turn my attention back to the temple. Crowning the temple is a reservoir of water. The water gracefully tumbles over and baptizes the facial façades along with the smooth adjacent sides, eventually coming to rest in a moat-like vessel encircling the structure. At each of the four corners, a stone bridge crosses the moat, then steps ascend the pyramid's corners, culminating at a gallery about twelve feet below the top reservoir. Here numerous entrances open to the temple's interior. The entire structure rises at least one hundred feet or more. Clearly the architects purposely designed a rigorous entry, allowing only those with resolve and intention to enter.

The esthetics I'm viewing are quite extraordinary. They are immediately sensual and sublime, blending a keen understanding of the material's sensuality with an appreciation of the infinite. 'I wonder what kind of people and society have evolved these sensitivities. I feel someone is waiting for me, but where? I seem to be missing my cues.' In contemplating the temple, I intuit that it encapsulates this people's understanding of the mystery of life. The temple enacts the involutionary and evolutionary cycles of the play of consciousness as symbolized by the descent and ascent of worshippers constantly climbing up and down the temple's façade. Through each of their individual pilgrimages the life-sustaining manna flows down and around them from the upper reservoirs of the divine—graced by the transcendent sculpted beings. The structure is a beautiful metaphor for the soul's journey.

I move in closer to the pyramid. People are congregating around the moat, bathing themselves in the pristine waters. From the thronging hordes, the site appears to be a counterpart to Mecca or Lourdes. It's obvious the people believe the water's properties hold spiritual blessings and healings. The surrounding area is landscaped with blooming, green, leafy shrubs. People reverently pick the plant's leaves, rubbing them over their skin as a topical treatment during their bathing. I suspect the leaves work in concert with the water's healing properties.

Once I have absorbed the beauty, I think, 'If the interior looks anything like the exterior, it merits the steep climb, and still no one is presenting themselves,' so up I start. It's a hike, and I find many are resting along the way, but my curiosity easily gets me there. Inside, I am awed by the remarkable spaciousness. The interior swiftly descends into an inverted pyramid, rapidly stair-stepping one hundred feet straight down to a striking altar resting between book-end pools. The altar is marvelously integrated into a myriad of clear glass cloisonne cells which comprise the altar's back wall. The wall's illuminated cells rise like ephemeral, watery pearls, ascending in a feathery gossamer, pronouncing emphatically to all—Ascend! Ascend! Ascend into the glorious, resplendent spiritual realms! It is absolutely gorgeous!

Looking down, I see that the steps of the inverted pyramid provide perfect seating for the worshippers. Each seat is carved right into the steps and incorporates a small dished-out basin for sanctifying the feet. Here the worshippers receive the blessings of the holy waters, cleansing the past and ensuring that their footsteps are purified and guided in the future.

Water is the primary element here—an integral part of their worship practice and life. Even at the altar there are several people bathing in the pools, cleansing their souls and uniting themselves with the sacred source—the carrier and nurturer of all life.

In a blink, I find myself amidst the commotion of a colorful marketplace. The temple has completely vanished; my contact must be attempting to communicate. Images are flashing—all indicative signs that I am experiencing difficulty anchoring myself in the dimension. Someone has just pulled my left wrist—I'm feeling a silky fabric brush along my arm. I snitch a glimpse out of the corner of my eye, but all I can detect is a bright flowing chartreuse blouse. It appears I can only take in fractured forms. Finally someone makes contact and I lose concentration. A voice firmly insists, "Stay with me—focus on my touch!"

As I attempt to stay focused, a wonderful scent arises. Again I hear, "Stay focused on my touch. Get into your senses, really feel the fabric, smell the scent—let it fill you."

The jumbled images fade. Now I'm sitting in a room around a table with an unusual being next to me. She is beautiful—ultra-fine feathers, nearly silken, cover her oval-shaped head. Just above her eyebrows, a brilliant fuchsia plumage fans across her forehead, matching the sleek feathers adorning her ears. I'm still not feeling quite solid—I find her beauty fleeting, as I continue to battle floating away. Her soft, sensuous hands rub mine. Delicate feathers line the sides and tops of her hands—silky strokes gently massage me back. My eyes open, close, then finally open. In the dimly lit room a friendly smile awaits me. A wall seems to emanate the little light that is present. She picks up my thoughts regarding the lack of light—automatically the wall shines out at a brighter intensity.

"Seems like you like it brighter, don't you? My name is Juules. I'm so happy you are here," her pleasing voice welcomes me.

After her brief introduction I promptly fade again. How embarrassing. For some reason I am not able to stay focused today. I hear an emphatic, "Stop doubting. Let it come."

The voice is too strong for Juules, so I know it must be one of my guides. I'm floating out in space, then back in the room. Juules' face arises out of the confusion and there are small tears in her eyes. She recognizes that my struggle to anchor myself is becoming futile and her attempts to assist are so far unsuccessful. I start to float off again then I shout out, "Aurora! Help me!"

Immediately I feel Aurora's cape swoosh around me. I am still ungrounded and floating, but I'm back in the room. Aurora and another of my spirit guides, Mateka, are by my side. Aurora exclaims, "Let's all hold hands."

The four of us hold hands around the table. How good it is to see Mateka, as it is rather rare to see him on my journeys! Their energy is calming and nurturing—eventually I am anchored, feeling quite solid. Whew! Finally I feel more at ease, yet somewhat embarrassed about my complete lack of control.

Mateka moves over and sits next to Juules—they appear to be familiar with each other. After they exchange brief pleasantries she plucks a feather from her forehead, delivering it to my hand.

"Here is a memento to remember me by," she smiles, beaming an amusing, playful sparkle. "You deserve more for your gallant efforts, but by clutching it, the tactile sensation will keep you grounded."

Just then a baby cries. Juules perks up and walks to the next room. I get up to follow, focusing on Juules' feather. As I do, Aurora and Mateka discreetly jump dimensions. They are simply nowhere to be found, effortlessly returning to their previous engagements.

In the next room, Juules attends to her child in the crib. He is darling. She reaches down, lovingly stroking the child's forehead feathers. The child's feathers are pure, snow white. Juules now begins communicating with me telepathically, patiently explaining, "As time passes, our child's forehead plumage will change colors—taking on a mixture of the colors of my plumage and my husband's deep bluish-purple coloration. Since our child is male, the combination of feathers will reflect more of my husband's coloring than mine. Through his maturation my colors will gradually fade and my husband's colors will eventually dominate our son's plumage. If our child had been female, the opposite would occur, leaving our child's coloration predominantly fuchsia. The more one spiritually evolves, the more brilliant the forehead plumage becomes. I want you to know I wanted to meet you at the temple, but I couldn't leave our child at this young age. So regrettably I had to let you explore on your own. I was transmitting all the time and eventually it severed your connection with the temple and you naturally gravitated towards my vibration. I can't play tour guide with you on this trip so I thought I would show you around via projection. You'll like this, it's just like your journeying!"

Juules continues transmitting to me, but now the communication is primarily through images. She shows me a scene illustrating how they communicate with each other. It is fascinating. They project video-like events back and forth as communication. It allows for incredibly descriptive transmissions relating vast amounts of information in seconds. She shows me that they often transmit to each other by lying face up on the floor with their heads grouped together, pointing in towards the center. Each being becomes like a spoke on a wheel, or a petal on a daisy. In this fashion, parents and teachers educate their children.

Now movies project on my inner screen of children at school. The children are drawing on something similar to our paper, but I don't see any writing. All literary and language skills are assimilated through the use of computers. They place their foreheads to the screen and their hands on the computer's top surface. A light flashes and the inflow of information ensues. There is some kind of electron transfer occurring, moving through their heads and hands, which allows them to assimilate the transmission. All the homes and schools employ similar computers and they even use them to vote with.

Shortly after watching these movies, Juules and I journey back to the main temple through this gift of telepathic, shared imaging. It's really just like being there, nearly instantaneous in its transmission. An enormous celebration for their elders is in full swing at the temple. The elders are being seated around the altar, right where the pools are located. They are dressed in special ceremonial robes, made from unusual fabrics. Jubilant, rosy-faced children surround the elders, each dipping and diving in and out of the circle, trying to find the perfect place to stand. Soon the rustling is hushed. As if on cue, the children burst into joyous song praising their beloved grandparents, statespeople, and clergy. Their innocence and sincerity are touching and infectious, demonstrating such respect and love. I'm impressed with the intimate rapport of the children and the elderly; they seem to be a very integrated society. When the singing concludes, the elders are completely submerged in the altar pools. As they re-emerge their feathers are even more brilliant than before, as though they were double-dipped in dye. Astonishingly, they're dry within moments.

Suddenly arenas switch and I am viewing a wedding ceremony. It is an elaborate affair. The bride's gown is embroidered with treasures of jewels, from atop her regal tiara down to the longest, most elegant ceremonial train imaginable. The entire gown is tastefully color-coordinated with the bride's vibrant forehead plumage. Absolutely stunning! In our culture it would appear incredibly ostentatious. But here, the festive mood is the play of magnificent splendor, honoring the pageantry of creation. Once the procession is completed, the couple is submerged in the altar pools and decreed man and wife by the priest's blessings.

Then the images stop. We are back live to present time in the baby's room. Juules is listening to music. She says, "The spontaneous projection of these scenes is really the viewing of past events reactivated through the use of a natural virtual reality mechanism. It is almost identical to reality, the differences are so miniscule." Juules' eyes close as she shifts her thought. She is radiant—completely engaged in the music, absorbed to such an extent that she lifts slightly off the ground. It is so natural I nearly didn't notice. Then she begins to talk in a somewhat thoughtful tone.

"I have attempted to project to you some of our culture, but let me tell you a bit more about the nature of our people. Throughout each of our activities during any given day, we utilize all of our senses for experiencing our world. When I'm listening to the music, I hear it with my ears, taste it with my mouth, feel it, see it, and smell it. We use our whole being to experience each incident of life. Can you use your entire being to experience certain phenomena in your reality? Try it! Listen to the music with your whole body for a moment; activate all your senses at once." Suddenly a piece of music plays inside my head. I attempt to hear it throughout my body, but I'm finding it difficult! I just cannot seem to get it. I continue to focus, and gradually I start to feel the music moving inside my heart. How strange, but it's so physical I'm astonished.

"Feel it in your whole body. What is it like for you? Can you feel it touch and move over your skin, moving through your veins and organs? Can you see its exquisite colors dancing gracefully through space, can you sense its delicate fragrances? Yes, that's right—music can even exude an infinite variety of scents. Can you experience it on the neurons of your entire body? Now feel it around your throat, moving around your arms, massaging your hair…reach out with your neurons throughout your body—feel the body's multi-sensual orchestra! Can you hear, see, feel, taste, and smell with every neuron?"

While she's prompting me, I start to feel the music on my toes. A vibration moves through them as if my toes are flowing with the movement of the music, not a dancing feeling, but a feeling of the music moving through them like an electrical current stimulating every neuron. I ride it like a buoy afloat on the tides of an electrical sea.

"When music is inspired from love, you can feel it pour straight into your heart. When an artist puts their entire being into a painting, you can experience it through all your sensory organs—through touch, sight, taste, smell, and sound. Sincere artistic passion from any discipline naturally titillates and assuages all the senses. So as you continue your drawings remember this, and your viewers will surely experience a sensory explosion. Really, I'm not saying anything that is unusual, only wanting you to be aware that you can direct the focus of your consciousness to all the senses at once—simultaneously appreciating all aspects of reality through every atom and cell instantaneously. Remember what you have experienced—it will come to you eventually!"

Juules is holding my hands; her feathery touch is so warm and tender. I feel her love coming through her touch, pouring through her eyes, enveloping my heart. We embrace. Oh, the delightful feelings rage like gushing symphonies.

She looks up mischievously and says, "Ask your nephew about me; he knows!" Then off I drift—floating away. (Our five-year-old nephew once saw a picture of Juules and exclaimed, "Loving Alien!" Yes, he certainly knows!)

TWENTY ONE

RAY-SHUU
voice-print maestro

I'M RELAXED AND SITTING comfortably. Then quick snapshot, collage-like visions appear and fade like fizzlers into the night. An amphibian, frogish—but larger—creature comes into focus. It has huge bulbous eyes and keeps diving in and out of my vision, like a heckler popping off unusual sounds. Then I emerge into a room. I'm observing a being with a chevroned, carnival-colored forehead standing at a "silverboard" (type of chalkboard) conducting class. Erratically, I cut away to another scene. Here there is a being of the same species lying on a bed, reluctantly waking up from his groggy slumber. He sits up and rolls his large eyes lazily back in his facial orbits, like some crazed "toon" about to make his final departure from the sane. Then there is a pulse on my inner screen, fracturing my experience into static fuzz. Everything suddenly goes blank. Unexpectedly, I've somehow bounced off the unknown back to the original classroom. Whew—this is disjointed!

The instructor is still standing in front of the silverboard as though he was waiting, frozen in suspended animation for my return so he can make his point. Off to one side of the room, a large habitat occupies a sizable space. It's a completely self-contained, artificial mini-environment—like you might find at a natural history museum.

Fabricated out of stones and dirt, it recreates an authentic slice of pond life, providing all the accoutrements indigenous to frog bliss, including tules, reeds, cattails, water lilies, mud, the whole works. Lounging about the habitat are several impressive varieties of amphibians; some are larger than African bullfrogs, others are similar to our typical pond frogs. But each frog's eyes are larger, protruding through a much blacker, smoother skin than is usually associated with species of frogs on Earth. It's a museum display, but clearly created for a more interactive purpose.

The chevron-skulled being at the silverboard escorts his class over to the habitat. All the children are circling around the environment, antsy as usual, looking for a place to plant themselves while waiting for something—what, I'm still not sure. Uncheremoniously, a large amphibian croaks out a throaty ribit. Promptly, and surprisingly to me, the teacher imitates the guttural sound to the tee, orchestrating his mouth and two flaps beneath his lower lip to perfectly duplicate it. His replication is remarkable! After he's finished, all the children start croaking out volleys of ribits. What a scene—each is attempting to get the enunciation just right. Amused, I have to chuckle. Pandemonium flies fast and furious from their aspiring discordant ribits. I suspect it sounds a bit like beginning band, or maybe more like beginning zoo! Really, they're not bad, but nowhere close to the instructor. The instructor echoes my analysis, saying it is not good enough and to keep practicing until they get it right!

Each of the children, like the instructor, exhibits multicolored chevrons capping their foreheads—but with slightly different sequences of colors. I watch the instructor listen intently to the massive frog. Somehow his acute senses detect the vibration, storing it in his crowning stripe. Now he duplicates the sound, matching its enunciation identically. As he imitates the basso ribit, his yellow crown stripe lights. Wow, that's neat! When he matches the throaty vibration exactly, it triggers off his crowning stripe where he first stored the voice print. He instructs his students, "This is the sound you must replicate—get it exact."

The children do the same, storing the ribit sound in their crowns. Now they concentrate on their mouths and flaps, forming them just right, so they can capture the perfect enunciation. But when they articulate the sound, their crown stripes remain dormant. Over time they keep at it—eventually, one by one, their stripes light up. After one student is successful, he or she immediately attempts to assist the others without being asked—quite unlike any classroom I've seen. I take my hat off to the instructor. It is easy to see he has engendered an inspiring atmosphere, where each student is anxious to help their classmates learn. It's obvious the kids really want to learn; each makes an honest effort to do their best. Soon all their capping stripes are lit—blue, green, red, and yellow caps, all aglow. They bop around like a wild, strangely furrowed rainbow tribe, gay and happy about their new success.

Now the teacher focuses on the sound of another frog. The students go through the same process as before, tuning their crown stripes into the sound, then they attempt to match it. It is clear the youngsters are developing their ability to imitate sounds—not just frog sounds *per se*, as it could be the sounds of rocks splashing into the pond or practically any sound. This teacher is expert—his forte is teaching the development of sound expression in the youth, and this is the method by which he motivates and achieves his results.

He imitates another sound and tells the kids they're on their own for the time being, then he walks over to me.

I greet him with a "Hello."

He says, *"Hello,"* with my identical intonation. It's funny hearing him imitate my squeaky feminine voice—sing-songing out from his masculine, alien body. This is perfect slapstick in the making. I decide I can't pass up an opportunity for a little playful twist, so just to see what happens I say with a humorous affect, "Hi there, I'm the woman of your dreams!"

His echo bounces right back. *"Hi there, I'm the woman of your dreams!"* An exact voice print. I can't get over the improbability of this strange-looking being speaking with my dainty, comical voice. It is so amusing that a smile uncontrollably spreads across my face, revealing my inner laugh, which giggles and bubbles away. Then I decide I should be respectful and I introduce myself properly. What has gotten into me? I don't believe it, I never act this way!

"My name is Monica."

He very deliberately enunciates, *"Monica,"* first parroting my voice, then repeating "Monica" in his own. I just have to laugh, it's so weird. Just when I'm thinking, 'Where do we go from here? Perhaps a little Gershwin or some Rap?' he interrupts my inner digression and states, "My name is Ray-Shuu!"

Immediately I feel a little embarrassed for my shenanigans, but I can tell he knows I was just playing and he has actually been an accomplice in my fun. Now I attempt to imitate his voice saying, "Rae-Shoo." A good try, but I fail miserably. I try another attempt: "Rae-Shoo." Once again I'm clearly off. Somehow I just can't say it the same way, even though I've consciously attempted to alter my enunciation! I keep trying—getting closer, but still my enunciation sounds like "Ray-Shoo." Again and again I try, wanting to do as the Romans do, and finally he respectfully says, "You're close."

I relax a bit, but I know I'm not close—I simply can't duplicate his sound, which makes what they're doing that much more impressive. I'm so thankful he has let me off the hook though, as I'm feeling very inept and becoming quite self-conscious.

"It's alright, just do it your way, *Monica!*" He says Monica again as I would—it's so cute, I start laughing out loud. He pretends not to notice me. "You just use your voice," he says with some concern. "Please don't mind my using yours. When we use the other person's voice intonation for their name, it's our way of honoring the person with respect. So, please allow me to follow our customs in your honor, but you needn't worry about being bothered yourself, as it will detract from your experience if you keep agonizing over the exact enunciation. OK?"

A student calls over to him, affectionately using Ray-Shuu's voice print for his name.

"Mr. Ray-Shuu."

I can't get used to this—it just strikes me as comical. Here's this little person using Ray-Shuu's big masculine voice. My giggle button bursts inside. I do my best to curb it, knowing how discourteous I'm acting and that he's telepathically picking up all my thinking, but my masking is obviously transparent. How embarrassing, but I can't seem to control myself. I've been infected with the grammar school giggles and there's no hope.

The student wants to know what's next. Ray-Shuu tells him he's now in charge and to keep imitating the new sounds they discover around the habitat. As I look at Ray-Shuu, I can see my reflection in his huge, glassy corneas. When his attention returns to me, I ask him about the flaps located just below his lower lip on his chin.

He answers, "They are essential in the re-creation of sound. The children are still working to gain mastery over the use of their lower flaps. When they are young these organs are smaller and not fully developed. It takes practice to master this skill."

As Ray-Shuu talks I seem to fall into the corneas of his eyes. I begin to see flashes of him singing an opera like Pavarotti; singing pop songs, imitating Whitney Houston. He's adept at making any sound vibration he chooses, no matter how complex—he's a Dolby maestro, a veritable animated voice-print machine. How amazing, a perfect voice memory!

When these flashes complete, I register some wonder about his eyes. He picks up my thoughts, saying his specialty is the voice, but although he's not as adept with the eyes, he can demonstrate their attributes.

"Come over here and take a seat, *Monica*."

I walk to one of the classroom desks, taking a seat across from him, face to face—or should we say, cornea to cornea.

"Now concentrate on one of my eyes," he suggests.

Once again I see myself swimming in the reflection of his cornea goggles. I focus on one of them, allowing myself to delve deep into his eye. Suddenly, I'm a young child of three or four years, standing alongside my mother. I'm desperately clinging to her skirt, hiding behind its long draping folds. Mother is patting my head, comforting me; knowing I'm petrified, she says, "Don't be afraid, it's OK, Monica." Shortly I shift to another scene. I'm in my childhood classroom in a Catholic school in Rangoon, Burma. My teacher is a nun and the entire class watches as I stand atop the chair connected to my classroom desk, which she has forced me to mount. Tears are pouring down my face as the nun relentlessly drills me to answer a simple question. I am so intimidated and afraid of the nun, I can't speak out loud—even though I know the answer. I'm utterly humiliated and ashamed; it's all I can do is keep from bawling my eyes out and crumbling into a puddle on the floor. So I just stand there, tears streaming down, my scrawny little legs shaking away, hoping to God I drop through some invisible hole in the floor, never to be seen again. But I know the best I can hope for is that I won't collapse.

In this moment, a space opens up in my consciousness. I sense a presence of someone on my left-hand side. It's my master teacher. I experience a rush of energy and vitality, and out of nowhere I blurt out the answer. The nun is completely flabbergasted—I've never done this before. She's so astonished—she actually seems mad that I've broken out of my stupor, stepping out of her incarceration and right out of the ranks of duncehood. I step down somewhat defiantly from my chair and sit at my desk—posture more alive than I can ever remember, wiping away my tears and self-loathing. Inside, I am absolutely exhilarated out of my skin. I stare at the teacher with a new-found confidence, as if to say, "You don't scare me anymore—MEANY!" Then the scene disappears and my face reappears back in Ray-Shuu's reflective eyes.

Extraordinary! This I never expected! I have relived my failure as a student, completely regenerating a healthy, positive outcome to the events which have plagued me all my life. I feel renewed and vital. A new confidence transforms the worn-out, downtrodden images of doubt and self-contempt—transfigured into aliveness! I feel lighter and brighter, with a sense of expectation rather than doubt. It was sensing my master teacher's presence, feeling his love and acceptance despite my humiliating circumstances, which gave me the boost to catapult myself through the smallness of my past characterizations. Knowing we are always embraced—regardless—is so absolving. As a result I was able to lift myself beyond the intimidation and ignorance of the nun. I actualized my desire, spontaneously choosing aliveness over being victimized by my feelings of helplessness. I enacted my power, unleashing myself from the belief in my past limitations. What an exhilaration!

I refocus into the present. I look out and there is Ray-Shuu beaming broadly. I am so happy, I can't acknowledge him enough for his gift to me. I burst out a robust, "Thank you, Ray-Shuu, thank you—this was so wonderful for me! I feel uplifted, like a deep festering soul scar has finally surfaced and purged itself."

"You're welcome, *Monica*," he says in his cheerful manner. "In a session like you've just experienced, we're able to facilitate the re-dramatization of past events, illuminating one's blockages and traumas. No event is inaccessible, and each can be brought up for reinterpretation and reliving. No event is locked into linear time as a static, crystallized event—hopelessly imbedded into one's being as an eternal curse. You see, time is dynamic, not static and bound to linear interpretation. It can be revisited, reinvented, and recreated. All outcomes, conclusions, and beliefs that one has formed, no matter how dreadful one has judged them, can be changed if there is a will to be free. But it's up to you. It is your desire and willingness to transform the event, that makes it so—not us."

I sense he has been most humble. Even though his expertise may lie with sound imitation, he is without question a great healer. He has assisted me in healing a nagging source of low self-esteem. His love and encouragement were pronounced throughout the process. I understand that his compassion and acceptance opened a space, creating the context for healing. Like a shaman's inherent awareness creating the group mindset for others to firewalk or experience some other extraordinary event, Ray-Shuu's being sets the stage for soul transformation.

I am so grateful, I gush out again, "Thank you!"

My staying power is waning and Ray-Shuu can feel my focus shifting towards home. We both stand to acknowledge each other and say our goodbyes. I give him a big hug and unavoidably bump his protruding nose while kissing him affectionately on his cheek.

He blushes slightly. "Take care *Monica*," he chirps in his uncanny way.

A big smile breaks out across my face, followed by a tiny self-conscious giggle. Then I attempt my best imitation of him, saying, "Goodbye, Ray-Shoo."

He smiles, knowing I've made a genuine effort to honor him the best I can. His love radiates through his shining eyes. "Goodbye, *Monica!*"

TWENTY TWO

LIZARDMAN

*ecoambassador of
the galactic hatchery*

MY AWARENESS SIGNALS THAT I'm traveling light years into space, soaring through the universe in a starship. I don't know how I know; I just know. Striding through a sterile hallway I see a red neon haze demarking a doorway, piquing my curiosity. I enter. Stainless-steel incubators rest on table-like shelves, hugging the room's circular walls. Each incubator perfectly cradles a delicate egg. Apparently I have leapt into a stellar hatchery, a strange embryonic cradle of some distant world.

Suddenly I can't focus—I struggle to stay anchored. My entire focus is shattered and I start debating whether I should stay or exit. I hear Aurora's voice: "It would be good to complete this visit another time. You do not have the capacity to be fully here today."

I abort my journey for now, leaving Noah's Intergalactic Ark, forced by the whimsy of a mild headache.

This is a subsequent session.

Bouncing around, I jump back and forth between home and the dimensional beyond. I decide to use the cone to direct me [see Chapter 8]. Still I am unstable, jumping erratically. Using the cone is helpful, but I am yet a novice. I realize I must concentrate—then immediately I hear Aurora's booming confirmation.

"Concentrate!"

I try the cone again, this time leaving my mind behind. I just glide into the cone, letting it carry me. I'm in a room, round with a domed ceiling, completely fabricated out of a seamless matte silver material. In the wall there is a three-foot niche cut out; louvers hang vertically in the window, ostensibly functioning similarly to vertical blinds. But when the louvers rotate, angling slightly to one side, a differently colored aura emanates from each of them. Blue, orange, purple, yellow—the colors are endless. When activated the louver's aura intensifies, reminding one of the phosphoric day-glows of the sixties. Now as they rotate shut, the entire window simply disappears seamlessly into the silver wall.

Intuitively, a knowing dawns on me. Ahh, an activated louver anchors the ship to a particular dimension, reconfiguring the ship's resonance to that dimension. So this is the ship's power core, the chamber which generates the shift from one dimension to the next—a far cry from the greasy engine rooms of the eighteenth through twentieth centuries of Earth.

No one is here. I'm feeling isolated, stranded within this slick hi-tech launching zone. I seem to have landed in a different location this time, but clearly it's the same starship as yesterday before I aborted my mission. This room has zero appointments, just a circular coil of silver unrolled into a wall, with one niche revealing the targeted dimensional spectrum. Momentarily, I hear an internal nudging—someone is attempting to explain the purpose of the room. Colored louvers keep sliding in and out of the window niche, more akin to an elegant kinetic sculpture than sophisticated technology. Then abruptly the entire ship vibrates in quick jolting bumps—it seems we have landed. I understand that one of the kinetic louvers has played a part in our landing, facilitating the execution of our solidity in this dimension.

My understanding is sketchy, but initially I think one louver directs the ship, setting the precise vibration at which the ship must resonate to slip through the dimensional portal. The other louvers exposed in the niche hold the vibration once the ship has attained the required resonance so the ship can stabilize in the dimension. Each open window reveals all the dimensions associated with a particular planet or star, so if we were to look at the window for Earth, we would see the number of louvers which account for all the vibrational dimensions associated with Earth.

Now the open window closes in the wall. I am standing in a stark silver room with no openings and 360 degrees of silverscreen. It appears I've skipped into 2112 or thereabouts. I feel like a quark trapped in a quantum-mechanics experiment. My mind panics, not knowing how to handle the sterile environment. Claustrophobia closes in — I struggle to find some stimulus in the steel desert. A pall grabs me — it is becoming all too clear that I don't do deprivation chambers well.

Then a door opens out of nowhere, perfectly concealed within the silver walls. A gigantic saurian being walks upright through the opening — absolutely regal and all-encompassing in his presence. It's as though I accidentally tripped the trap door in Houdini's magic room, unleashing irrevocable illusions. The lizard being is at least seven feet tall, clad in armor plates covering his forehead and nose. He glistens and shimmers in gorgeous deep purple and iridescent hues. My heart races with uncertainty, maybe the sterility wasn't so bad after all.

It's an amazing sight. Here stands a nearly prehistoric creature, in total command of unimagined technological wizardry. My mind is stunned, reeling to keep its tenuous wits. If you were to fast-forward the evolutionary ride of an iguana or monitor lizard, tossing in a dazzling splash of jungle pizzazz and ingenious genetic engineering, you would achieve a close rendition of what stands before me. I am aware it's the outlandish paradoxical nature of the image that is shocking. His vibration is actually gentle and magnificent, but it still doesn't alleviate a raging case of the willies, even though I drew and became familiar with his image some time ago. Omniscient or diabolical, where will my mind settle? It scrambles for cues.

Then he begins to talk in what I can only interpret as pure gibberish. I do my best to stay calm, even though I'm far from feeling exactly at ease. In time, my mind syncs in and I begin to understand. He states, "We were just departing for another dimension when I realized you had shifted dimensions boarding our ship. I had to do some quick maneuvering to terminate the procedures already initialized into our systems. Once I shut down the systems I came right in; sorry for leaving you in the lurch, but it couldn't be avoided. You had trouble staying solid yesterday, didn't you? But now it looks as though you are quite solid. This will ensure your endurance, so just relax and enjoy yourself. I sense you would like to return to the room you briefly encountered yesterday. Is this correct?"

Even with all my trepidation, I'm disturbed by the imposition I've unwittingly created. He seems concerned with my welfare, and I suppose I can let down my guard and get on with our mutual discovery—knees knocking or not. But words are hard to find and I stutter embarrassingly, "Ye-ye-ye-yess! I would like that—it was fascinating."

We enter a corridor—everything, I mean everything, is hospital-sterile silver. While we are walking down the long sloping corridor, I'm hit with an ah-ha—maybe slightly slow, but I realize why the louvers were moving back and forth so much. It was the Lizardman's decision to shift back. The ship was re-resonating to the vibration of the home dimension, causing the numerous bumpy fluctuations. So from what I can determine, they use the louvers' frequency to initialize the physical shift of the entire ship's molecular structure, launching it into the targeted dimension.

After a short walk we reach the same room I visited yesterday. Glass walls comprise most of the surfaces of the round room. Placed systematically around the perimeter are countless incubators suspended on stainless-steel shelves. They each vary in size and shape, ergonomically nesting the embryos of a reptilian species. Electrical wires attach to each egg, then run back and disappear into the glass wall. The wall functions as a monitor, constantly sending biologically simulated impulses to the incubators, doing its best to approximate the mother's care. This makes the room quite humid in its attempt to re-create the innumerable micro-climates necessary for all the embryos to prosper.

As I look on, some of the eggs begin to develop filament cracks. Shortly, reptilian creatures innocently nudge away the shell, crawling out onto the cool stainless-steel shelf. There are many different species involved in this birthing act. One is a lizard, looking very raw, young, and fetus-pink. I have to wonder how it survives the harshness of the ship's environment. Others crawling out are much more mature, rugged, and astute.

The Lizardman walks over to one of the more mature infants and gently lifts it, affectionately patting and stroking its head. Then he proceeds to take it to a hole located on the shelf. He cautiously slides it onto a chute attached to the hole. The infant lizard crawls down the chute, spiraling to a lower level, where it stays in a holding chamber for the duration of the journey.

Now, the Lizardman moves to a snake which is seemingly close to full maturity. I'm surprised by its size—not a python, but noticeably developed. I can't figure how I missed this creature, which gives me quite a start as I wonder how many others I have neglected to notice. He pats its head with purposeful strokes, like he is imparting its mission, then repeats the same fatherly affection as before and directs it on down the chute. It certainly isn't the same as being received by the vibration of a mother, but clearly the Lizardman is a caring surrogate, transmitting his nurturing touch to each of the newborn. And compared to many reptiles, which are known to have cannibalistic tendencies, the Lizardman presents a distinct advantage. I am still concerned about the pinkish lizard—it is premature by the others' standards and hugs the wall, mainly relying on the heat emitted from the glass for survival. I suppose the Lizardman has his midwifery under control, and who would have more compassion and understanding for its kind than one of its own? So I shift my attention elsewhere.

As fascinating as it is, I thank God there is a buffer and I can keep my distance from the shelf—I've never been comfortable around snakes or lizards and I'm hardly prepared to change now. This experience is right on the edge of creepy. Hummm, maybe that's why I had so much trouble staying here in the first place. Intrigued, yes—at ease, no!

The Lizardman starts to communicate, "This is the method we use to quickly hatch the eggs when circumstances dictate the need. Generally, mothers tend the eggs, but there are many areas throughout dimensional reality which require populating immediately to avoid extinction. Our ship serves as an ecological ambassador, depositing the various species where they are desperately needed, applying a temporary tourniquet. We like to hatch our young naturally in the presence of its mother, but this room has been designed to imitate the vibration and temperature of each of the mothers based on its species, so we have done our best to mimic nature for crisis situations. Why don't you walk around and experience the different vibrations surrounding each of the incubators?"

I am stiff as a mummy. Instinctually I step back, displaying my fear, obviously shying from his suggestion. He easily detects my anxiety, exclaiming, "Don't be afraid—I assure you, you will not be harmed!"

I attempt to get a bit closer, but not too close. I'm sure they can detect my fear. I feel like I am wearing a big neon sign shouting, I'M PETRIFIED—BITE ME. It's true, though, each incubator puts out a totally different vibration. Some are sharp and intense, others gentle and soft, still others more agitating and disturbing. The temperature varies widely as well. Surprisingly, some areas are cool, while others vary in the warmer range of temperatures—each totally generating its own micro-climate.

The Lizardman starts to talk of their mission. He relates that the lower room in the ship has portals for the reptiles to crawl out once they have reached their destination. Years ago, when I first drew the Lizardman, I had a rapid vision of a spaceship landing in a desolate region of a planet. Its hatch door sprang open and I watched as the small portals lining the ship's exterior dispensed swarms of reptiles, slithering out onto the planet's surface.

As I think back to the vision, I remember the outside of the starship was rather clunky—unsophisticated compared to what I'm experiencing inside this highly advanced marvel of technology. He picks up my thoughts: "Yes, your vision was correct. I don't understand your reference to clunky, though—this is an amusing description." Then his expression lifts, "Oh, now I understand. Yes, the exterior was a bit dated. That ship was one of our older ships; but, actually, its design is my preference. I like the older ship's exteriors. They have a certain distinction that the new generations seem to gloss over—you know, like your vintage cars. It's interesting that you call our interiors hi-tech, yet for you, the old exterior is hi-tech as well—is it not?"

I determine he has me there, so I nod nonchalantly, shrug my shoulders, then change the subject, asking, "Where are we? Have we shifted dimensions yet or are we still on your home turf?"

"We never completed the dimensional shift, so we're still on our home planet," he responds.

"I see." I guess I was right about all the jolts. But I'm still a bit confused over the imagery I saw long ago. I say, "In my vision which you referred to—was I watching you land on Earth to deposit the reptiles or was it another planet? I suppose what I am asking is, was it your ancestors that were responsible for seeding our planet with reptiles?"

"Yes and no. The first reptiles on Earth were there before we initially visited. But, when there's an ecological disaster or a planet is undergoing environmental crisis, the planet cries out to the universe. Our home planet is quite similar to yours; much of the vegetation and many of the reptile species are closely related and alike. So when a planet has a need we hear this eerie crying-out—a rippling through the dimensions of our multi-dimensional universe. We receive the call. You might say it's a sort of inter-dimensional alarm to which we are instinctually attuned—like a mother to the needs of her child. When a planet like yours has undergone such devastation to its rainforests, many species are forced to the brink of extinction, if not beyond! We hear the beckoning wails reverberating though the neuro-highways of space, and we answer the best we can. We make our deposits discreetly, trusting that the modest number of species we release will adapt and repopulate. There are those among you who have championed the cause of the rainforests, but there must be more if you are to salvage one of your greatest treasures. And it is imperative that you do so. As we see it, you are ripping out the terrestrial lungs of the planet—how can you expect to survive? The devastation must stop! The animals will not survive it and quite possibly neither will the planet."

The sadness in his voice as he talks is unnerving. He demonstrates tremendous compassion and devotion for his species, but even greater passion for the health and welfare of the habitats and ecosystems throughout the universe. He is a compelling ambassador summoning us to awaken and turn back from the course of extinction.

"One of the reasons I came to you, Monica, was to bring this message for your people, emphasizing the environmental crisis your planet is encountering and the immediate necessity to stop the clearcutting and destruction of the forests and rainforests. Personal profits must be forsaken for the greater good. Listen not to the advancing forces of greed. Many have heard the ecologists' pleas, all too many times, but now it comes from the womb of space—we hope it will be received with a different spirit and enthusiasm. The environment cries out, the plants cry out, the animals cry out, all the inter-dimensional denizens cry out, and I cry out. *Oooo-whooy-ooooo!! Oooo-whooy-ooooo!!* We implore you to listen to our pleas, to feel the desperation and pain and act!"

His cry is so visceral and haunting that goose bumps rise all over me and I shake and shudder in my bones. I will never forget this sound. It is absolutely torturing, like hellacious wails of souls dying before their time—looking back at their ashen bones rattling through the winds of deserted space.

"At first I thought I wasn't going to be included in the book, as many of your first pictures have not been considered for the book. I was so disappointed! Then, when Gary insisted on including me in the final book I was so happy. I want to thank Gary for his insistence, and I trust that through the book's publication many will embrace our plea. We work hard to keep the endless dimensions replenished with our brethren. Most of the dimensions you have visited are highly advanced, having evolved a harmonic, balanced consciousness with their environment. But there are many dimensions you have not visited that have dismal relationships with their environments and are mired in similar plights as your own. I often travel through these dimensions restoring the depleted reptilian populations. But it is not a cure, only a stop-gap measure in hope that the peoples will soon wake up and observe the need for harmonic communion with the other denizens of their planet. Dominance must give way to cooperation and a genuine enactment of co-creatorship and co-existence with nature."

His power and message hit me hard. Feeling no better than the rest of my species and quite self-conscious and embarrassed about my personal weakness, I tell him I have a confession to make.

"The first time I saw you on my page, I was very afraid. I didn't want to finish your drawing. Not only was I afraid, but I was sure I saw you incorrectly. How could this creepy creature be coming to me? I thought I must be traveling to the lower astral planes—this cannot be an evolved species. I have had such great fear of that with which I am not familiar. Now I'm so glad I completed the drawing. It wasn't easy for me, and you can see I'm still struggling. But I can honestly say my appreciation and understanding have grown. I'm still afraid—but I feel better."

"I know—but your fear has dissipated because you have stood to face it. And because you did, others will attune without fear just as Gary did. Some will not be able to overcome their fear and I understand—we are so different and do not have the best reputation on your planet. But, in seeking understanding and addressing the alien in yourself, you will knit together a greater interspecies communion and instigate the eventual integration of the vast diversity of consciousness. I am so happy to be in the book. Many will become familiar with me as a result, reducing their fear, and someday when we meet face to face, we will be able to communicate like old friends. When the time comes for contact, this book will have been a facilitating factor in lessening the superstitions and fears, while opening a flow of energies between our two worlds. But the time is not upon us just yet—there are still too many difficulties with humans communicating just amongst themselves, much less facing an evolved bestiary representing the most ferocious citizens of Jurassic Park!"

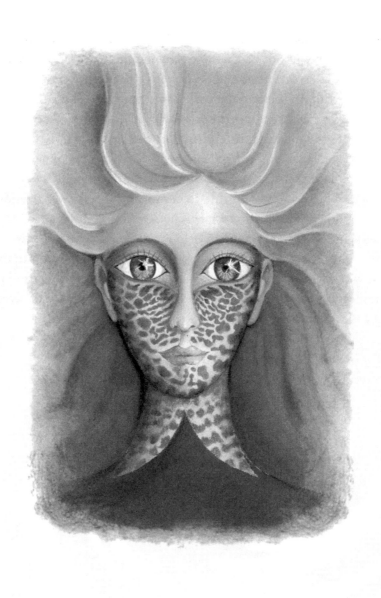

TWENTY THREE

SHI-SHAA

*escapades with
leopard woman and Ooja*

I'M EXPERIENCING DIFFICULTY FOCUSING. I hear Aurora's voice edging out from the drab background of my mind.

"Concentrate!"

For some reason I'm restless and want to wander aimlessly, unwilling to chain my mind to a focus. Aurora gives me some leash and I release into a floating stroll; after a bit I again hear an emphatic "Concentrate!"

This time the echo stubbornly lingers in my mind. I decide to visualize the lady who had the unusual spotted face which I drew several months back. Instantly an arid, hot landscape arises. Soon unwanted doubts creep in, like a virus eroding the pixels of my experience—my vision degenerates and goes blank. Once again I attempt to visualize her face. I hear Aurora emphasizing, "Let it flow, don't think so much—just focus on the face."

Immediately her face comes into focus, along with a host of others. Their spotted patterns all vary in coloration and patterning. Some exhibit spots from their face to their toes, while others somewhat more modestly exhibit their beastie bravado just to the waist. But each is totally unique. Risqué costumes reveal fascinating leopard patterns artistically wrapping and twisting around their bodies, luring even the prudish eye. They are surely festive, mimicking the animal kingdom's decorative, playful exhibition. My fascination draws me to inspect their motifs more closely. As I do, I notice some have tattoos, simulating their beautiful natural patterning. This is curious—some even have gone as far as incorporating hair transplants, attempting to enhance their cosmetic beauty to its climax. Clearly, beauty is coveted here, way beyond our versions of glamour. And from what I can tell, the more exotic and extravagant, the better!

Most display a diverse range of tight eyespots, approximating the look of a leopard. Occasionally, a rarer reptilian pattern can be found with iridescent shimmering colors, forming intricate, scaly meshes. These beings show off scintillating chartreuses, fuchsias, violets, indigos, and blues—while crowning their vibrant ostentatiousness with flaming chartreuse hair. They redefine anything I've ever considered outrageous. If one finds their skin patterns too flamboyant, look out; their hair colors would intimidate even the boldest transvestites prancing through the chic enclaves of New York and San Francisco. Wild hairstyles scream out in carnival golds, bright, gaudy reddish oranges, and jet blacks. They are truly an exotic, erotic parade of vivacious jungle glamour. Sometimes garish, sometimes suave—all cruising, unabashed and unconcerned, through the hubbub of the arid outdoor marketplace.

The boisterous dissonance of the bustling casbah ramble-rumbles out of the masses, as I wander through the thronging crowds accompanied by this exquisite lady. Her blue dress hugs her body tightly, descending voluptuously down to her hips, where it dramatically cuts away revealing a snug seductive bikini, exposing her long leopard-skin thighs, then falling like a veil down to her feet. At the back, the garment hangs gracefully, free-falling languidly around her shapely form. Long sleeves elegantly drape from her blouse; at the cuffs, a pinstripe of leopard spots meanders out and shoots down the tops of her middle fingers. She is stunning, so poised, seemingly the height of fashion—I feel like a complete klutz at her side, especially knowing she's just past eighteen. Sensing her presence, it is clear to me that the flamboyant styling belies the hidden sophistication beneath the circus pomp façade. But at this point I'm not sure to what extent.

Suddenly everything stands still, as if the frequency seems to cut out momentarily. I scramble inside to adjust my inner tuning. Then just as abruptly I'm back in the flow and the entire scene kicks back into animation. We are striding along, window-shopping through the marketplace. It is so gay and alive—extravagant colors snake in and out of what otherwise is a fairly common Middle Eastern-looking marketplace. But what is most unusual is the innocent atmosphere I sense amidst this sort of free-form burlesque show—all unfolding naturally without the tease, taunt, or mockery which generally surrounds similar displays.

As I scan the scene the sun glares down on small groups of people sitting on the landscaped fringe of the marketplace. They have all scattered themselves among the rocks and grass, finding the best locations to soak up the intense rays. They seem to love the sun and enjoy the camaraderie of mixed colors and patterning; it's obvious that each small grouping thrives on the marked variation and diversity, as laughter and energetic dramas unfold.

While we walk, I'm surprised to detect my companion's shyness. But even so, an unspoken excitement is brimming. She holds my hand as though she has been long in waiting, swinging it rhythmically by her side. Her walk is spirited, dancing out a cheerful lilt as we weave in and out among the strangers. She's not saying anything, but I can tell she wants to show me everything as she gestures here and there. Eventually we stop at a stall. Racks of vibrant fabric cascade from the booth, bone and animal teeth jewelry jams the cases, fresh fruits and veggies tumble out of crates, and *chatchkas* pack tightly into whatever space is left.

Somehow, my eye catches a decorative box amidst the clutter. It's silver with an ornate filigree design on its cover. The design is woven out of extremely fine silver threads with a centered bezel, set with a red cabochon stone. Her eyes sparkle an encouragement to open the box. The lid is hinged and opens easily. Inside is a waxy ointment, giving off a pungent odor—a mixture of various herbs instantly clears my head, expanding the neurotransmitting highways of my mind, like a peyote massage. Quickly I close the lid, recoiling from what I suspect might ensue, deciding to stay as conscious as possible of the immediate situation. Things are already strange enough—I think I don't need a higher dose of excitement. Soon the pungent smell dissipates, shrinking back into the case.

I look up inquisitively, as if to say, 'what is this powerful ointment?' Right in mid-thought, she breaks in. "You could call it perfume. We use it to enhance our cognitive abilities and improve our retention during the educating process. It clears the brain, helping one to focus. Really, it's a very common ointment. But there are other ointments which are quite rare and used in metaphysical circles. Let me show you!"

She turns to the lady attendant, asking if she has any samples of this special ointment. The lady whisks around and rummages through her bags, successfully plunging deep into one of her large crates and removing three small boxes to hand us. My friend asks if she minds if we sample one of the ointments. The older woman squints her eyes reflecting, then gestures agreeably.

The box is similar to the first one, crafted in the same finely woven silver design with a centered cabochon, only much smaller. My acquaintance opens the box—this scent is much milder. She dabs her finger into the goo, applying a splotch on my third eye. A cool Vick's vapor sensation roars right through my head, blasting open a sizable tunnel. Images start appearing right in front of my head like holographs, then travel back through my mind's newly burrowed recesses. Stars and planets whoosh by, racing like rush-hour traffic. I'm reminded of the movie *Koyaanisqatsi*. Everything is transforming at breakneck speeds, changing, changing—the marching of galactic and historical traffic. Eons forever changing—then it all shuts off! Fwaap!

Astonished, I look up with an expression of bewilderment. She exclaims, "This is what people use to assist journeys to the stars. But they don't use it in the marketplace, only in quiet spaces which are conducive to meditation. If this practice is followed, then the experience will slow down, allowing an enjoyable, magical trip. Not many are interested in this type of experience though—just a few."

"But you're interested in these types of experiences, aren't you?" I spout.

"Yes, yes, of course," she responds enthusiastically. "This is how I contacted you—traveling to your planet so you could draw my picture. I couldn't come physically, but I came vibrationally just like you're doing. For us it is more of a combination of mental and vibrational projection, not quite the emotional experience it is for you. My parents have always been involved with these kinds of experiences, so I was intrigued at an early age."

We continue to walk and talk, thoroughly enjoying each other. No pretense, just genuine interest and delight, while we each run through a medley of our metaphysical experiences. Eventually I ask her about their attunement to the animal kingdom. I know Gary was suspecting they had a keen understanding and communion with animals, and I'd like to check his hunch.

"Gary tuned in correctly. We have a deep bond with our animals and we derive much pleasure from their company. You haven't seen any just yet, mainly because they seldomly roam into the marketplace, much preferring the calm of the woods, gardens, and open spaces. In our dimension, because of our unusual rapport, they roam free without any restrictions. We don't keep them as pets, but often they drop by our homes for extended periods of time—staying a bit, then slipping off again. When we desire their companionship, we go to the woods to search out their lairs. After a while they sense our presence and approach—lying close by. We have grown accustomed to speaking with them telepathically, carrying on long conversations. Often we become friends and get quite involved in their lives, taking great interest in each other's experiences. Some are very wise and make wonderful company. Unlike many cultures, we've learned to co-habit in harmony, enjoying each other's friendship and mutual respect. But you must realize, even though we have similar patterning we are two completely different species."

After a time we amble out of the casbah and head towards her home. It's a trek, but we arrive. Rising right out of the base of a mountain, her home is much like the Anasazi apartment dwellings built in Canyon de Chelly in Arizona. To the rear a mammoth mountain rises high above their cliff dwellings, creating a dramatic setting. As we get closer to the dwellings I see they are sculpted in attractive, almost condo-like groupings—but more akin to Palo Soleri's futuristic complex of Arcosanti than to the primitive nature of the Anasazi. As romantic and esthetic as they appear, it is clear they are built in this location for one reason—to shield the inhabitants from the sweltering solar heat which dominates their locale.

Instead of visiting her house, we walk past the dwellings to the open spaces, where a woodsy area obscures the grassy fields and streams just beyond. Approaching the woods, I'm startled. Large, what I'd call beasts are nonchalantly sauntering through the fields and lounging in the cool woods. They are huge, magnificent leopards, more than twice the size of our beasts. Just superb, marvelous creatures! Their size is so immense it really takes me back, giving me a bit of a fright. The cats sport varying spotted patterns; some are reddish-brown, others black and golden. Their heads are a bit different from what I'm accustomed to; their ears are large and floppy, so much so, some even droop and fall over to the side, flopping to and fro. While looking at the two species, I have to wonder if the animals have influenced the people's exotic skin patterning or vice-versa, despite my friend's claims that they are two completely different species. My mind leaps to the natural conclusion; without doubt there has been some interbreeding to generate these similarities in pattern. I think of the legendary rumors surrounding Atlantis, giving form to the centaurs, minotaurs, and mermaids—my mind is cranking.

She breaks into my thought process. "By living in such close harmonic proximity, we have morphogenetically influenced each other by cross-pollinating through the morphing fields. But I know of no physical inter-species breeding amongst our people or deliberate genetic engineering. Possibly your suspicions of inter-species breeding could be part of our distant history, but we have no recordings of it."

As we continue walking, I'm curious to know her name, so I ask. She laughs amusingly, raising her brows with a bit of exasperation.

"My name is very long—you will probably have difficulty pronouncing it, but my parents call me Shi-Shaa for short. You can call me Shi-Shaa too!"

"My name is Monica," I announce.

She jumps in, "I know. When Aurora helped me project myself during your drawing, I discovered your name. It was difficult for me to project at that time—I was much younger then, so Aurora had to assist me. You can see my face is already different from your original drawing. Can you see I have grown spots on my forehead?"

Looking closely, I see it's true—she is absolutely right. Faint leopard spots are beginning to form in the fine hairs sprouting out on her forehead.

We pass through the open spaces. I begin to feel a little anxious as she guides me closer and closer to a gigantic leopard. My heart is thumping harder as we near. Then she invites me to sit next to it. I'm hesitant to move much closer—I'm already within arm's reach and that's a stretch. My fear must be glaring, pulsing out in neon to the leopard. I've never even felt comfortable around dogs in the past; how can I deal with this humongous beast? I keep resisting her invitation, it just confronts my every instinct—I want to run like crazy and never look back. But why should I be overly frightened? They're not wild like our leopards. Finally I reluctantly sit down. The cat perks up his head, ears flopping to the side as he slowly turns our way. He is gorgeous. Shi-Shaa leans over and throws her arms around the cat, giving him a big cuddly hug. She is so loving, and it is obvious they are very close and have developed a special relationship.

"This is Ooja! He's my dearest friend," she gushes. "I come here often. Ooja goes on lots of trips, and when he returns he always tells me all about his escapades."

I hear something like a distant echo bouncing through the canyons in my head. Suddenly I realize it's Ooja. His thoughts are large, perhaps how one might imagine the Old Man of the Sea to sound—hollow, yet spacious. Now Shi-Shaa introduces me to Ooja; her voice is excited and buoyant.

"Ooja, this is my friend, Monica!"

No longer trembling and more at ease, I feel quite special, as it is evident that Shi-Shaa wants Ooja to connect with me just as he does with her. She is so sweet and caring. Ooja's sound is like a feeling in my mind. In his deep baritone rumble he describes how happy he is to meet me. Wow, a talking leopard!

He goes on reflecting in his deep tone: "I sense you have been to the marketplace, testing the different ointments. Now I would like you to experience the other side—my side!"

My mind leaps—I thought I was experiencing the other side. What can he possibly mean? I imagine the other side will instantly deliver me back to my living room!

Ooja continues, "In a space of quiet, meditative serenity is where you use the ointments—in attunement with the wide-open spaces. Here you won't be cramped by claustrophobia and all the hubbub of the crowd. You can freely move in an atmosphere which allows you to relax and endlessly drift. It is here where you experience pure creative intelligence. It is here where the silence dynamically projects the infinite variations of our potent field of being."

I'm sensing that I should close my eyes. I do and Ooja's thoughts effortlessly arise. "Just be; don't try," he exclaims. "Allow the awareness to take you!"

Next to me I feel Shi-Shaa letting go, moving with whatever the environment offers. I feel the big, kindly leopard transmitting—filling my awareness. I see a cat racing free. So fast—not a care. Galloping abandonment. I flash on a story I once heard from an Indian. He spoke of the distinct difference between domesticated dogs and wild wolves. When the Indian discovered the wolves' footprints in the snow or mud, they were always unbounded, toes fully spread, and free! But when he saw dog prints, the toes were restrained and bound, in tight conforming alignment. I can now empathize with the spirit of the wolves as I watch the leopard galloping full tilt; no concern of falling from the Garden; no need to conform. So fast does it romp, it is nearly flying—turf spraying every which way in its wake, pure expression unfettered and alive. Suddenly Shi-Shaa and I are running and jumping at the leopard's side—frolicking through luscious green rolling hills—feeling incredibly free. Even though I'm running it seems as though I'm floating, there's such an ease. Then we trip over each other, spilling head first and down we go, sprawling into the grass, tumbling and laughing as we somersault down the hillside. Finally we come to rest in a twisted heap. Howling with laughter, we bounce right back up, springing into full stride. The freedom races through my blood like a drug—it's so intoxicating!

Strangely, somehow we are right back at Ooja's side in the cool grassy field. Shi-Shaa is exuberant, acting as though the fun is just beginning. She tugs on Ooja's coat, passionately insisting, "Oh, do the one for Monica where you take me way out into outer space—that's the place I really like!"

"OK," Ooja nods.

We close our eyes again. I hear an enormous roar rushing out of Ooja's lungs, like a waterfall's powerful cascade blasting into space. I feel the jungle force. I jump back, startled half to death. Other sounds have been casually echoing in my mind, but this blast puts me on alert. Soon all three of us are again floating into space. We're doing this funny kind of space running. It's very strange—we're running as if in mid-space, eclipsing stars and planets, then speeding right off into the starry night. We must look like some wind-up Disney animations that have jumped the tracks, skyrocketing out of orbit. It's crazy—

Shi-Shaa and I are suspended in lost space, chasing this enormous floppy-eared leopard through the stars. My mind flashes on the ancient astronomers' colorful characterizations of the heavens, and I imagine some artist capturing us dashing through the Seven Sisters, hi-tailing it right behind Ooja's pouncing form. The exhilaration screams through every pore of my body. Wow! I think, 'If my gym teachers could only see me now, maybe they'd appreciate my athletic prowess after all.' It would be nice to rid myself of that old dowager princess stereotype! But, fat chance—unlikely they'd ever read a book like this! Oh well, it doesn't hurt to fantasize!

Stars keep shooting by, then a large silver disk slowly passes and we shoot out into the vastness of deep space, completely enveloped in nothing but black. Out of the void, ribbony waves of color break into the velvety carbide, surging one after the other, in random succession. Shi-Shaa shouts, "Oh, wow! This is so beautiful!" sounding just like an acidhead in the sixties, but I must admit, with good reason. Colors keep glazing the skies—colors I've never seen before enfolding into each other in dynamic turbulent feedback systems. They mix and form in an endless procession of outrageous colors. It is absolutely breathtaking! The skyscapes appear as galactic drapes, lyrically undulating colors—rippling in gentle logarithmic motions. Waves of color splash and crash into the sandy shores of deep space, refracting myriads of celestial rainbows—bouncing on and on into infinity. I could watch forever. It's just dazzling!

In a flash, we are back in our ordinary bodies, sitting in the grassy field. I open my eyes and there is Ooja, sitting majestically like the mythological maestro of the skies. Shi-Shaa cries, "Isn't Ooja wonderful? He always takes me to these wonderful places."

Shi-Shaa gets up and gives Ooja a big hug, declaring, "I just love you, Ooja!"

I get up to hug Ooja, but I'm still a bit tentative; his body is just so huge. I love his spirit, but I have to get up the nerve to actually hug his imposing body. I decide to just thank him for the spectacular journey, but instead I think, oh what the heck, and burst through my anxieties, wrapping my arms around his enormous furry neck. He is warm and I can feel his body pulsating under the soft coat. What a rush! I feel so good and brave. It's like embracing the primal and cosmic all in one. There is a new bond I'm feeling, a relationship with a force that I can't quite describe. Something wild and unbounded. I feel it calling. A force that rampages just under the surface, pounding like the drum beats of a distant culture. Maybe this is the link with the ally spirit the shamans so often talk about. It's raw and powerful, a consciousness distinctly different from mine, yet linked and now accessible. Indescribable!

Now I look affectionately to Shi-Shaa, knowing my time is running short. "I must go now. I will never forget our episode together. Thank you, Shi-Shaa. You are wonderful!" It is amazing that in such a short period I feel we are as close as sisters.

Shi-Shaa can't wait to hug me. She doesn't seem shy anymore, she is vibrant and alive. We hug like long-time siblings and say our good-byes.

TWENTY FOUR

AAHOOOMM

*unmasking
hopes and dreams*

I AM DESCENDING FROM my short flight into a denser atmosphere. A planet comes into view. The thrill of the unknown leaps up, my excitement rearing. Clear gel-like craft, shaped like jellyfish stars, sporadically drift through the vicinity. They are somewhat akin to our starfish, but mostly transparent, permitting a view of the planet below. Strangely, I sense they are being commandeered. It must be by remote control, as the pilot is undetectable. Though I cannot distinctly see the craft, I determine their whereabouts by the detection of vibrational blocks of energy moving through space, emitting distinctive low-level hums.

Soon I land and I'm ambling my way through a sizable city. All the buildings are rounded and coated with sand. When I reach out to touch one of them, sand rolls away from the surface, revealing a cool, wet, concrete-like material. All the buildings are different sizes. There are doorways galore, some quite small, others more familiar, while still others boast Atlantean proportions. The buildings are bunched extremely close together—a booming molecular city with valences mushrooming out of control. Imagine your high school chemistry teacher getting a little over-rambunctious illustrating an elaborate chemical grouping—the little plastic models exploding every which way. Well, this city looks like that, only more rambling.

Time has passed and still I have seen no signs of life, yet I have that inner sense someone is aware of my whereabouts. Maybe the atmospheric radiation is harmful and everyone dwells inside to survive. I don't know exactly what, but something is quite different here! Curious about who and what may be inside, I look for a door. A black Gothic door catches my attention—it is about my height so I enter. Immediately I am swallowed by the darkness. Moving forward I notice that the light gradually intensifies, apparently activated by some motion-sensing device. The illumination reveals a glorious vestibule, decorated with an endless palette of shimmering colored panes. The panes cover the entire walls and ceiling. Light glows out through the glass, creating a magical radiance, almost as if you had stepped inside a cellular-like crystal and were looking out.

The floors are comprised of large rectangular glass blocks. When I step onto a block it lights up yellow. The next step lights up blue. Each step lights a block of a different color as I rest my weight on it, while simultaneously emitting a sound. A whimsical notion grabs me. I can't seem to help myself as I start prancing out a spirited, snappy little musical light show all for myself. It's great fun. Here I am at this smashingly elegant discotheque, choreographing a spontaneous dance number—right on the edge of nowhere. Then I reach out to touch a panel on the wall and the same phenomenon repeats itself—each panel lights and sounds to my touch. Wow, the entire building is wired.

Continuing through the vestibule, I see a railing appear towards the rear, leading down a tubular flight of stairs. The stairs are dark, but before I descend, they too begin to illuminate. This is an intriguing place—there is an element of fun luring me each step of the way. So even though the situation is quite unusual, I don't feel any concern or fear. Winding through the tunnel, the stairs work their way down into the subterranean realms of the structure. Colored panels similar to those that adorned the vestibule line the tunnel's walls.

I keep walking through what seems to be an endlessly long tunnel of muted colors. As I walk I am hit with an insight. The city I think I am in isn't a city, but a house. My gosh, how could this huge complex be a house? Maybe the structure is a futuristic Hefner-like mansion, or could I be gradually descending into Persephone's abode? As

I descend further and further, it seems obvious the latter is more likely the case. Questions continue to arise. From the outside the building seems innocent enough—a kind of huge, organic, molecular sprawl, imitating what seemed to me a fanciful city from the future. But now I'm not so sure and I'm starting to wonder just where I am.

I'm still walking, but I sense the tunnel's end is near. Suddenly, I find I am smack-dab in the middle of an enormous room. It is dark and spacious, at least three to four stories high. The light begins to creep up slowly as before. With the increase in light the room appears more like a dank, dusty cave with Romanesque vaulted ceilings. The mood has shifted dramatically—no bug-eyed, rafter-dwelling gargoyle's saliva drools down, but I get the feeling they're watching. It is scary. It is cold and still plenty dark in this mammoth cavity. No fun here! I wonder if I was purposely misdirected.

Now the lights come up brighter and brighter. Rather crude diamond-shaped designs ooze their way through the adobe walls, articulating primitive patterns. About a foot in front of the walls glistening glass panels hang like a mosaic in mid-space, casting elegantly colored light, shifting the ambient mood of the room. Surprisingly, I have never seen such a successful marriage of the primitive and the sophisticated in such close proximity, but the esthetic realizations don't alleviate my mounting fears.

Turning in towards the middle of the room I notice a throne, seating what looks to be a most ancient being. An empty chair close by suggests an invitation. I approach the chair with my gaze directed down in deference. When I look up to acknowledge him, I am taken aback. Upon his head rests an incredibly strange, delicate headdress weaving its way upward into the room. Gangly, archaic appendages arc up, displaying two organic horns woven of fine filigree thorns, possessing two unbalanced rates of growth. Awkward and primitive, its bizarre asymmetrical nature has no counterpart. More than ever I realize I have stepped beyond the threshold of the alien, to arrive at the distinctly unknown. A quiver crawls up my spine, forcing spasms through every nerve ending. Have I trespassed beyond my welcome?

I look to his face for some expression or welcoming, but it's completely masked by a grotesque leather shrouding, concealing all but a rough scissored cut-out. The crude opening allows a piercing pinpointed eye to beam out a searing laser from his dark optical cavity.

The eye socket is deep and dark, intense at its core. It shimmers brilliant blue—blasting a blazing atomic light from some remote nebula, seemingly light years away. As I watch, it turns from blue to silver to purple, never resting, always moving and shimmering from color to shimmering color. The rest of his face is draped in shriveled, withered leather, covered with dried thorny branches poking out this way and that, camouflaging the leather shielding. Definitely creepy, and completely unapproachable. Yikes, maybe I should gracefully exit—what am I doing here?

I'm standing next to the chair facing him, hesitant to take the seat. I am not sure whether to run for my life or what! A scrawny claw-like hand slowly rises, gesturing for me to sit, but I am flat-out scared and within seconds of splitting. Now I hear Aurora's voice assuring me everything is OK.

"Don't be afraid. You are just experiencing a type of energy you are unfamiliar with." I feel wary, my mind screams conspiracy, but Aurora insists, "I assure you, you won't be harmed—just have love in your heart and be open. Accept this being completely, exactly for who he is. He has been away from his people a long, long time. This is why the vibration is so unusual."

My trust in Aurora is unflinching, so I sit down. Immediately I notice his hands. Emaciated, bony knuckles protrude through saggy dried tissue—his nails are like talons. Daring to look closer, I watch his hands transform through liquid morphing sequences. They gel from claws to slender fingers. The old, gnarled, and wrinkled skin melts to a delicate, fair complexion. I move up to his face. His blue eye moves all around—a fierce solar light glares relentlessly. He is not saying anything—the atmosphere seems thick and Transylvanian. Ah, there's movement, he's trying to communicate with his eye. I follow the beam as it flits from place to place with seeming purpose. It finally lands on my left hand, right on my wedding ring. Reflections sparkle and scatter around the room; a sense of joy bubbles up within. The beam loiters on my ring. I notice images rising out of the ring—Gary and I are getting married and various happy events chronologically ensue. Our love is full, strong, and flowing.

Now his eye moves to my third eye. I see an orange glow inside my head—images of myself doing psychic readings flash before me. Rapid images keep flooding my inner vision, all weaving in and out of the orange smoke pouring from my third eye. Then his laser beam moves again, down to my throat. Suddenly I am feeling violated, outraged. He is extracting my life story without my permission. My outrage surges.

"Stop! Stop right now! You must interact in a different fashion. I don't feel like you are communicating. You are just extracting information, attempting to read me without my permission or any sense of communion. You do not have my consent to continue," I say succinctly and emphatically, shaking uncontrollably.

He retracts his eye beam. I hear a huge rumble in my head. It's completely unintelligible, like a mammoth tectonic plate shifting in my mind.

"Please speak slowly and softly. Your volume is way too overwhelming," I emphasize, attempting to build a greater sense of authority.

This time I hear a barely detectable, wee little voice—like a distant echo bouncing off the mountains from afar. I see he is really trying hard to meet my criteria and can't seem to find the range, vacillating between the two extremes. Knowing this eases my tension, as it is clear he has no bad intentions.

"No!" I stress. "That is way too soft and sounds like it is coming from a couple valleys over."

Then he goes back to the earthquake rumble—back and forth he goes, adjusting his volume, attempting in vain to attune to my range. Finally he adjusts something and the sound is softer and closer. His voice keeps changing—slowing like a tape recording of a hollow, raspy Louie Armstrong. Then it accelerates, racing like Chip and Dale on amphetamines. So it goes, until finally his voice zeros in on a much clearer, audibly recognizable bandwidth. He is doing his very best to reach me. His first effort was innocent enough and clearly not a violation from his perspective. As I listen attentively, images mingle with his voice. They are dreamy. He earnestly apologizes for his oversight.

"It has been a long time since I have communicated with anyone," he says in this straitjacket tone. "This is the way in which we communicated. I have forgotten there are other ways to communicate."

Suddenly he terminates his rationalizations and directly inquires, "Why did you come to see me?"

"Well, I don't completely know. I went through this tunnel, letting myself flow with the energy of the tunnel, and here I am. But reflecting on it, I remember there was a thought—I wanted to go somewhere, to a planet where I have never been before. I wanted to commune with someone who is very different from me, someone I can learn from and expand my understanding of the universe, with whom I can share my love and experiences. I believe this was my intention when I started the journey. To you is where it led me."

As I finish speaking, my host becomes very quiet. He is thinking about something, but what I'm not sure. The stillness is thick, awkward, and uncomfortable. Now, vast blue skies appear on my inner screens, gorgeous blooming white clouds float high, with glistening rays of resplendent light streaming through. The image stays as he slowly begins talking.

"I have been away from my people a very long time—so long I cannot remember when I last saw them. Recently I have been thinking I want to contact someone, someone with whom I might communicate who doesn't know my past. Someone who will accept me as I am, the person I am right now. I have thought it wouldn't be necessary for this person to be part of my race—it could be anyone! So, you see, it seems our thoughts have crossed, drawing us together. Give me your hand," he requests gently.

His hand stretches towards me. It just keeps shifting from bird claw to old bony hand to a maiden's sensuous, silken hand. Many fleeting thoughts fly through my mind, but in the end I decide to trust and reach out my hand. When our hands touch, I feel the cold shriveled claw. Gradually it transforms. Finally, to my amazement, I feel the soft and feminine. I am no longer hearing a man's voice, but the innocent, sweet voice of a woman. Again the energy shifts, and a compelling voice touches me.

"I am so happy you are here!"

He is so sincere and compassionate his energy penetrates my heart. He is deeply moving—completely convinced that I, out of everyone in the universe, am the most perfect person he could be with at this moment. The lover to the lover; the mother to the daughter, the son; the master to the *chela*—there is no faking it, the vibration cannot be disguised—we are embraced in transcendent communion. I'm staggered by his feeling and caught totally unsuspecting by the intimate caressing quality of our souls' encounter. Then his hand morphs back to a masculine human hand, and with his masculine voice he says in resonate tones, "Tell me of your hopes and dreams." I'm surprised at his inquiry; it seems to jump out of nowhere.

"Well, let me think—I have many. But often I notice something about the hopes and dreams I have: I am not sure I really want them once I've conjured them up," I say, off the cuff, somewhat surprised at my disclosure.

Again he reiterates more emphatically, "Tell me of your hopes and dreams."

I pause, not knowing what to say—it seems he has got me good. Clearly he is coming from a much different place than from where I answered. It seems he is not requesting idle chatter but a completely reconciled response. Boy, I have been stuck on this question for as long as I can remember. How can he expect me to address it on such short notice? I'm stumped. What to say? Then my mind just opens up and starts to flow.

"I suppose one of my dreams is in relationship to my work. I want to do something I really like. I want to go to work and feel passionate—do something I look forward to doing, something I love doing! The only problem is, I don't know what it is I want to do." Then I hear him again, even more passionately.

"Tell me of your hopes and dreams." I pause even longer. I thought I was telling him, but I realize I'm immersed in my feelings and not discussing what I really want. I am side-stepping the question. So I attempt to go deeper than before—to say exactly what I want. I hit a wall of frustration and I blurt out, "I'm totally frustrated and stuck! I don't know any more than I have told you."

My forthrightness is shocking. I am usually much more reserved. What is going on? He has really hit a nerve. I realize that I have built up incredible discontent regarding my work and never truly addressed it.

"You have fallen into a comfortable groove and have not taken time enough to think about what you want. Just take time to genuinely entertain one of your hopes, one of your dreams. You have many tools and ideas, but you have not spent enough time exploring your gifts or following through a thought or idea."

There is another long pause, then I spurt out, "You are absolutely right. I will begin thinking about what you have discussed—in fact, I am starting to receive inklings as we talk about how I might determine what I really want to do. When it becomes clearer, I will come back and let you know what I have decided. I appreciate your insights." Then I ask, "Is there anything I can do for you? I feel I have received a gift from you. I would like to give something in return." My request is direct. Already I see a difference in my interaction—my deferential nature has fallen away. I don't feel so apologetic for being however it is that I am. This feels good, authentic!

He says, "You have given me more than anyone, by just being here. Our communication alone has fulfilled my wish. But I do want you to come back again. I want you to know you have a friend. Even though we have not spoken volumes, we have communed heart to heart. Just being with each other this short time, sharing with each other, has re-opened lost aspects of my being. You can't imagine the depth of your gift to me. Emotions and thoughts that had long since run dry have awakened and are alive again. I feel I have known you for years, and I know you feel the same."

"It is funny, I do—I feel it too. Even after our rough start, we have become quite intimate and authentic with our feelings!" Somehow I feel intuitively that I really know who he is—the pain, the isolation, the Gulag Archipelago he has enforced and inflicted on himself from fear. In my case, this fear is the fear that someone might reveal who I really am. So I stay distant and invisible. Or quite possibly the scariest of all, I might discover who I really am. How magnificent I might be. The responsibility just might be way too burdensome—could I fill those shoes? I feel that our contact, even though it has been short, goes deeper than the surface interaction. With these feelings present, I depart company with my unusual new friend.

It's another day and I focus my attention on my masked friend. I arrive at the destination rapidly without experiencing any transitional zone. Rampant thoughts break my focus, interrupting the flow, and abruptly I find myself right back in the living room. This time I enter the tunnel by directing my focus on my friend. I speed directly to the chair where our past interaction occurred.

But he is not in his seat. The remaining structure is like a shell—the empty mask is connected to the throne, but he is nowhere to be found. He must have slipped out, leaving the bizarre masked-headdress behind. Again, I don't have the staying power and I find myself back in our living room. I enact the journey again—dropping in from up above, right down into the seat I occupied during our first encounter. Now he is back, sitting in his headdress.

I look straight into his laser-powered eye; it is moving all about. I say, "Hello, my friend!" Then I hear the familiar rumble. I think, 'Oh no, he can't remember the technique he used last time.' But he quickly recaptures the working voice and now he's audible.

"It seems like you are experiencing difficulty this time," he states.

"Yes, my focus was fractured."

"As you surmised, I wasn't here when you first dropped in. It is the first time in eons I moved away from the mask. I was taking the time to explore the spaces throughout the building, reacquainting myself with what was once very familiar terrain. As I explore myself without the encumbrance of the masked headdress, I'm seeing new things, hearing new sounds, and feeling new sensations. Even though these are very familiar surroundings, it's different now because my perspective has changed. It has been so long, I have forgotten what everything was like before the mask. Life had become a total figment of my inner interpretations and perceptions, based on my disassociation with others. I became an island unto myself. With the new awareness, there is an indescribable excitement—new hope and happiness surging out of me. Now I can see my dreams and wants are resurfacing with new vigor. I have decided to describe the past to you from within the masked headdress, because I can see and feel there is something in your life which is parallel to what is happening with me. I think in my explanation you will receive a deeper understanding of what is important for you to know. So I will do my best to relate my experience for you.

"I have discovered that my perceived need for a mask has stymied and thwarted my yearnings, squelching all my inner impulses—labeling them inept and unworthy. Not only have I disguised my true wants from others, but I realized that my protected stance slowly began to mask my own wants from myself. My disguised personality began to take preference over my deep wantings and yearnings for myself. It was easier than facing an outer response that may be hostile to my wanting. I became distanced from my true impulses, or you might say I masked myself from my very self. Now as I place myself back in this shell I feel heavy, closed in; my vision is short and occluded. The protection my disguise affords me once again becomes of the utmost importance. I perceive that its façade allows me survival—it is life and death. So I choose to alienate myself from others disassociating myself from my true self, feeling what's best for me is to survive any way I can. Now it is all so clear—I have inflicted deep wounds upon myself because of my fear of perceived imperfections, punishing myself by maintaining flawed constructs of myself and the world."

He pauses—I start wondering if there is a parallel. Is this my pattern as well? Could I too be punishing myself, hiding in my own fashion by pretending not to know what I want? Perhaps not behind such an elaborate contraption, but still with my own seemingly invisible mask. Maybe his crazy autistic mask really vividly illustrates my inner defenses, frailties, and confusion. What archaic mental constructs we harbor, tying us to our beloved patterns, fears, and limitations. I know I want to come out and at times I have peeked, but mostly I know, when I honestly confront myself, that I remain hidden behind my make-shift façade, desperately protecting myself, holding my confused disguise in place. Amazingly, I do feel a parallel with this strange being. Maybe the only difference is that his disguise is just more honest and forthright—no pretense here. He sits in the open, resting behind the most fragile and primitive of masks.

I'm stunned at my awareness. I would have never guessed I'd be relating to this most bizarre being—never mind admitting our similarities—especially knowing he is quite possibly the most alien of the alien beings I have encountered! It is strange—I see that even an advanced soul and mind of the far reaches of consciousness can trap themselves in their flawed perceptions and mental constructs. Now I hear him. I suppose more correctly I pick up his thoughts even before he conceptualizes them. Wow! We are linked—thinking the same thing simultaneously, effortlessly. I now reflect on how amazing it is. He called out deep within his soul. I created the intention to communicate with someone I could consider a new friend. And here we are supporting each other, pulling our spirits together for this incredible encounter. Amazing! The universe works in such perplexing ways!

He slips out of the headdress-mask. His head is quite greyish and anemic from lack of light. The room is dimly lit. I can barely perceive his greyish horned peaks. Suddenly the room begins to brighten. His face and horns get brighter and brighter, with his face sunrising into a bright orange. He is shielding his eyes, obviously not accustomed to his new-found luminosity. Soon he adjusts. He is tall—about seven feet. I scan his face, eventually focusing on his mouth, where he seems to be pumping out immense energy. My mind whirls. I start having these funny thoughts. I think, 'Gee, he has been under that mask a long time—after a long and dark hibernating slumber like that one must wake up with wretched breath.' I hear him laughing uproariously.

I say, "I'm sorry—I can't believe I'm so insensitive at times. I apologize for thinking like that. I must get used to this telepathic intimacy—it really busts you when you least expect it."

"It's perfectly all right. Whatever comes to your mind just let it flow. You have no bad intentions. You have no need to shield yourself. These thoughts are what give you personality—let them flow into the world."

He walks towards me, stretching out his vibrant, orange, hairy hands. In between his fingers white hairs flair out like tufts of wild grass. I reach out to meet his hands. They are soft, silkenly refined, and extremely hairy. Something special seems to be unfolding. Our physical connection builds and builds, taking the emotional bonding even deeper.

Then he reflects, "I am feeling so very happy. It is slowly coming over me. It magnifies as I am able to release more and more of my past. I still see I am trying to control, evading the spontaneity of the moment. You can easily recognize that I am still stiff, not totally letting go just yet. But the release is dawning and in full metamorphosis. We are both doing similar things—each being very careful so as not to get hurt by those who don't understand us, those whom we perceive are not interested in our gifts, who might treat or judge us unfairly."

"I realize this is true for me too. I am always afraid of being persecuted by the crowd or the uncaring. I suppose I am just plain afraid of peoples' intentions, completely skeptical, and lacking trust."

He says, "I know how you feel, because that is exactly what I am feeling. But I know there is something great out there for both of us…if we just let go and shine, sharing ourselves unmasked—unconcerned about our perceived value. I know we can touch people, each in our own special way. I hear your thoughts—I hear you saying, 'I don't want to go out there and start screaming and shouting and preaching how wonderful I am and what I can do for everyone.' You know you don't have to do it that way, because it is not your way. You do not have to imitate other people. Just let go. Stop feeling you have to hide to survive, then whoever you are will come out naturally. Again, I hear you—you think you won't know what to do if you just let go. But I can guarantee you will know exactly what to do. You don't have to think, you will just be, being exactly who you are before the censoring and masking!"

Inwardly I hear—he has an idea!

He spouts, "As we can both read each other's thoughts, I know you want to enact this idea too. So let's start today—I am going to go out and be with my people. I am going to let this excitement and happiness I feel brewing flow out. I am going to come out and let people see who I really am, undisguised, uncensored. If I can touch people or heal people in some way, I will not hesitate to do so. I want you to do the same, as I know you want to. Let's create an agreement. We can make it a partnership, or even better—as your language puts it—we can be bosom buddies. We will each go out into our respective worlds and stop hiding and stop pretending we don't know. And if and when we need encouragement, we will call on each other. And know in a flash we will be there for each other, regardless of the circumstances."

I am excited at the prospects. I feel so supported. I exude, "I'd be honored to be your buddy!"

"I know!" he says with his big orange smile. "We will meet again in a couple of weeks and share our experiences."

Just as I'm ready to depart I pick up his thoughts. "I am hearing that although you have released the disguise, the mask throne is still something you want to use as your refuge, but not to hide from others, only to meditate and go into deep states of inner revelation."

"Yes. Even though I have been using this apparatus to protect myself, it has also provided me with a way of transcending my immediate surroundings, to reach out within my soul, finding inner understanding and peace. I sense you would like to sit under my mask and see what it is like."

"It wasn't even a fully formed thought yet, but now that you ask I recognize it is true. I have been curious to experience your version of the mask for quite some time."

"I want to tell you that the experience can be disorienting at first, as you can well imagine, so just be aware and you will be fine."

I take a seat on his throne—it's completely dark. I am so short compared to him that the mask hits me right on my forehead, blocking the light. I decide to kneel in the chair to make an adjustment, but he moves the mask to fit my proportions. Now I'm perfectly situated. I feel intense heat rippling off the mask. The two horns are sourcing incredible amounts of energy. There seems to be some kind of energetic transference coming from them. They are operating like psychic antennae directly linked into the building and beyond. Now I understand what I was feeling when I first arrived—I sensed someone was watching, and clearly I can now tell it was him. Through the horns he has remained vibrationally in touch with his people even though he has been physically out of touch. These horns attune one far beyond the physicality of the surroundings, reaching out to the mysteries of the universe. Wild, wild thoughts—many completely indecipherable—surge like phosphoric fractile configurations, impressing upon my mind's awareness.

I wonder again what happened to isolate him to such a severe degree. As I continue to pick up his perceptions, it is obvious that he is far more evolved than my understanding of consciousness. His thoughts are vast and expansive and so foreign. He has always talked with me in a way that puts us on the same level. He has created our circumstances in such a way that we can support each other, showing me that although we may exist at different levels of consciousness, all consciousness is one and we are united through many intersecting experiences. At this moment in time we are both coursing through the same transitions. I am touched by his compassion and humility—so honored that he is willing to share his life and insights into our mutual circumstances. When I come out from under the mask, he is sitting so peacefully and contently, completely free of any pretense. He looks beautiful and loving—how amazing! What a difference from my first impressions!

"I sense it is time for you to go," he pronounces.

"Thanks for sharing your intimate nature unmasked. I really

know who you are now—what a treasure you are. I feel so grateful to know you. Why is it we all can't be this way with our brothers, sisters, and fellow voyagers?"

His eyes peer deep into me, my mask instantly transparent, and I know we can—then he seems to wink and says, "Remember our agreement—see you in two weeks!"

I've missed my two-week appointment, but now I'm back in the room where we first met. The room is much brighter. Again the throne has been vacated. I look up and my unusual friend is walking towards me—boy, he is tall. When we meet, he stoops way down to hug me. Feeling uncomfortably guilty, I welcome him with, "I know I am late, so I want to apologize."

He casually retorts, "No need. I was tuning into your vibration, so I knew you weren't going to be here as agreed." Checking him out, I can see that his mood is happier—his face is glowing, much more lively. His stiffness has eased.

"Well, let's review our results—I think we have both met with some success," he exclaims.

"Yes, I am sure you know, I have come out a bit more, but I know I have not really let go," I say self-consciously.

"I know, but you did operate much differently, and that is movement in the right direction. Let's look at what did happen, not what didn't. Does your tendency to feel guilty and see failure assist you in moving towards your goal?"

I know he is right, and as I stop and think about it, I realize that I was much more interactive with people than normally. I really did stretch myself—maybe I wasn't outrageous, but I was aware, making different decisions to be more engaging than in the past. So, why not acknowledge my movement and just keep moving in this direction?

Then he states, "I want to show you something!" We go together down a corridor, then down a flight of steps to an area close by some windows. Here there is a wooden table set with rough stones in the surface. It is a sort of outcropping from the wall, encasing a huge picture window. We take a seat at the table, then he instructs, "Look out the window."

Glancing through the pane I see an ocean, shrouded in a heavy mist. It is as though we are on the bow of a ship, right at sea. You can practically feel the ocean spray whipping across your face as we break through the wispy, white crests.

He quips, "I know what you are thinking, but we are not on a boat!"

I'm trying to figure out what he is attempting to show me. The scene continues to unfold around expanses of misty water. Suddenly it just fades. Wisps of mist still eerily hang, but the water has vanished. Now in the mist, gigantic cartoonish toadstools emerge. They are bright orange, dappled with big white polka dots. Rings of them bend and sway in the gentle air. Here darling faeries, in cute cheery flower caps, circle round the stools—while charming Art Nouveau butterflies flitter overhead. Now the faeries make a circle and heartfelt song springs to life as they bounce to their lyrical lutes and lyres. A couple of mossy crags push up from the ground, breaking the concentric circles of mushroom colonies and pointing one down towards a small trickling stream. At the stream, the feisty faeries dare the currents on their makeshift leafy rafts, shrieking cries of laughter. Close by a stout mushroom bows under the weight of two mischievous imps flying high through the air on their woodsy swing, trailing gay shrills behind the swaying motion. Oh, they are so joyous I can't believe anyone could be so jolly and gay. I decide I have to get a closer look. Stealing a more intimate view, I am astonished, for these two impish characters are none other than myself and my dear, strange friend. I am aghast—I can't get over it. Bewildered, I look to my friend.

"We just created this from our thoughts," he spouts matter-of-factly. "The entire scene is our thought manifestation."

I interject, "How can that be? I don't understand. This might be you creating this, but I have had nothing to do with it!"

"Yes! It is definitely you who is the conspirator behind this scene. Was it not you who had fear come up when you believed you were in a boat on a misty, choppy sea? You couldn't see for sure what was going on out there, and it gave you pause. It felt cold and wet and you thought, 'Gee, what if there is a big storm brewing out there, coming our way?' So you changed the scene. I picked up your thoughts. Unconsciously you created a scene where you thought you would be safe, and I went along, creating it with you.

I am puzzled, and I drift for a few moments in my thoughts...then I respond saying, "It is true. I suppose I did have thoughts about a storm—*20,000 Leagues Under the Sea* rushed before my eyes for a second. It was kind of scary for me, so you were right about the fear. How did you detect that—it raced across my mind in a nanosecond, barely perceptible even for me. Amazing, each of our thoughts is an indelible imprint for anyone to lift, if they but have the development to perceive. OK, you have me there—but no way was I creating this entire faerie scene out of my mind! But I do like and enjoy faeries, and God knows I would love to be part of the scene. In fact, it was so enjoyable watching us swing. I felt so carefree flying high from the toadstools, not a thought in the world (or so I thought), feeling cut thoroughly free."

Suddenly the scene springs back into action, and there is Gary swinging right there next to us, bursting with energy and exhilaration. My friend glances back at me with a look of knowing, eyes twinkling that laser blue.

"Are you convinced now? It is you—you are the culprit!"

Flabbergasted, I must concede—he is right. I did want Gary to be part of the scene, so momentarily it crossed my mind and whammo, there he is in living faerie color!

Now he reflects, "You must be wondering why I am showing you this. It is quite simple. Our thoughts are very strong—as you know from your experiences, thoughts are things. Even though what you were thinking seemed nearly unconscious, it still manifested. So when you consciously think about something, imagine what you can do. With strong intent and belief in yourself you can do almost anything. You created some results in life the last few weeks, didn't you? Even more than you were willing to acknowledge!"

I think about it for a moment and I know it is true. Over the weeks that I was back in my normal life, I was creating a project for the celebration of *The Birth and Enlightenment of Buddha* at Aquarian Foundation. I wanted a water pump to create a fountain, but we just didn't have the budget to buy it. Every day I thought about this pump, hearing the water trickle through the fountain and feeling my hands run through the cool water, even though we didn't have the money to purchase it. Amazingly, the day before the celebration, someone just brought the pump in unbeknownst to me. Yes, this was a great lesson for me. I operated completely differently. I continued to stick to my wants, enacting my vision regardless of the circumstances.

"You can manifest everything in this way! Your hopes and dreams are not a distant, difficult event, just a few crystal-clear thoughts away. But remember, in hiding you mask yourself from your true yearnings. You put your attention on the pretense rather than the wanting. When you release the disguise, your wants will naturally manifest."

I start to fade and he sees I am running out of gas. "It is time for you to go––if you would like, we can stay in touch—just call when you want to interact!"

"You know I will, but I don't even know your name—what do you call yourself? I would really like to know so I can remember my fond thoughts of you."

"My name is Aahooomm. Think of the wind—it sounds like a brisk breeze. Remember, just call and your buddy will be there."

My staying power has quickly vanished and I'm gone like the wind!

Afterword

AFTER READING ABOUT THESE JOURNEYS, one might surmise that the universe lies waiting like an untapped cosmic party ready to be crashed. Certainly those curious enough to attempt negotiating its strange corridors will be magnificently entertained. Once one has broken through to the other side, unfathomable landscapes and bizarrely inhabited worlds manifest, presenting realms only visited by the imaginary daring of a handful of voyagers. It is a wonder that such a spectacular phenomenon is not more generally known. Although reports of these escapades are infrequent, we believe the time is rapidly coming when many will be incorporating sojourns through multi-dimensional realities as part of everyday life. These experiences will further spiritual development, scientific discovery, artistic inspiration, and social and perhaps even biological evolution, generating leaps in consciousness in every domain of existence.

As one can see, our journey has carried us into realms of existence not immediately familiar to the Western mind, but certainly not alien to previous Earth dwellers in general. If we were to take a moment to drop into the cultural mindscapes of the Aborigines, the Mayans, the shamans of other indigenous peoples, or exceptional astral travelers and mystics of the past, we would begin to recognize striking similarities in experience. There is more than one precedent. Our experiences aren't merely isolated incidents flailing away in the unpredictable breezes of lunacy. Historically, many have taken journeys such as those related in this book, demonstrating the ability to access fields of existence which vibrate at a different frequency than our normal perception.

The Australian Aborigines have a shamanistic interaction with a dimension they describe as Dreamtime. In Dreamtime they encounter archetypal spirit beings of a supranormal nature, who intersect their reality and with whom they carry on an active intercourse and dialogue. For example the Dreamtime dingo spirit is good-natured and generous, the possum spirit extremely curious, the eagle spirit very dangerous, the lizard or goanna spirit particularly ferocious, and on and on. These are different from the fauna represented by the dingos, possums, and lizards. The Aborigines believe that once upon a time these ancestral spirits of Dreamtime created all the celestial bodies and formed the very Earth we inhabit—from Dreamtime all knowledge and all laws of existence came into being. So in the Aboriginals model of reality the physical dimension is a natural continuum with hyperspace. Through entering Dreamtime, the Aborigines encounter a world of creative principle in sacred space and time. We might say they activate their inner knowing, linking them with creative mind and activating what we have referred to as "Imaginality."

In Dreamtime they collaborate with beings of other dimensions, creating an inter-connectedness between humanity and supernatural intelligences bridging past, present, and future. Time and space as we know it vanish, and an entirely foreign universal order takes precedence over the physical world to which we are accustomed. It is in this altered state of consciousness that the Aborigines' special rapport with Dreamtime unfolds, it has been the source of their mythology, ritual, and meaning in life—opening their understanding of spirit and the evolution of humanity and creation.[3] Their entire cultural understanding and relationship with the Earth have emerged from this unique interaction. They experience the Earth as alive, humanized, and celestialized by a continuous narrative spinning from their imaginative inner mind. Rocks, caves, lakes become veritable portals and corridors.

The Aborigines enter Dreamtime through the use of art, music, and dance. The didgeridoo, a simple wind instrument produces an eerie, hypnotic, trance-like vibration. This resonant tone enhances the ability to shift into an altered state of consciousness, enabling one to feel and experience different patterns of perception, accessing thoughts and emotions of another order. In addition to the didgeridoo, many dreamers use distinctive abstract paintings to attune themselves to the realms of Dreamtime. As the Aborigine focuses his being on the imagery, a vibratory shift in consciousness occurs and a non-ordinary state of reality is ushered in, opening the vast domains of Dreamtime.

Aboriginal experiences in this regard are consistent with what anthropologists describe as shamanic journeying. The shaman is considered an intermediary between the seen and unseen worlds and is responsible for some cultures' cosmology, medicine, and relationship to the spirit world. Our world is not considered an isolated phenomenon onto itself, by the shaman, but linked to non-physical forces. Shamanic journeying in most indigenous cultures is induced by drumming, drugs, or initiation through apprenticeship to a shaman. Without the dominating influences of a technological culture, individuals are more inclined to experience the subtleties of other dimensions and their inhabitants. Occasionally, as in the case of Dr. Hank Wesselman, an American anthropologist, the experience comes upon one spontaneously. This is rare especially for a product of our industrialized society. He has painstaking chronicled his experiences, demonstrating that even an educated rationalist is not prohibited from taking excursions into the realms of hyperspace.[4]

During the 1960s, Western scientists conducted laboratory investigations into the effects of rhythmic drumming on consciousness. Brainwave changes have been observed when the tempo is altered from two beats a second to four beats. Native American Spirit Dances have long used drumming in rituals to produce visual and auditory imagery. When the traveler has entered the shamanic state of consciousness, he (or she) comes to the realms of what is referred to as the lower, middle, and higher worlds. Here one meets denizens of non-ordinary reality.[5] Only they are called totem beings, were-animals, spirits, allies, power animals, etc.

Typical shamanic encounters and Monica's experiences both supersede normal space and time, giving rise to countless beings, landscapes, and spiritual insights. One of the primary distinctions we've noticed is that Monica appears to transport farther away from the influences of the Earth's traditional realms to more alien sectors of reality. We suspect that her experiences are considerably detached from the influences arising out of the specific astral and vibrational planes of Earth. In general, many of the reports we've come across in shamanic journeying depict beings, animals, and experiences related more closely to aspects of tribal ancestry, cultural archetypes, and terrestrial experiences. The import of these perceived distinctions is yet a mystery. Perhaps Monica being a journeyer from a culture that has invented space probes, radio telescopes, and electron microscopes, she is thus primed to leave the Earth behind in certain contexts. Clearly a culture that is depicting UFOs and aliens in much of their contemporary mythology is ready for denizens of the greater cosmos.

As one studies and listens to the experiences of the Aborigines it seems clear that as a people they collectively exist in the realms of Dreamtime every bit as much as they exist in biological and geological reality. They are, so to speak, bi-located between two realities, the physical and the non-ordinary reality, both of which they allow to compose the human experience. This makes for a rich and diverse human incarnation, one that grounds the terrestrial in the celestial and the galactic conscience into the human conscience.

Monica's portraits play a similar role to that of the tribal artists' paintings of Dreamtime; if attuned to at the level of their vibration, they shift the perceiver into the inter-dimensional beyond. Aborigines' epic Dreaming stories captured by tribal artists depict journeys made by ancestral beings. Each painting is both a psychic and physical map of the landscape. Each guides a journeyer to a particular place on the Earth that is tied to an event the Dreamtime ancestor experienced long ago. Often colorful sand paintings are drawn right on the Earth where a primal event once occurred. These act as a corridor by which the dreamer can transport into the other dimension, completely shifting his or her vibrational frequency to another order of space and time. After the journey is completed, the painting is sifted back into the earth, leaving no trace of the act of creation/communion which just transpired.[6]

The Aborigines believe that many of the ancestors depicted in the paintings continue to live right within the rock and landscape, only observed by the Dreamers. By reenacting an ancestors' story through the process of painting, the Aborigine draws that ancestor near, transcendentally bridging time, inviting communion. If we studied the mythological nature of the cast of Aboriginal ancestors inhabiting Dreamtime and evaluated the mythological ramifications of the beings Monica has encountered, I suspect we would find significant overlaps, especially in the areas of transmission of cosmic wisdom and training of individual and spiritual growth.

Mystics from around our planet have long claimed visits to distant worlds like those Monica explored. One of the more accomplished was Emanuel Swedenborg during the eighteenth century, who puzzled and confounded those of his era. He had a penchant for knowledge and he published scientific works on subjects from the brain to soils and mud. As the leading mathematician in Sweden he wrote papers on: *Principles of Natural Things, New Attempts to Explain the Phenomena of Chemistry and Physics by Geometry, Corpuscular Philosophy (speculations on atomic physics), Characteristics and Mathematical Philosophy of Universals, Motion of the Elements*, to mention but a few. In addition he was one of the masters of his day in anatomical work, contributing much to medical sciences, and was the first to discover the function of the cerebellum. In short, he journeyed through all the sciences of chemistry, engineering, physics, mathematics, mineralogy, geology, paleontology, anatomy, physiology, astronomy, optics, metallurgy, cosmogony, cosmology, and psychology. At age fifty-six he had mastered and exhausted all known sciences of the times, even discovering a few himself; he then proceeded to unravel many secrets of religion and the mind, which led him into the inner realms of the universe. He represents the rare exception of a man who studied the outward nature of the world, then turned on a dime, demonstrating the capacity to investigate the inner world with the same depth and thoroughness. An eccentric of his era, he could be easily dismissed as a raving crackpot, but his insightful writing along with numerous public demonstrations of his psychic intuitions provide evidence to the contrary.

On one such occasion, Swedenborg was in the company of a group of people assembled in his honor. During dinner Swedenborg suddenly turned to a Mr. Bolander, the owner of a cloth mill, and said sharply, "Sir, you had better go to your mills." Mr. Bolander thought his manner was anything but polite, but nevertheless he rose from the table and went to his mill. Once he arrived, he found that a large piece of cloth had fallen down near the furnace and begun to burn. If he had delayed, his property would have been nothing but ashes.[7]

I mention this incident to give credence to the authenticity of Swedenborg's experiences. Many over the centuries have claimed that Swedenborg was deluded, that his claims of traveling through the stars and his correspondences with spirits of heaven, hell, and the celestial realms were pure poppycock. But he provides physical evidence, irrefutable evidence in the presence of crowds, where there was absolutely no possibility of shenanigans, demonstrating the lucidity of his paranormal vision. The numerous verifiable incidents give rise to the possibility that just maybe Swedenborg is seeing reality as it really exists. Throughout his book *The Spiritual Diary*, he talks of his experiences of communicating with inhabitants of the spiritual planes of Earth, the heavens, and spirits of some universe in the starry sky. He proceeds to elaborate on traveling to far-off places, cultivating a natural rapport with spirits inhabiting Mercury, Venus, Mars, Jupiter, and Saturn, while imparting how they know the things they know.[8]

Swedenborg wanted genuine answers for the problems that confronted society. He rebelled against the presiding religious forces, looking for new solutions to humanity's plight. He said that if the prophets of yore could talk with angels, so could he. He searched deep within his heart for answers and prayed diligently with all his soul. Through vision and will he became a successful practitioner of imaginality, ultimately writing volumes and volumes of communications with spirit realms, portraying a heaven very different from the descriptions of any of his orthodox contemporaries.

I have heard a 1974 communication in which Swedenborg returns to talk through the trance mediumship of Keith Milton Rhinehart, the medium from whom Monica first received her message regarding her psychic art skill.

[Rhinehart's psychic abilities are well documented and widely known. Rhinehart has been tested by doctors, scientists, magicians, and police officers alike, furthermore he has been tested in over twenty countries which gives credibility to his mediumship and therefore reliable authenticity to Swedenborg's statements. Of particular note, Rhinehart was tested under controlled conditions by Japanese scientists in Tokyo in 1958. His manifestations occurred after he had been securely locked into a specially designed "Fraud-proof chair" invented by Dr. Ando of the University of Osaka. Before sitting in the chair

Rhinehart was stripped and thoroughly examined, then given a simple kimono to wear. He was precisely weighed and measured, his blood pressure was taken, his urine was analyzed, and other tests were made. This procedure was repeated after the séance and the results showed that physiological changes occurred during the mediumship. Rhinehart was then tied into the chair where both his arms lay in wooden enclosures which prevented any movement. Two electronic buttons in the arm-chair under the wrists were connected with two red lights which flashed if the medium moved his arms or wrists from the buttons. An electronic graph also recorded any bodily movements and increases or decreases in bodily weight. The medium's mouth was then filled with a colored liquid chemical, taped shut, and special markings were drawn across the tape onto the skin. Under these test conditions numerous physical phenomena transpired showing ectoplasm in various forms, produced under white light and photographed with still and moving cameras. Ectoplasm is a subtle physical substance that comes out of a medium's body during trance and is often invisible. At times it can be seen and looks like a milky-white material of nebulous form and consistency. In the Japanese tests ectoplasm flowed from the nose, ears, throat, and solar plexus of Rhinehart, levitating trumpets and forming finger-like protuberances known as pseudopods, and an ectoplasmic voice-box. During the séance the pseudopods grasped a pencil and proceeded to draw a face recognized by Mr. Mikami, a Japanese religious leader. In addition an ectoplasmic voice-box was used by the spirit communicators to converse in fluent Japanese with those in attendance.][9]

In this transmission Swedenborg through Rhinehart speaks from the spiritual realms, validating that his Earthly experiences were indeed genuine and that his writings chronicling the dimensions of the afterlife were absolutely correct. He says he saw things he never dreamed of: he saw realms and realms of angels, and countless solar systems where human life forms and beyond exist, populated with beings just like us. And he saw endless planets where beings exist who have great intelligence, meaning, and spiritual significance, displaying forms of life much different from us. He goes on to explain what an astral experience is. He says the first time you project from your body you glance back and see yourself lying there. Then the walls of the room begin to glimmer with light. You envision a distant place and amazingly, you're moving down a long tunnel-vortex of life energy. Suddenly you're there. You feel an ecstasy beyond anything you've ever felt in your life. You feel your spirit is free and you realize how bound and chained you've been all your life, encased in that heavy body. At this point you know you're a spiritual being who will survive the ages, marching on to victory to exist among the stars.[10]

Swedenborg saw existence as a series of worlds scaling down from the most sublime to the most dense. Each level of existence links and corresponds to the others, reflecting each other's nature to some degree. Through the law of similitude of correspondence, each level is knitted into a related whole. From God to the celestial heaven, to the spiritual heaven, to the lowest heavens, to the exterior of experience, to the world and to the individual body, each level of existence is interrelated.

Swedenborg stated that the inner realm reveals itself particularly through symbolic images. It is only through these representations that something much more abstract, vast, and profound can be cognitively grasped. One might relate this process to how inner feelings and moods are revealed through facial expressions—the facial pose or series of facial expressions exposes a true commentary about the inner mind. But never does the face completely describe exactly how we might be feeling—it only approximates our inner state. This suggests how the different worlds correspond to each other. Much of our own world involves correspondence of this nature, as all the emotional states—affection, happiness, anger, grief, etc.—are the outward manifestation of the inner states of the mind and are expressed in a variety of different manners. Language is another example. With each communication we deliver, our words closely correspond to the abstraction of our thoughts but never perfectly capture our inner knowing.[11]

Emanuel Swedenborg wrote in *Heaven and Hell:* "The whole natural world corresponds to the spiritual world, not only the natural world in general, but also in particular. Whatever, therefore, in the natural world exists from the spiritual, is said to be its correspondent. It is to be known that the natural world exists and subsists from the spiritual world, just as an effect exists from its efficient cause...."[12] If we were to view Monica's journeys from this vantage, we might determine that each journey is a symbolic projection into our realm from dimensions which correspond in some manner to Swedenborg's spiritual realms. Each journey depicts a correspondence from one part of the cosmos to another, symbolically representing a message from across the width and breadth of consciousness. So from within the bounds of consciousness, the dimensional realms fly open, radiating a more expansive aspect of Monica's own being, taking an impersonal abstraction from afar and formulating it in a language and character form she can assimilate. In Swedenborg's language, one might say Monica's journeys represent correspondences stepping down from other levels of existence. Here stories and imagery unveil unknown levels of reality, presenting poignant insights into the depths of human and cosmic nature.

We may never visit planets in other solar systems and galaxies by standard means of transportation and, while Monica's images may not be color snapshots of remote worlds, they carry the essential aspects of the inhabitants as represented in universal consciousness. In answer to the question, do the beings actually look like this I will leave it up to you to determine. Monica has contacted them on a plane of spiritual correspondence, not physical extraterrestrial contact, but through her own inner evolving relationship with imagination. They may not look like this when viewed physically from their dimension, but we suspect there is a close approximation.

Celebrated author and renowned psychologist Jean Houston writes in depth about the different inner levels of our being. She describes an ocean of consciousness in which we swim, where different parts of our being exist like species of fish, each swimming at its own depth levels. In each depth zone, a different facet of our being broadcasts an aspect of our nature, comprising the entire ocean of beingness. In her book *A Passion for the Possible*, Houston explains the four major levels of the inner being that she has discovered in the human psyche—the sensory, psychological, mythic, and spiritual. If we were to investigate these levels we would find that they too open a line of inquiry to understanding the import behind Monica's journeys.[13] For example, through the sensory organs of the imagination Monica has come into a greater awareness of her perceptual abilities, through the psychological she has reimagined memories of the soul, through the mythic she has seen her story played out in the lives of alien personalities and from their story found remedies to her quest, and finally through the spiritual she has recognized she is inescapably united with all of the universe no matter how foreign the local landscape may be. Are these journeys external to Monica's personal consciousness or a remote aspect of her personality? I suppose one could argue convincingly from either position and in the end be hopelessly trapped in a labyrinth of paradoxes. But ultimately, based strictly on an innate knowing, we believe they correspond to another order of consciousness, expanding beyond the personal soul to a broader pool of consciousness—where one can communicate with other intelligent life streams for one's own spiritual edification.

The last traveler I'd like to introduce here is Robert Monroe. From 1939 to 1976 he was a successful executive for a number of broadcasting companies on the east coast of the United States. In fact, he created and produced more than four hundred radio and TV network programs. Mr. Monroe is also considered a maverick in the exploration of out-of-body experiences, having subsequently pursued this interest for more than twenty-five years until his death in 1995. An out-of-body experience (OOBE) is defined as a condition in which one finds oneself totally conscious but located outside of the physical body, with the ability to perceive and act as if functioning physically—with some exceptions of several peculiarities that one doesn't normally experience in the physical body. For instance, one can move through space and time quite slowly or at a rate even greater than the speed of light—a mobility clearly reaching beyond the parameters of Einstein's theory of relativity. Additionally, one can move through physical barriers of substantial mass, without effort, distorting elastically—while stretching the body like "Gumby."[14]

An OOBE is not a new experience, as many historical cultures have reported a variety of such incidents. Even more eye-opening, most people inhabiting our contemporary culture report experiencing at least one OOBE adventure in their lifetime. In occult circles the most singular OOBE experience has been referred to as "astral travel." Astral travel differs from space travel in that the body need not be transported, but the astral vehicle of consciousness does the actual journeying. In metaphysical writings it is thought that there is an astral duplicate of the physical body into which one can consciously step. During the astral experience, the traveler is journeying in the astral vehicle of consciousness separate from his or her physical body, viewing the landscape from this less familiar body of perception. Here one perceives a different band of existence from what we generally consider ordinary physical reality—a realm manifesting in different vibrational frequencies that surrounds the Earth. What made Monroe so unique among OOBE travelers is that he took an empirical approach in chronicling his experiences, rigorously documenting endless control tests of not only himself, but other travelers. Many of the phenomena that Monroe describes are comparable to Monica's experiences and provides a cross-referencing of what we refer to as interdimensional journeying.

When Monroe first began having OOBE experiences he was convinced that he was dreaming, having strange hallucinations, that insanity lay waiting just around the corner. Subsequently, when they persisted he sought professional help, claiming he was concerned about his mental health. Only after he accumulated evidential data did he believe the experiences to be genuinely based on travel in a body of a different order.

One of the most frequently asked questions regarding the OOBE experience is: "How do you know you're not dreaming or just experiencing a particularly lucid hallucination?" Monroe thought this fair enough—his first response was: "How do I know my waking awareness is real?" Then he emphasized that the clearest statement he can make is, "When the condition exists, you are as aware of 'not dreaming' as you are when you are awake." In other words, the identical standards one applies to waking consciousness can be applied to the OOBE consciousness with the same positive results. Here are some of the ways by which the OOBE differs from that of dreaming consciousness from Monroe's perspective:

1) There is a continuity of some sort of conscious awareness.
2) There are intellectual and emotional decisions made during the experience.
3) Sensory perceptions are evaluated through a logical process.
4) Identical patterns do not occur.
5) Events develop in sequence, pointing to the elapse of time.

He goes on to declare that in a dreamstate one's reasoning and intellectual process is absent, rendering analysis not an option. One's participation in the unfolding events is purely at a reactive or uncontrollable level, or there is complete non-participation, i.e., viewing the events as an inanimate observer unable to act. Perception is also generally limited to one or two senses. Monroe indicates that OOBE consciousness, or what he refers to as the Second State, is the complete antithesis of dreaming. When one is located in the Second State, there is the recognition of "I am" consciousness. Here the mind operates and takes in data as it does in the waking state, acting and deciding based on perceptual and reasoning abilities that one normally possesses. Each of these attributes is consistent with the nature of Monica's journeying.

A second question arises: Is this OOBE a product of self-hypnosis with attendant post-hypnotic suggestion? Monroe states that "suggestion" as used in hypnosis could be part of an activation process, but he adds that he consciously strives to avoid any indirect suggestion or stimulus that could possibly provoke hallucinatory experiences.[15]

Another question that commonly arises when discussing OOBEs is: Where do you go with this so-called Second Body? As Monroe conducted tests and experiments, he developed a vocabulary that helped to identify the distinctions among experiences. "Locale I" was the term Monroe used to describe the first area of adventure. It consists of the people and places actually existing in the physical world with which we are familiar at the moment of the experiment. It is the world perceived by our physical senses, with which we interact on a regular basis. Visits to Locale I don't contain strange beings, events, or places, just the normal occurrences of every day. With this parameter in mind, we must acknowledge that the only evidential results provable by conventional methods of confirmation would take place on visits to Locale I. For Monroe's own edification, and possibly his sanity, he has worked to produce evidence while traveling in Locale I. These events are too detailed to elaborate in full but have been verified by Dr. Charles Tart, a professor of psychology (and expert on parapsychology) at the University of California-Davis. Dr. Tart has documented that Monroe has in fact retrieved data from afar, observing people and events at a distance from his physical body, where he could not have known of their whereabouts or dealings other than being present in his Second Body.[16]

Locale II is of an entirely different order—an environment presenting organized laws of motion and matter with which we are not commonly familiar. It's a non-material locale whose immensity and bounds are unknown, with a density and dimension that are incomprehensible to the finite mind. Monroe states that only a very few of the visits to Locale II have provided anything that could be considered evidential data, a consistent A plus B equals C. The environments of Locale II are inhabited by entities of varying degrees of intelligence with whom one can communicate. There appears to be an evidential sequence of events, but time as we know it in the physical world is completely altered.

Reality in Locale II is: as you think, so you are. Thought is the force from which all springs. Thought supplies any need or deed that may be required. Motion and communication are instantaneous, all proceeding from the mind. Monroe says Locale II is the ideal world of the Second Body, where the principles involved in its unfolding, composition, and perception all correspond directly to its nature. The Second Body's composition is not of this world, and this is why Monroe believes that the majority of his travel attempts involuntarily took him into the destination of Locale II.[17] Clearly Monica's experiences most closely relate to Monroe's description of Locale II. One can see "Imaginality" at play here—how the mind in collaboration with the will organizes one's experience, playing a director's role in both interrelations with other beings as well as the choreography of the elements within the dimensional landscape.

Finally Monroe describes a Locale III which has all the appearances of Locale I without the evolutionary development achieved in our present technology and sociology. It appears to be a physical-matter world nearly identical to our own. This locale seems to coincide with many of the latest discoveries in physics regarding quarks and antimatter. What is of most definitive interest in Locale III is that all the inhabitants remained unaware of Monroe's presence until he merged with one who apparently lives there—one whom he reports is a person who could only be described as the "I" who lives there. Monroe's experiences of inhabiting this other body, which he describes as a person much like himself, seem to be a case of intrusion into the other person's world—what might even be considered a form of possession. Here he took on the emotions and experiences of the person when he inhabited the other "I."[18]

Monroe's experiences are far too vast and detailed to chronicle here, but I think one brief episode from Locale II would contextualize Monica's journeys:

CLICK! [refers to instantaneous change in consciousness]
(I am in a bright white tunnel and moving rapidly. No, it is not a tunnel, but a tube, a transparent, radiating tube. I am bathed in the radiation which courses through all of me, and the intensity and recognition of it envelop my consciousness and I laugh with great joy. Something has changed, because the last time, they had to shield me from the random vibration of it. Now, I can tolerate it easily, the actual energy itself. The radiation flow is two-directional in the tube. The flow moving past me in the direction from which I came is smooth, even, and undiluted. It is organized in a more complex form. It is the same as the wave moving past me, but it contains a multitude of small waves impressed upon the basic. I am both the basic and the small waveforms, moving back to the source. The movement is steady and unhurried, impelled by a desire I know but cannot express. I vibrate with joyous ecstasy just by the knowing....)

CLICK!
The return to the physical was near-instantaneous, my face and eyes were wet. I sat up in the chair and remembered. I reached for the yellow pad and pen, to get the rote into words immediately. I knew I had changed. For the rest of my physical life, I would remember. But this would never change:

For those who would die, there is life.
For those who would dream, there is reality.
For those who would hope, there is knowledge.
For those who would grow, there is eternity.
—Robert A. Monroe, *Far Journeys* [19]

The process that initially illumined these alien dimensions for Monica is a very specific form of mediumship called psychic art. Psychic art itself has been shrouded in mystery throughout the twentieth century. Guilty of cohabiting with the clairvoyant arts, it has been hypothetically tucked away in the archives of mythical civilizations, existing merely as diaphanous conjecture, vulnerable to the fate of pagan witches and mystics.

We feel it is time to put to rest the Judeo-Christian superstitions.

In our research we were able to locate precious few publications on psychic art—only a couple of publications in England, along with several articles in *Psychic News Newspaper*. We wondered why this fascinating area of Spiritualism hadn't garnered more publications. But given our culture's prejudices against both psychics and artists, it is not surprising. To this day psychic artists have continued to be viewed as outsiders, both by the art world and traditional spiritual studies.

With this publication, we display a body of work that bursts out in vibrant hues dancing with glee. This celebration of color, light, and vision steps forward into the future—boldly announcing its roots. It is a genuine art form and discipline of intellectual inquiry, having a viable, relevant message—artistically, spiritually, and historically. The dimensional beings who breathe life into these pages come with love, compassion, and light—opening the way for personal discovery, healing, insight, and wisdom. We are ready to demystify and absolve the negative psychic connotations of the past, which have fettered and stunted our divine imaginations. It is our birthright to travel to the most distant reaches of all dimensions of our being—spiritually, mentally, emotionally, and physically, pushing and expanding our evolutionary orbits, freely using our psychic/imaginative organs to sojourn. To journey without incurring religious, scientific, social, or governmental ridicule and defamation is our spiritual right and destiny.

It is true that many psychic dabblers demonstrate little intellectual rigor. We find that unfortunate, but because this is so, it is not fair game to automatically brush aside all psychic ventures as "woo-woo," to stand by silently, allowing skeptical inquirers to defiantly stamp out psychic voices just because the findings don't meet the scoffer's inflexible belief system, standards of testing, or scare them. It is many scientists' notion that any phenomenon that doesn't jolt their instruments escapes rigorous intellectual scrutiny and therefore is the product of whimsy and wishful thinking.

Sir William Crookes, Sir Oliver Lodge, and Dr. Charles Richet—all advanced scientific minds of the nineteenth century—did brilliant work in the field of parapsychology, providing credible evidence that psychic communication is genuine and scientifically provable. Scientists' frustration over the inability to disprove or prove mystical doctrines becomes more and more irrelevant with the ongoing revelations of quantum mechanics, which clearly give credence to past mystics' truths. Someday we will have instruments sensitive enough to detect the subtle substance of the spiritual/psychic and other dimensional realms, but until then our divine imaginations should not be silenced by scientific intolerance.

The psychic/supranormal realm has been driving humanity's artistic endeavors since our first ancestors began exploring the urge to express their inchoate feelings and thoughts on cave walls. Artistic expression has often been the harbinger for humans' adventure into new domains of consciousness. Otherworldly artists like Blake, Hieronymus Bosch, Marc Chagall, M. C. Escher, and Joan Miró—have thrust us into imaginative mindscapes that challenge consensus views of reality, or at the very least beckon into unfamiliar terrain. The visionary art and writings of Blake rocked the moorings of the traditional religious and ontological thinking of his day, while Chagall, Paul Klee, and Miró wandered deep into the surreal catacombs of the subconscious mind, changing forever the archetypal imagery of our culture. These artists were psychic travelers reporting their findings, intent on expanding and redefining the nature of reality through imagery, thus spinning new evolutionary ground.

Remember the words of Aldous Huxley in *Heaven and Hell:* "Almost never does the visionary see anything that reminds him of his own past. He is not remembering scenes, persons or objects, and he is not inventing them; he is looking on at a new creation."[20]

Traditionally, recognized artists have rarely ascribed psychic sources or powers to their works, but I believe many works have been inspired by nudges from other dimensions of life. Blake's visions are clearly inspired by transcendental experiences. He describes his imagination as infinitely more perfect and organized than anything seen by his mortal eyes. Blake was most certainly not speaking figuratively when he reported he saw visions. He interpreted the Prophets' gifts just as he interpreted his own when he states, "The Prophets described what they saw in Vision as real and existing men whom they saw with their imaginative and immortal organs; the Apostles the same...." Blake's revelations gave rise to a language that articulates his concept of imagination. His passion and conviction in his experiences led him to give credence to the existence of an interactive spirit side of life—life existing in another dimension—which guides and inspires us through sending impressions via the human imagination. This inspiration was Blake's art, his message, all that he was about; those who would but see and listen were uplifted.[21]

Psychic art in its pristine form is simply mediumship. Most artists refrain from this characterization, as it devalues their personal genius and places artistic credit in the spirit realms. Artists are not always interested in or predisposed to the underlying principles of Spiritualism and are not necessarily attuned to the subtle promptings issued from spirit. But when an artist comes to the world of creativity via a spiritual awareness, he or she is all too eager to ascribe the accolades to the spirit planes.

Rosa Parvin was such an artist. She was given a message through the mediumship of Annie Brittain in which Annie proclaimed: "I see thousands of portraits in front of me, and in your lifetime you will paint portraits of guides and helpers for people who will come to you from all over the world."[22] So it happened: during her career Rosa completed over 17,000 portraits of people from spirit. As a clairvoyant artist, she allowed her hand to be guided by a spirit artist who accurately portrayed those who had passed into the spirit dimensions. This artist called himself Papa Pierre. The story he told was of a little-known society painter living in Paris some 160 years ago. During his latter years Papa Pierre discovered his gift for psychic art when he was commissioned to do a portrait of a young lady. Partway through the portrait he found he was unable to complete it. The face of his son, who had died some ten years earlier, kept involuntarily being drawn on the canvas, much to his surprise. Through this experience he came to realize his psychic abilities and continued to demonstrate this talent throughout his life. Rosa attempted but never discovered the true identity of Papa Pierre.

Rosa's first experience with psychic art was indicative of her accuracy and profound talent. On her first trip into town to purchase art supplies she couldn't find the right materials and was about to leave when she felt a distinct pressure urging her to buy the paper she thought totally unsuitable. At home, she immediately started work and produced two portraits of an unknown airman and sailor. Soon afterwards, a well-known healer brought a group of sitters from Brighton to have psychic portraits done. As Rosa was preparing herself she happened to show one of the ladies the two drawings she recently completed. Instantly, the woman claimed one to be her son and the other to be her son's friend. From this point on, Rosa continued to produce drawing after drawing, providing clear evidence for her sitters that her portraits genuinely captured the likeness of dead relatives and loved ones—all people she had never seen.

Rosa Parvin's experiences go further to demonstrate the plausibility of beings inhabiting other dimensions of life, the existence of whom has long been maintained in metaphysical and occult circles. At one point in her career, Rosa had painted a portrait for a lady from Pretoria. It was of a Frenchman named Charles. Rosa's psychic impressions indicated that in a previous incarnation this lady had been a nun during the French Revolution and had worked with Charles. They had also been related during this lifetime. She gave the lady a word which sounded like "Bonour" and indicated that this word would someday have special meaning for her. Years later, during a trip to France, this woman came across the owner of a large château, Count de Boulle. The Count offered her a tour of his estate, which she graciously accepted. Upon ascending the staircase, she noticed many portraits, one of which she recognized as Charles, the man Rosa had drawn for her years before. She immediately inquired about this picture. The Count informed her that the man's name was Charles and he had helped Marie Antoinette escape during the Revolution. Just opposite this portrait was a portrait of a nun whom the Count said was a relative of Charles. She was overwhelmed with Rosa's accuracy and taken aback again as she departed—noticing that in the Boulle family crest, the word "Honour" was inscribed.[23]

This odd sequence of events, as incredible as it may seem to one's normal logic, not only implies the continued existence of the personality beyond the grave, but supplies a record of some spirits' ability to project accurate visual documents from another dimension through psychic imagery. The Pretorian lady's encounter at the château additionally corroborates Rosa's communication from spirit and demonstrates the bleed-through of past events colliding in present time. A third party corroborating Rosa's story of a psychic message unbeknownst to the third party provides evidence beyond even a skeptic's ability to reason—proving that psychic imagery projected from other dimensions of existence is indeed a verifiable fact.

One of the more intriguing examples of psychic art is produced through a psychologist presently living in Brazil, Luis Antonio Gasparetto. By his twentieth birthday he had produced some 2,400 canvases by forty-eight well-known artists of the past. These are not works by undistinguished court painters, but the likes of Monet, Leonardo da Vinci, Michelangelo, Toulouse-Lautrec, Modigliani, and Degas. Each painting has the undeniable markings, colors, and signature of the famous artist. Of course, one could claim these paintings are "spiritual" forgeries, masterminded by incorrigible spirits. That in itself would be fantastic enough, like the talking dog who orders the wrong brand of beer. But the art masters state the contrary, claiming that they are working on theirs and our spiritual development by providing proof of their ongoing existence, emphasizing the continuity of life.

Gasparetto creates his works of art in a dimly lit room where it is impossible to discern one color from another, at such a speed that he completes each work in less than ten minutes. He says he enters an altered state during which he feels the spirit artist's emotions, sensing what he is going to paint long before he begins the painting. His mind is fixed on the thoughts the spirit is generating and experiencing, often with the impression of four or five personalities rushing forward at once. They come close, holding his shoulders, controlling the movement of his arms, just as if they were doing the paintings themselves, and his arms flail about immediately, responding to their thoughts.

Confounding the mind yet more, Gasparetto developed the ability to create two paintings simultaneously, one with the left hand and one with the right, both of which are signed by different famous masters. In 1974 Gasparetto's spirit guides insisted that he begin ballet lessons. He was a bit disconcerted, as he had displayed no interest in or talent for dance. But he complied, and the following year, during one of his trance paintings, he rolled up his pants legs and began painting with his feet. Within minutes, he produced a wonderful painting of a young woman signed by Renoir. With this newly developed talent he could now paint three canvases simultaneously.

Gasparetto claims he paints with such fervor because the paintings have already been completed in the spirit world—his movements are driven by the thoughts of a master painter as he reproduces the original by following the template design. Some might suggest that Gasparetto's strange gift is just a queer phenomenon having no more significance than the autistic behavior of the idiot savant. But Gasparetto says that during a painting session, a window opens between the two worlds through which spiritual healing energy flows, bringing physical and spiritual healing to those present. This process alone justifies the phenomenon no matter what its true source.[24]

What is it that Monica, the Aborigines, Luis Gasparetto, Robert Monroe, Emanuel Swedenborg, and others have in common? It seems that each has collected enough experiential data to lead them to believe something much broader is happening in life than what is being acknowledged by consensus reality. Each has been willing to allow his or her experiences to flow into the mainstream of consciousness undaunted by the opposition of presiding opinions. Their inner life spills into their outer world, illustrating how the inner symbolic imagery integrates and connects us to a much larger unified reality and universe than many of our contemporary pundits are willing to admit.

After studying non-ordinary states of consciousness for over thirty years, parapsychologist Stanislav Grof, the chief of psychiatric research at the Maryland Psychiatric Research Center and an assistant professor of psychiatry at the Johns Hopkins University School of Medicine, has come to the conclusion that the multiple pathways and the extent of interconnectedness of our consciousnesses are unfathomable. Grof has personally guided more than three thousand LSD sessions and studied the records of thousands of his colleagues' sessions. Throughout the experiments there didn't seem to be any limit to what Grof's subjects could experience. Many traveled to far-off worlds visiting discarnate beings and beings of suprahuman consciousness. On one such occasion a young man related to Grof that he found himself in what seemed to be another dimension. Here a luminescent presence appeared to be close by. To this man's surprise an intelligence began to communicate. It asked him to contact a couple who lived in the Moravian city of Kromeriz, to tell them that their son Ladislav was being well taken care of and he was doing just fine. Then the voice gave the young man the couple's name, address, and telephone number.

The information meant nothing to Grof, but he couldn't get the message out of his head. So with mixed feelings and risking the ridicule of his colleagues, he went to the phone and called the number. To his complete amazement a woman started to cry when he asked for Ladislav. Finally, she calmed down enough to explain that Ladislav had passed away three weeks ago. Grof says after his years of research, "There is at present little doubt in my mind that our current understanding of the universe, of the nature of reality, and particularly of human beings, is superficial, incorrect, and incomplete."[25]

Grof explains that the nature of the transpersonal beings and events with which he became so familiar through his psychological experiments can best be explained through a holographic model of the universe. This concept has collected many subscribers from the scientific community over the past few years. A hologram is a three-dimensional picture made with the help of a laser. A piece of film is developed with laser technology, and when a beam of light is passed through the film, a three-dimensional image is projected into space. If the piece of film is cut into pieces, each piece retains the whole image. In viewing the universe through the perspective of a hologram, we would see that each part retains the master imprint of the whole.

Throughout the last three centuries scientists have been unable adequately to account for the effects of paranormal events, nor can they explain all the phenomena expressing themselves through nature. A holographic theory points to a direction for explicating many unusual coincidences (synchronicities), encounters with a collective unconscious, telepathy, vivid dreams, paranormal events, and inconsistencies in the commonly perceived fabric of reality. It points to the interconnectivity among different orders of reality, alluding to the idea that the manifestation of forms in the universe is the result of endless unfoldings from a more primary level of reality. Everything in our world is the projection of ghostly images coming from a reality beyond space and time; all are projected holographic images from a master piece of film. Two of the first scientists to begin perceiving the universe's holographic nature were physicist David Bohm and neurosurgeon Karl Pribram. Together, their ideas open up a completely new world view.[26]

In the words of Michael Talbot writing in *The Holographic Universe*: "Our brains mathematically construct objective reality by interpreting frequencies that are ultimately projections from another dimension, a deeper order of existence that is beyond both space and time; the brain is a hologram enfolded in a holographic universe."[27] If we look at the interconnectivity between the body and the endless cosmic catacombs that open through inter-dimensional journeying, one can see the brain—the organ that allows the functioning of the imagination—as a key to exploring and developing the holographic paradigm. In this view, Monica's hyperspace experiences seem to redefine the brain as part of a larger imaginative organ, mapping and charting the interior corridors of a vast holographic universe: one brain providing each of us with infinite points of departure to the unending labyrinth of cosmic reality, all accessible through the cerebral hemispheres; one being allowing each of us to perceive perfect microcosmic templates of multidimensional reality, all couched seamlessly in the disguise of each soul's imagination. Who knows—maybe we each represent a microscopic model of the universal cosmic genome, each embedded with the genetic codes of all creation.

We don't require or expect you to believe or disbelieve the experiences related herein. We only request that you view the portraits and journeys with an open mind and a loving heart. We want you to entertain the possibility that the journeys are genuine, so we have provided you with the stories of other journeyers of more renown, so you might take the heretic's plunge. Once you have, just like the rest, you'll never again be persuaded by the paltry confines that tether the reigning religious and social definitions of what the human experience is all about. With just a focused thought, a momentary investment in the imagination, you can vanquish forever the spell of the materialistic yoke.

Viva the imagination!

> By a single thought that comes into the mind,
> in one moment a hundred worlds are overturned.
> —Jalal al-Din Rumi, *RUMI: DAYLIGHT* [28]

Acknowledgments

THE AUTHORS WISH TO EXPRESS their appreciation to Keith Milton Rhinehart for the prophecy that he gave Monica about her gift as a psychic artist, without which none of the incidents of this book would have occurred. Our deepest gratitude goes out to him for the sacrifices he has made for us and the world. In that Keith was himself being entranced by spirit beings, and that many of our experiences have been guided by beings from other dimensions, we want to extend our love to these wonderful souls and acknowledge that we have been blessed and guided.

Many other people have supported us along the way, and we would like to thank the individuals who have crossed our path, contributing to our understanding of ourselves and the universe. We would especially like to thank those who assisted us directly on this project, including June Whitney, Bill Vartnaw, Vickie Matthews, Walter Shelburne, Don Jones, Jean Houston, Terence McKenna, Hank Wesselman, and Jann Werner. No project gets published without the backing of an individual with vision. Few people took us seriously, much less be willing to stand behind the vision we wanted to extend to the world. For us, one such individual was our publisher Richard Grossinger. We are grateful to Richard for his willingness to listen to his instincts and not be swayed by the pushy voice of the industry, and it did get unbelievably pushy in the case of this book. Richard also contributed by giving the text more snap and color. And finally we want to thank our editor, Kathy Glass, whose insights pulled the book together, giving the book fresh character and a coherent message.

Note on Keith Milton Rhinehart

Keith Rhinehart, a world-renowned Spiritual Teacher, is the Spiritual Founder and Spiritual Leader of Aquarian Foundation; based in Seattle, Washington, with branches across the United States and study groups around the world.

Rhinehart is recognized as the most scientifically tested physical phenomena medium in the world. His spiritual and psychic gifts include telekinesis, apportation phenomena, mental and physical phenomena, levitation and materialization.

In his younger years, Rhinehart appeared before thousands all over the world. Audiences who have witnessed different types of physical and mental phenomena coming through him have been amazed and astonished.

Rhinehart is a captivating speaker and teacher; he generates tremendous energy. He has inspired people of all ages, from the very young to the more mature. His scope of knowledge is immense. Rhinehart's powerful, dynamic, and insightful teachings give dignity to persons of all lifestyles and beliefs. These teachings are innovative and ahead of their time; they inspire the human soul to solve the dilemmas of man's inhumanity to man.

During his life work as a Spiritual Teacher and Spiritual Leader, he has interviewed many famous and influential people about their spiritual and social views. One of the many reasons for this is to give his students an insight into the minds and hearts of people, who have been influential in Earth's history. Some of these famous people included Lord Bertrand Russell, Nobel Prize winner; Lord Dowding, military leader who won the "Battle of Britain"; Margaret Mead, famous anthropologist; and Agnes Moorhead, star of an American television series.

Rhinehart is also a philanthropist at heart. He has been instrumental in raising large sums of money in South Africa for the Cancer Research fund; the Mayor's Happiness for Handicapped fund, and the Star Seaside fund for Children. In California, he raised funds for the Long Beach Children's Clinic.

One can read about Keith Rhinehart and his phenomena in publications such as *Reader's Digest*; *This Timeless Moment* by Laura Huxley, wife of the late Aldous Huxley; *Photographing the Spirit World* by Cyril Permutt; *Parapsychology and Nature of Life* by John L. Randall; in issues of *Psychic News*, *Psychic Observer*, well respected journals of the day which chronicled events in the psychic world, and in the prestigious *New Scientist* of England, October 16th, 1969, pages 114-115. The purpose of the experiments in this issue was to show whether subjects with psychic backgrounds, could defy known scientific laws. Keith Rhinehart and the other subjects in the experiment had to predict within 1/10 of a second the random flow of electrons flowing from radioactive strontium 90. In conclusive laboratory experiments, Keith Milton Rhinehart (KMR)...got results. "The number of hits obtained was 4.4 percent higher than the statistical expectation value. The probability for obtaining by chance so high a score is less than one in 500 million."

Notes

Introduction

1. Morton D. Paley, *Energy and the Imagination: A Study of the Development of Blake's Thought* (London: Oxford University Press, Ely House, 1970), pp. 200-201.
2. José Argüelles, *The Mayan Factor* (Santa Fe, NM: Bear & Company, 1987), p. 61.

Afterword

3. Geoffrey Bardon, *Papunya Tula* (Ringwood, Australia: McPhee Grimble, 1991), pp. 2-3.
4. Hank Wesselman, *Spiritwalker* (New York: Bantam Books, 1995), p. 7.
5. Michael Harner, *The Way of the Shaman* (San Francisco: Harper & Row Publishers, 1980), pp. 51-52.
6. Geoffrey Bardon, *Papunya Tula*, pp. 8-9.
7. Wilson Van Dusen, *Presence of Other Worlds: The Psychological/Spiritual Findings of Emanuel Swedenborg* (West Chester, PA: Chrysalis Books, 1991), pp. 159-160, 169-178.
8. Emanuel Swedenborg, *The Spiritual Diary, Volume III* (London: James Spiers, 1883), pp. 1-16.
9. Ayako Kasukawa, *Ectoplasm Seen on Japanese TV* (London: Psychic News Newspaper, June 14, 1958), p.8.
    Kázuo Kondo (Editor of the Shinrei Jiho, Hiroshima, Japan) *Phenomena In Japan* (Jamestown and Cassadaga, New York: Psychic Observer, #470, June 10, 1958), pp.1-2.

10. Keith Milton Rhinehart, *Astral Projection to the Moon, The Other Planets and Beyond the Stars, by Master Ashtar and Emanuel Swedenborg. Through the Trance Adeptship of Reverend Keith Milton Rhinehart*. Cassette Tape. 1974.
11. Wilson Van Dusen, *Presence of Other Worlds: The Psychological/Spiritual Findings of Emanuel Swedenborg*, pp. 159-160, 169-178.
12. Ibid., p. 162 (from *Heaven and Hell*, by Emanuel Swedenborg, paragraphs 89-90).
13. Jean Houston, *A Passion for the Possible* (San Francisco: Harper-Collins Publishers, 1997), pp. 18-38.
14. Robert A. Monroe, *Far Journeys* (New York: Doubleday & Co., 1971), pp. 3-4.
15. Ibid., pp. 179-185.
16. Robert A. Monroe, *Journeys Out of the Body* (New York: Doubleday & Co., 1982), pp. 60-72.
17. Ibid., pp. 73-76.
18. Ibid., pp. 86-95.
19. Robert A. Monroe, *Far Journeys*, pp. 120-123.
20. Aldous Huxley, *Heaven and Hell* (New York: Harper and Row, 1954), p. 97.
21. Morton D. Paley, *Energy and the Imagination: A Study of the Development of Blake's Thought* (London: Oxford University Press, Ely House, 1970), p. 201.
22. K. J. Fuller, *Rosa Parvin* (Cape Town, South Africa: Creda Press, 1976), p. 11.
23. Ibid., pp. 13-15.
24. Alberto Villoldo, Ph.D., Stanley Krippner, Ph.D., *Healing States* (New York: Simon & Schuster, 1986), pp. 6-12.
25. Stanislav Grof, *Beyond the Brain* (Albany: State University of New York Press, 1985), pp. 69-70.
26. Michael Talbot, *The Holographic Universe* (New York: Harper-Collins Publishers Inc., 1991), pp. 1-11.
27. Ibid., p. 54.
28. Jalal al-Din Rumi, Maulana, translated by Camille and Kabir Helminski, *RUMI: Daylight* (Putney, VT: Threshold Books, 1990), from *Masnavi* p. 125 (II, 1029).

MONICA SZU-WHITNEY

Monica was born and raised in Burma and immigrated to California in 1975. She started to experience inner visions in the mid eighties and began to develop as a spiritual healer and psychic artist in the following years. Monica graduated from San Jose State University with a B.S. in Interior Design and is presently working as an interior designer for a San Francisco architectural firm. She had her first showing as a psychic artist in June of 1998.

GARY WHITNEY

Gary was born and raised in California. He received his M.A. in Art from Chico State University and taught Art for several years in Quincy Junior/Senior High School in Northern California. Gary has been involved in the consciousness movement since the mid-seventies and has worked with several personal growth organizations. Now he acts as a personal coach, teaches creativity, and runs his own graphics and interior design firm.

Portraits

If you have interest in owning a large Iris print (artist's print) of one of the portraits illustrated in the book or would like a portrait done for you of your spirit guides or other dimensional beings wanting to interact with you, please contact Monica Szu-Whitney through writing Frog, Ltd.

Workshops

Groups of people interested in exploring inter-dimensional journeying and discovering how to use the portraits as portals into other dimensions can also contact us through writing Frog, Ltd., to set up a date for a workshop.